Fast Forward

The Harvard Business Review Book Series

Fast Forward

The Best Ideas on Managing Business Change

Edited with an Introduction
and Epilogue by
James Champy
and
Nitin Nohria

A Harvard Business Review Book

The *Harvard Business Review* articles in this collection are available as
individual reprints. Discounts apply to quantity purchases. For information
and ordering contact Customer Service, Harvard Business School
Publishing, Boston, MA 02163. Telephone: (617) 495-6192, 9 A.M. to 5 P.M.
Eastern Time, Monday through Friday. Fax: (617) 495-6985, 24 hours a day.

The paper used in this publication meets the requirements of the American
National Standard for Permanence of Paper for Printed Library Materials
Z39.48-1984

Library of Congress Cataloging-in-Publication Data

Fast forward : the best ideas on managing business change / edited with an
introduction and epilogue by James Champy and Nitin Nohria.
     p.   cm.—(The Harvard business review book series)
  Includes index.
  ISBN 0-87584-673-4 (alk. paper)
  1. Organizational change—Management.   2. Reengineering
(Management)   3. Business networks.   4. Creative ability in business.
I. Champy, James, 1942– .   II. Nohria, Nitin, 1962– .   III. Series.
HD58.8.F37   1996   95-46548
658.4'06—dc20   CIP

Contents

managers, by virtue of its skills, resources, and motivations, uniquely positioned to shape and deliver on the company's strategy—and shows how networks can significantly change the behavior inside companies.

Successful companies increasingly go beyond adding value by reinventing it. Looking at European businesses in Sweden, Denmark, and France, the authors show that a company's strategic challenge is the continuous reconfiguration and integration of its competencies and customers—changing the roles and relationships among its "constellation" of key players.

Percy Barnevik, president and CEO of ABB Asea Brown Boveri, is the quintessential global manager. Barnevik has worked aggressively to build ABB into an organization that combines global scale and world-class technology with strong roots in local markets. In this interview, Barnevik explains ABB's matrix system that leverages global power while maintaining local presence, and he describes the new breed of global managers that is making such an organization work.

Part II   The Process of Change

While organizational change efforts have gone under many labels in recent years—total quality management, reengineering, restructuring—the basic goal is almost always the same: to cope with a more challenging market environment by changing fundamentally how business is conducted. Having observed more than 100 companies attempting to reinvent themselves into better competitors in the past decade, the author provides his own insights and valuable lessons for any organization trying to transform itself in an increasingly competitive business environment.

Companies often make the mistake of using information technology to speed up business processes that are themselves decades, if not centuries, out of date. The author explains that the power of computers lies in the freedom they provide managers to break away from work routines based on objectives, beliefs, or technologies that no longer prevail. Only by rethinking their business processes can managers truly benefit from the power of computers, creating significant savings and efficiencies for their organizations.

Managers seeking a fundamental shift in their organizations' capabilities need to focus on the challenge of reinventing themselves; the authors argue that reinvention is not changing what is, but creating what isn't. They show that reinvention requires confronting what might be an organization's deadliest problem—the hidden assumptions on which all decisions are based—and suggest that only then can the organization gather the courage to leave behind what is for what might be.

relationships, seeking out new sources of ideas and opportunities, and brokering deals across internal and external boundaries. They must rely on new tools of leadership and motivation as their companies transform for greater flexibility and innovation, in effect transforming the nature of managerial work itself.

Acknowledgments

We would like to thank Bob Gilbert, Bob Buday, Allan Cohen, Diana Line, Scott Snook, and Rakesh Khurana for their suggestions and help in the development of this book.

Into the Storm: The Cycle of Change Quickens

James Champy and Nitin Nohria

Without doubt, today's ever-quickening cycle of change is unprecedented. Change today is faster, more erratic, more elemental than ever before. A collision of technological, competitive, and cultural pressures is forming the vortex of what we have begun to call the "information age." At the eye of the whirlwind sits management, sometimes creating, sometimes reacting to, and sometimes being damaged by swirling change—change that is marked by chaos in markets, businesses struggling to redefine themselves, organizational forms that no longer work, and management thinking that is quickly outdated.

Futurists have seen the clouds gathering for some time. And management thinkers have invented terms to explain and navigate these changes: "paradigm shift," "transformation," "reinvention," "reengineering," and "revitalization." All these are straws in the wind of a storm with origins that are now becoming clear. Three major drivers are stirring change faster: technology, the changing role of government in business, and globalization.

Technology, particularly information technology, is transforming business in dramatic new ways:

- A "virtual bank" in Brazil, with hundreds of thousands of customers, is not much more than a logo. The bank owns only an electronic network and its customers. Other financial services companies supply the products. There is no headquarters building, branches or "bricks and mortar."

- A mom-and-pop retail store in Maine offers its products over the Internet. Now, with no investment in capital, it has moved from a regional to a national business.

- A publisher of professional journals is changing the meaning of publishing. Its output is now more than 60% in digital form. Not only has this publisher dramatically changed the speed with which research is disseminated and commented on, but it has changed the nature of professional discourse itself.

What's important to recognize about the role of information technology today is that it is not only changing how we do our work, *it is changing the definition of the business.*

Then there is **government**, dramatically rethinking its role in business. On a worldwide basis, we see deregulation, privatization, and increasing free trade:

- Once-protected U.S. utility companies are now subject to open competition, while local utility commissions restrict the companies' operations and pricing.

- Government-owned European airlines and telecommunications companies are being spun out to compete with American companies that are pushing their way into European markets.

- With the creation of new institutions such as the World Trade Organization, falling trade barriers are allowing new players to enter markets and change the basis of competition.

All of these sometimes quixotic government actions are forcing businesses to rethink their purpose, their organization, and the way they manage. And for some companies, there is for the first time the need to learn to compete.

Finally, there is the phenomenon of **globalization**: companies from all parts of the globe competing to deliver the same product or service, anytime, anywhere, at increasingly competitive prices. Globalization is forcing companies to organize themselves in radically different ways. For example:

- A software firm in India operates a virtual office in New Jersey. Customer service representatives in India respond 24 hours a day to calls directed to their office in New Jersey. By collapsing turnaround time and employing less-costly local developers, this firm is able to offer software development services at a fraction of the cost of its U.S. competitors.

- AT&T, Dun & Bradstreet, General Electric, and the U.S. Chamber of Commerce have formed the International Business Exchange to let businesses electronically line up suppliers, negotiate contracts, make and receive bids, and arrange the delivery of goods and services around the globe. If the world was already a global village, it just became smaller.

- Giant multinationals such as Asea Brown Boveri (an interview with its CEO, Percy Barnevik, is included in this book) have become truly global, as opposed to being tied to any particular nation-state. ABB manufactures and sells around the globe, has senior executives and board members of all nationalities, and its stock is listed on several national exchanges.

If there is one inescapable conclusion, it is that all companies and institutions (including governments) now must redefine themselves. The fundamental forces at play are too compelling to deny the future.

Change can be a powerful energizer and a creative force, which is to the good. But there are hazards as well. Our intent in this book is to present some of the best ideas on managing change in this turbulent environment, one that holds great opportunity yet feels as if it is relentlessly moving ahead at fast forward.

We have organized these ideas into three sections, to answer, in turn, three questions we believe are fundamental to navigating this storm:

- Where are we headed? Or, what will our future organizations look like?

- How will we get there? Or, how can we manage the process of change?

- What new personal skills and capabilities will we need? Or, what will become of the work of leadership and management?

We hope our readers will discover their own answers to these questions by reading the seminal articles that we have included in this book. We have learned much from these influential thinkers, and we expect you will as well. Metaphorically standing on their shoulders, then, we want to offer our own perspective on each of these questions.

The Future Organization: Where Are We Heading?

Twisted into a new shape by fierce global competition, changing markets, and technological breakthroughs, the business organization of the future is emerging with distinct characteristics. It will be

- information-based,
- decentralized, yet densely linked through technology,
- rapidly adaptable and extremely agile,
- creative and collaborative, with a team-based structure,

- staffed by a wide variety of knowledge workers, and
- self-controlling—which is possible only in an environment of clear, strong, and shared operating principles and of real trust.

We hold in our mind's eye a fluid network, where connections form and reform almost organically, like the branches of the human nervous system. There will be authority, of course, and some hierarchy, but gone forever is the archaic organizational shape: the pyramid.

As we enter the second half of the 1990s, most would agree that the apogee of centralized "machine age" management and organization passed in the 1980s. Hierarchical, bureaucratic, and characterized by the specialization of labor, this pyramidal structure was a metaphor for its era of one hundred-plus years. It arose in the United States in the late nineteenth century, and, in Europe, reflected the staff system of the Prussian army. Some argue that this command-and-control model grew out of the vastness and complexity of its undertakings. Certainly, a great many complicated steps were involved in going from the red iron ore of the Mesabi Range to the millions of gleaming cars produced annually by General Motors. And this management model was indeed perfected by GM's president, Alfred P. Sloan. From the top down, this machine model required countless levels of management that acted as valve lifters and connecting rods to pass down concepts and report back real-world information. Annual product cycles provided the spark.

While nineteenth-century hierarchy combined with bureaucracy to give us the machine model, business today is no longer "simply" big and complicated. It must operate under extremely dynamic conditions. Today's business requires a huge amount of information exchange. Management finds itself needing to be creative and collaborative. It needs to be nimble and fast. Obsolescence is no longer planned on the inside, it comes winging in from the outside.

Centralized organization has become too slow, too costly, and too inefficient. It is, in fact, outdated in its very structure: An innovation of the old GM was to separate strategic planning staffs from operating managers, isolating conception from execution. In fact, some cynics even believed that intermediate management was there only to serve as "translators" between top management, who talked of numbers, and workers, who talked about things. This is not to pick too strenuously on GM, which, like the rest of the world, has flattened its organization. GM also has moved away from vertical integration. Formerly, it internally produced 90% of the value-added components in its cars. GM has reduced that to about 40% and it sources the rest from a network of firms that are viewed not just as suppliers but as genuine business partners. We mention the old GM to point out the need for a new metaphor of management and organization.

If the dominant product of the first half of the twentieth century was the automobile, the second half belongs to the personal computer. The computer's ability to perform tasks in ever smaller, less expensive, and more powerful ways, extending its tendrils to outside networks of information, feels symbolically like the increasingly rapid evolution of our business organizations.

Think of the tempo of change in networking technology itself. Not long ago it was the province of specialists who talked of SNA and "topologies." At the mass level, Windows 95 and the Internet are making such arcane knowledge unnecessary for most of us. In the past decade or so, new computer operating systems, graphical user interfaces, and point-and-click "mice" have obviated the users' need for machine language and complex user commands. In the very same way, we believe electronic commerce along the Internet will sweep away the old idea of Electronic Data Interchange (EDI) among private networks. With network services now priced as commodities, the era of dedicated networks between business partners may soon be gone. New organizations will plug into new networks and drop others at will. *Any to all* is the goal. And even once-staid AT&T is betting that the "mother of all networks" will turn the delivery of computing services into a utility that will be wired into every home and office.

Again, if one posits that management's world views at any point in time grow out of the underlying technologies of that age, then there is one more factor. For, in addition to computer technology—with its message of the computer is the network—we also have the new biological sciences, with their message that all living organisms are fashioned from twisted strands of DNA and that intelligence emerges from patterned interconnections in evolving neural networks. The Internet and the "neuralnet" are the dominant technological images of the latter half of the 1990s. All of which suggests what we believe to be the most appropriate metaphor for the future organization: the *adaptive network*.

Think of the parallels in organization: management networks, or project teams, that form, reform, or rapidly die out from disuse. One does not imagine a well-oiled machine, one thinks of electrical impulses, of dialogue and constant re-creation. One does not imagine an entity impelled by command from the top. One thinks of an organization kept in constant motion by information flows that cross levels and boundaries.

A network structure differs from the traditional machine model in several other ways. Labor in a network structure is not *divided* but rather *shared* among "knowledge workers," who may act either as individual contributors or as part of a team.

Work in a network structure is performed primarily by cross-functional teams that can be more or less permanent. Such teams bring together different combinations of knowledge workers and operate under with little formal supervision. Some teams, such as autonomous assembly-line work groups or order fulfillment teams, are relatively permanent. They are responsible for the production of a complete product or the execution of an end-to-end business process. Others, such as product development teams, oversee the creation and introduction of a new product, forming and disbanding according to the life cycle of the product. Still others form on an as-needed basis, focusing on a specific problem or customer need.

Decision making in a network structure moves as far down as possible. With the help of technology, information is available to support decision making by the knowledge workers instead of by managers higher up in the organization. Middle managers, who traditionally relayed information up and decisions down the organization, are redundant in network organizations. This change leads to flatter organizations with fewer levels and broader spans of control.

A network structure blurs the boundaries between the organization and its environment: vendors, customers, and competitors. Old walls dissolve between companies and customers, value-added partners, strategic allies, and competitors. Also melting the inside/outside line are customized products and services for specific customers and just-in-time production techniques. The production process thus moves to the boundary of the company in real-time interaction with vendors and customers. This is quite different from traditional hierarchy in which production is viewed as a core that is buffered from the environment by parts and finished-product inventories. Everyone in the network organization is expected to deal with the environment. There is no core that is sealed off from the world to keep uncertainty at bay.

The network structure also overturns the superiority of the formal over the informal organization. While the informal structure was undoubtedly important in the traditional organization, today it dominates. There is no time for formality in a fluid structure that changes so often and is so dependent on personal relationships to mobilize people for action.

Network organizations are also much less politically fragmented than traditional organizations. Given the fluidity of network structures, political coalitions organize around work units that have real purpose. Also, authority derives less from one's formal position than from one's on the expertise and resources.

The main advantage of the adaptive network structure is its capacity to unleash the power of the individual. It gives the organization *agility*. The adaptive network organization enables fast, creative responses to ever-changing market conditions. However, the dark side of individual power and quick decision making is the potential for lack of control. The Barings Bank debacle is a cautionary tale. One trader brought down a huge worldwide organization. Obviously, as companies become more global, as decision making moves farther down into the organization, more of the company can be jeopardized by the errant actions of any one of its nodes. This begs a couple of obvious questions: Where is the locus of control in such an organization? How does a manager know what's going on in a dispersed organization comprising self-managed individuals?

In 1988, Peter Drucker anticipated these problems as he envisioned information-based organizations replacing the circa-1950 manufacturing organizational structure. In his seminal *Harvard Business Review* article, "The Coming of the New Organization," which we have included in the first section of this book, Drucker suggested that the organization of the future would be much like a symphony orchestra. Here, one leader works with a team of superb specialists, and everyone knows the score, in both senses of the expression. To maintain control, Drucker argued, "an information-based business must be structured around goals that clearly state management's performance expectations for the enterprise and for each part and specialist and around organized feedback that compares results with these performance expectations so that every member can exercise self-control."

Self-control is indeed the goal, for it is the only viable choice in an adaptive network organization. But what if the group has to make up new music as it goes along, like a jazz quintet, which is the more actual state of business?

Going back to the network metaphor, if improvisational jazz rather than a classical symphony is the music of our times, we must move toward an organization with multiple centers and instantaneous communications, the equivalent of servers in a distributed network. Each server will have its own local network, and each network will be connected to the others. Complex operating protocols allow disparate computer networks to exchange data. Likewise, the new organization will not emphasize a hierarchical center, but will stress the shared operating *principles* that permit local action, yet ensure coordinated effort. To hold the network organization together, the management team must clearly define the organization's shared purpose and operating principles. Operating principles help define standards and codes of conduct. Ideally, such principles applied locally generate the collective result senior management wants. Or, in somewhat existential terms, these principles describe how any member of the organization should act during so-called moments of truth—for instance, the length to which one should go to satisfy the customer.

As certain as we are that the organization of the future will inevitably look like an adaptive network, we must add that there is an almost generational resistance to this form of management and organization. While our sons and daughters feel very comfortable about plugging into the Internet and living in a world of virtual organizations and relationships, most of us grew up in bureaucratic organizations. We still seek the comfort of knowing where we fit on the organization chart. As for the too-human need for strong direction, consider the lingering sense of loss for a centralized economy in the former Soviet Union—despite the gain of freedom! Uncomfortable as we might feel about losing the familiar, we need to remember that the future doesn't wait. Indeed, it is already here.

Starting With Purpose: How We Can Get There

In a storm, one can lose sight of one's destination—the purpose of the journey. Like a compass check, we believe that managing through today's turbulence must start with an inquiry into purpose—knowing what lies true north. From that knowledge flows the essential course-setting work of

- developing a new business model and aligning senior management around it,
- resetting the business fundamentals, and
- creating a culture that stimulates renewal and growth.

In all of those, we have a bias toward radical approaches that focus on results—on getting big change fast. But deciding on a direction can be hard when change is fast and choices are uncertain.

For example, if you were to ask a group of newspaper owners what business they are in, there could be a series of varied responses: "We provide advertisers with potential customers—our readers." "We select and analyze the news." "We expose the public to important ideas and provide context for events." "We print and distribute time-sensitive information."

Those statements, in turn, might lead them to consider a series of questions about the basic nature of their business: Do we need to own all of the manufacturing and distribution channels—from printing presses, to trucks, to people delivering and selling on the street? Does word-based information necessarily have to be provided on paper? Would advertisers and subscribers pay for the content we provide if someone else packaged and delivered it? What will happen to the collection and shaping of the news in an information superhighway environment with many specialized media outlets and topics that interest groups select themselves?

There are no easy answers for publishers. But those questions exemplify the questions that those who seek to manage change must ask first: What is this business's purpose? What are its fundamentals? Where do we need to go? How do we get there in a hurry?

Answers are needed urgently to the question of purpose because, as has been noted, not only are the winds of change blowing faster, but the number of variables are increasing as well. Thus the consequences of actions are not only harder to predict, but their potential penalties are also greater. Rigid organizations get flattened in a market landscape that Peter Drucker has described as "re-arranging" through technological change or new entrants into the markets.

Look also at the utility industry. Just as cheaper MIPS (or computational power) spelled trouble for IBM and a wonderful business opportunity for Intel, the successful effort by big power users to negotiate cheaper kilowatts from new independent power producers (IPPs) may mean deep trouble for the biggest utilities. Large power providers are in the midst of a re-arranging of their market that may soon become full-scale deregulation. Indeed, a decade from now, of today's two hundred investor-owned, integrated U.S. public utilities, no more than 20 may exist in their current form.

Of course, no one has a crystal ball. Looking ahead just 20 years ago, how could the publishers of *Encyclopedia Britannica* have known that they would have to compete with a product on a CD-ROM that sells for $100—and soon will cost even less? A compelling sense of purpose can start with a shrewd hunch, a bold assumption, or the experience gained in a prior defeat.

The personal history of Gordon Moore, one of the founders of Intel, started with all three. Back in 1968, when Moore and Robert Noyce left Fairchild Semiconductor to start their company, Moore recalls, "It was very useful to be able to start again, start with a clean sheet of paper."[1] As he told *Forbes,* he spent little time studying management theory. He had already learned enough by observing his former bosses' mistakes. Nor did Moore push to an illogical extreme his extraordinary vision for the future of integrated circuits (now called Moore's Law, which says the number of transistors per chip would double every 18 months, while costs would fall at a like amount). Rather, he adapted an extremely pragmatic approach to achieve an audacious end. Moore calls this his "Goldilocks strategy."

The nascent Intel "had a choice of three technologies, an easy one that could be quickly copied by Texas Instruments and Fairchild; a complicated one that might bankrupt them; or a moderately complicated one. 'They, like Goldilocks in the fairy tale, concentrated on the middle course. The key was the right degree of difficulty. Too easy, you get competition too soon. Too hard, you run out of money before you get it done,'" Moore explained.[2]

Moore was ahead of his time in several ways. Intel's success shows that the ability to manage change must start with a compelling sense of purpose that enables one to fast forward—by starting the planning at the end instead of the beginning. We call this "right-to-left thinking." It forces change in big chunks; it is learning by doing rather than analysis and prolonged study. It is a predisposition to invent the future as one goes along rather than to react after the fact.

The danger, of course, is that a company can be too visionary and lose sight of financial realities. Indeed, our own research of companies that attempted to transform themselves shows that every change program was doomed unless the business fundamentals were reexamined and the under-performing assets trimmed.

This lesson is underscored by one of the masters of change, Al Dunlap, a former CEO of Scott Paper Company. Dunlap came to the helm of Scott at a difficult time in the company's history. He quickly reshaped Scott and prepared it for a merger. His comments in *Forbes* provide a succinct view of the importance of pragmatic fundamentals.

Asked how he had pumped new life so quickly into Scott, a company that was on a credit watch, Dunlap replied:

> Scott is just a microcosm of corporate America. Everyone thinks a restructuring is just cost-cutting. Nothing could be farther from the truth. We had a simple, clear, four-part plan. First, what business are you in? Sell off the other assets. Second, get new management in there. Third, make one-time major cuts. Fourth, develop and invest in the right business strategy.
>
> You will have a window of one year, and I passionately believe at the end of a year the window comes down like a steel door. If by then you haven't shown great leadership, dealt with the restructuring, and determined what business you're in, it's over.[3]

In fact, to stop financial hemorrhaging immediate action is often unavoidable. For example, Corbin McNeill, CEO of PECO Energy Company in Philadelphia, approached a large-scale reengineering effort by implementing an immediate 30% staff reduction. Yet it was not a case of mindless downsizing. Rather, McNeill decided to take inevitable action first and have it done with. His action immediately energized the utility and set the stage for a new identity and sense of purpose based on those who believed in the new future. There is often no mild alternative for companies in dire straits.

Next comes the hardest part, the part that many "turnaround artists" fail to accomplish: the task of creating a culture that stimulates renewal and growth. Cultural change requires challenging deep-seated beliefs, habits, and practices. It requires a commitment to alter "the way things are done around here."

This was well recognized by Sir Colin Marshall, who is credited with having transformed British Airways from having its initials stand for "bloody awful" to "bloody awesome." When he joined British Airways as CEO, the process of resetting the business fundamentals had already been initiated by Lord John King, the airline's chairman. Between 1981 and 1983, King had taken what he called "tough, unpalatable, and immediate measures" that included reducing staff from 52,000 to 35,000 and closing 16 routes. He also halted cargo-only services and inflicted massive cuts on all forms of perquisites.[4]

Marshall recognized that necessary as these changes were, they were not sufficient to transform British Airways. He made customer service a personal crusade. He devoted his energies to creating an "enabling culture" in which employees "feel they can actually come out with ideas, [in which] they will be listened to, and feel they are much more a part of the success of the company."[5] In addition to becoming an active role model, Marshall invested heavily in a series of corporate renewal programs. The Putting People First program emphasized the value of positive relationships with people in general. Marshall also introduced a management program that emphasized the importance of trust, leadership, vision, and feedback. Managers said the program profoundly changed the way they viewed their roles and responsibilities. Marshall gradually created a culture that enabled the firm to renew itself by focusing on global marketing and customer service. British Airways went from being one of the world's least profitable to one of the most profitable airlines. It also became one of the best liked.

To recap, the process of managing change must start with a clear sense of purpose. Frequently, it is important to introduce cost-cutting programs immediately, just to reset the business fundamentals. But at the same time, there must be a committed effort to revitalize the company through initiatives that create a context for renewal and growth. A word of caution: Organizations can get caught in a downward spiral if the cost-cutting phase lasts too long or is perceived as having been done with little sense of humanity. Frank Borman never realized this at Eastern Airlines. Each time the airline faltered, he tried to cut costs by seeking yet deeper wage concessions from the airline's unions. Eventually, Borman lost his credibility and couldn't get any more out of his unions. The resulting stalemate between Borman and the unions drove Eastern into bankruptcy.

Similarly, organizations can get caught up in useless flavor-of-the-month change games if renewal initiatives are not tied to the pursuit of demonstrable business results. For a long time, this was precisely the problem at Northwest Airlines. There was no shortage of programs designed to change the corporate culture and the way things were done at Northwest. Still there was no improvement in business results. It took a disastrous plane crash for Northwest's managers and employees to recognize that these change initiatives were only meaningful if they were tied to quantifiable performance outcomes, such as improvements in safety and customer satisfaction.

Another lesson: Throughout the change process, at every stage, companies must take a radical approach instead of an incremental one. Radical does not mean outrageous. Radical does not mean impractical. The word is from the Latin for root, and in our usage means getting to essential issues with as little delay as possible.

Today, because of the habits left over from the good old days of stable markets, most managers still prefer to approach change incrementally. The how-to goes like this: First, you determine where you think you are. Next, you determine where you think you're going. And then you ask what steps you need to take to get there. Finally, you change some things and check their effectiveness. In practice, this is like that old conceptualization of being unable to reach the wall by continually pacing off half the distance to it. In other words, over time, change becomes more and more minuscule. Incrementalism is a luxury that's no longer affordable. If nothing else, the last half-decade has amply shown that the rearranging markets reward speed and an inclination for action.

There are two other problems with incremental approaches. The first and most common trap is that participants get hung up in the process and lose sight of results. The change process becomes an end in itself. The second problem is that incremental changes are often restricted to local initiatives. They affect small parts of processes that cut across departments and business functions. Thus a bit of a core process, inside a function, might be improved. Yet those initiatives fail to realize the often greater benefits that lie in making changes that cross functional and other organizational boundaries.

A radical approach runs fewer risks of suffering from these problems because it starts by setting ambitious and indeed seemingly unachievable goals. If you say to an organization, "We must improve the performance of this part of the business by 10% a year," its people will normally just change the current work processes until they run out of options. But if you say to an organization, "Look, our industry is changing so quickly that we must improve the performance of this business by 100%, and, by the way, we must do it within 18 months," its people will quickly realize that they cannot accomplish that result with the current operating models. They will be more likely to undertake the radical work process changes that will yield the desired improvements in performance.

The key is to have relentless ambition for performance improvement. Total quality programs, which are often seen as intrinsically incremental, can in fact be radical when they are driven by ambitious goals. One has only to think of Motorola and its commitment to improve quality tenfold every few years to see how this can be the case. Similarly, reengineering programs, which are viewed as intrinsically radical, can be little more than incremental tinkering. For example, we have seen one large financial services company declare with pride that it has 300 reengineering projects, simultaneously. We fear most are on the scale of reengineering the pencil-ordering process.

In a phrase, then, the choice is either to fast forward or fall behind.

The New Responsibilities of the Executive: How We Must Change Personally

In the new organization, management will no longer be the primary generative force. For the most part, self-organizing network organizations will mobilize *themselves*. Meanwhile, the distinction between manager and worker will erode further. Management's role will evolve beyond its classical functions of planning and budgeting, organizing and staffing, and controlling and problem-solving. Likewise, the functions of the executive will stretch beyond today's traditional leadership tasks, defined by John Kotter as visioning, aligning, and motivating.[6] We believe executives will increasingly have to embrace three additional responsibilities:

- The establishment of a company's *identity*, which illuminates its purpose
- The nurturing of *initiative*, to tap the wellsprings of creativity within the organization
- The pursuit of *integrity*, which creates trust and serves as the basis of organizational control

Embracing this new view of the functions of the executive will be the most challenging of the numerous changes we have identified so far. The most virulent resistance to change exists not on the assembly line or in the field office but rather at the top of the organization. Forty years after W. Edwards Deming's quality-improvement teachings first fell on Japanese ears, and nearly a decade after the introduction of more radical ideas such as reengineering, most managers have fully accepted the need to overhaul the processes of work. Yet very few have successfully steered their organizations into the future. Why?

The reason has to lie within. Or, in the words of the comic strip character Pogo, "We have seen the enemy, and it is us." Into the twenty-first century senior executives still bring the managerial mindsets of the twentieth century. That mental image of what it means to be a manager—how to lead, how to understand markets and devise strategy, how to structure the organization to pursue those markets—

is now obsolete. Flatter organizations, in which people collaborate across functional areas, have left many hierarchy-minded managers in a daze, as Rosabeth Moss Kanter points out in "The New Managerial Work," the essay we have chosen to introduce the section on the changing role of leadership and management. How do such managers mobilize staff who no longer automatically follow a marching order? How do they motivate those who fall outside their authority or those who must be won over through reason and negotiation?

The answers, we believe, lie in recognizing that executives of leading twenty-first century corporations must embrace three new fundamental managerial responsibilities: *identity, initiative,* and *integrity.*

Responsibility for defining the firm's identity includes, but goes beyond, establishing a vision of the future. Simply put, *identity* involves asking what the enterprise stands for in the broadest sense: Where did we come from? What are we distinctive at? Where are we going? At the core of identity is understanding of an organization's distinctiveness. Managers who lose sight of what the company has done and can do distinctively well have unwittingly cast it down the road of mediocrity, to wage a losing campaign of mimicking the strategies, products, and processes of competitors.

Identity brings into the future what an organization has done well in the past. It uniquely recognizes that a firm's history is important and cannot be cast away entirely. It encompasses the shared values and beliefs of the organization that have served it well over time. Despite finding itself in an increasingly competitive market for the best business school students, the Harvard Business School, for example, can never afford to respond to these changes simply by emulating Wharton, Northwestern, MIT, or whichever school is atop the current business school rankings. Harvard's identity—and its professors' skills—revolve around the classroom and the case study method. Any reinvention of the business school must recognize these core aspects of the school's distinctive identity and heritage. Yet the school must change and its identity must evolve in response to the new realities of the market for professional business education.

Therefore, one new role of managers is to understand the firm's identity in their own eyes and the eyes of their constituencies. What do employees think they're coming to do when they walk through the door in the morning? What do customers really think they are buying when they purchase your product?

While understanding the core competencies of the past is critical, it must not constrict management. That is where thinking about purpose becomes important. The purpose of an enterprise is the essential function it serves for its customers—and if that purpose changes, it must change with great clarity. Purpose is the inner compass that steers the corporation through the turbulent waves of regulatory, political, competitive, technological, and demographic change.

The second managerial mandate—*initiative*—calls for increasing the generative capacity of management. How do managers unleash the firm's creative energy to seek new markets, products, and processes? The command and control model of management, with its one-directional communication patterns and its culture of obedience, has resulted in managers tapping no more than 10% of employees' productive capacity. That was acceptable when markets were stable, competition was gentle, and products lived on for years. Now change occurs so rapidly that top management must rely on frontline employees as their window on the world. In a world where product cycles are measured in months, a key role of the new manager is to get everyone in the organization to monitor the marketplace closely.

Generating initiative demands undoing decades of ingrained managerial habits that assumed that the generative capacity of the organization lay at the top. Managers plan, workers execute. In the new organization, the entire organism must be recognized as having generative capacity. Gordon Binder, CEO of biotech powerhouse Amgen, thinks constantly about maintaining an atmosphere in which initiative flourishes. So does Michael Bloomberg, who has built a half-billion-dollar information service business for securities traders that employs state-of-the-art technology. Said Bloomberg recently: "Our ideas don't all come from our 'smart people.' My main job is to keep us from developing a structure that will preclude a kid we just hired from walking through the door and saying, 'Why not try this?' "

To unleash initiative throughout the organization, management must be willing to create discordance. The main enemies of constructive change are orthodoxy and dogma. Debate must be encouraged—to a point. And then decisions must be made. The new organization is always moving forward in a state of tension; managers who are uncomfortable with ambiguity will not be able to function. The process of creation is far less predictable than the process of cost-cutting. Volumes have been written on how to pare fat from the corporate body. There is no cookbook on invention.

Managers have one other essential role. While nurturing identity and initiative, they must also relentlessly pursue *integrity*. Integrity lays the foundation for trust, which can be the only meaningful basis of control in an adaptive network organization. Integrity demands that all communication be authentic, that is, honest even if it reflects badly on management or reveals that the managers don't yet have the answers. Integrity also implies that my word is as good as a promise. If I say I will do something, you can trust that I will get it done. If the integrity of anyone's word is in doubt, coordination can easily break down in an organization where everyone can—and indeed must—take local initiative based on their best judgment.

Lawrence Bossidy, CEO of AlliedSignal, exemplifies such integrity (see "The CEO as Coach"). He believes in answering tough questions directly. Further, he solicits them. "It's good if people go home at night and say, 'I told that son of a bitch what I thought about him today.' " Yet executives like Bossidy and IBM board member James Burke, who was CEO of Johnson & Johnson during the Tylenol scare, are still in the distinct minority. Burke, who was part of the search committee for IBM's new CEO in the early 1990s, publicly acknowledged that the IBM board missed the boat when computer technology was changing. That showed integrity.

Integrity is also about establishing, communicating, and, most important, exemplifying a set of core values and operating principles. Such lasting values and principles guide people's behavior no matter what the condition of the business or the market. Indeed, it was the conviction with which everyone at Johnson & Johnson held the values and principles embraced in its credo that enabled the company's unflinching response to the Tylenol poisoning tragedy. Nobody needed to be told what to do when it was discovered that some Tylenol packages had been tampered with and poisoned. They knew the right thing to do. The product had to be recalled, whatever the cost. And around the globe, it was done. Here we see the power of control based on integrity rather than authority.

"Going to work" no longer necessarily means "going to the office." So, such standards of integrity take on unprecedented importance. Managers now guide their employees who are out of sight in the new networked organizations. In their influential role, senior executives must embody such integrity more than anyone else.

The successful managers of the twenty-first century will bear little resemblance to the cream of the twentieth century crop. As Bossidy says in his interview: "We need [managers] who are better at persuading than at barking orders, who know how to coach and build consensus. Today, managers add value by brokering with people, not by presiding over empires." The day of the commanding and controlling manager is over. In a stormy era, managers must get centered in their new roles and in themselves. All managers must stretch themselves to take personal responsibility for shaping the evolving identity of their enterprise, for stimulating initiative, and for upholding unifying standards of integrity.

After the Tempest

We are at just the start of a new management era. Alfred Sloan's vaunted managerial model arrived many years after the introduction of the automobile and Henry Ford's revolutionary process for assembling it. Similarly, the predominant managerial framework for running today's corporation is trailing the introduction of the technology that is reshaping our era: the computer and the communications network. This delay is perhaps just the time it takes for managers to come to grips with change and regain their balance. More pessimistically, we fear that the changes required are beyond current management's ability and await a new generation of managers.

Much change will undoubtedly occur before the skies clear. Yet not everything from the past will be swept away. The German philosopher, Hegel, held that history bumps along on triangular wheels of change—thesis, antithesis, and synthesis. We believe this famous dialectic will play out again as we move in organizational thinking from the model of the machine to the network, from incremental to more radical views of change, and from a conception of management based primarily on authority to one based on personal responsibility.

Notes

1. Robert Lenzinger, "The Reluctant Entrepreneur," *Forbes*, September 1, 1995.

2. Ibid.

3. Dana Wechsler Linden, "You Want Somebody to Like You, Get a Dog," *Forbes*, August, 28, 1995.

4. John P. Kotter and John L. Leahy, "Changing the Culture of British Airways," Case No. 9-491-009, Boston: Harvard Business School Publishing, 1991.

5. Ibid.

6. John P. Kotter, "What Leaders Really Do," *Harvard Business Review*, May–June 1990, p. 103–111.

Fast Forward

PART

I

The Future State: Where We Are Heading

1
The Coming of the New Organization

Peter F. Drucker

The typical large business 20 years hence will have fewer than half the levels of management of its counterpart today, and no more than one-third the managers. In its structure, and in its management problems and concerns, it will bear little resemblance to the typical manufacturing company, circa 1950, which our textbooks still consider the norm. Instead it is far more likely to resemble organizations that neither the practicing manager nor the management scholar pays much attention to today: the hospital, the university, the symphony orchestra. For like them, the typical business will be knowledge-based, an organization composed largely of specialists who direct and discipline their own performance through organized feedback from colleagues, customers, and headquarters. For this reason, it will be what I call an information-based organization.

Businesses, especially large ones, have little choice but to become information-based. Demographics, for one, demands the shift. The center of gravity in employment is moving fast from manual and clerical workers to knowledge workers who resist the command-and-control model that business took from the military 100 years ago. Economics also dictates change, especially the need for large businesses to innovate and to be entrepreneurs. But above all, information technology demands the shift.

Advanced data-processing technology isn't necessary to create an information-based organization, of course. As we shall see, the British built just such an organization in India when "information technology" meant the quill pen, and barefoot runners were the "telecommunications" systems. But as advanced technology becomes more and more prevalent, we have to engage in analysis and diagnosis—that is, in "information"—even more intensively or risk being swamped by the data we generate.

So far most computer users still use the new technology only to do faster what they have always done before, crunch conventional numbers. But as soon as a company takes the first tentative steps from data to information, its decision processes, management structure, and even the way its work gets done begin to be transformed. In fact, this is already happening, quite fast, in a number of companies throughout the world.

We can readily see the first step in this transformation process when we consider the impact of computer technology on capital-investment decisions. We have known for a long time that there is no one right way to analyze a proposed capital investment. To understand it we need at least six analyses: the expected rate of return; the payout period and the investment's expected productive life; the discounted present value of all returns through the productive lifetime of the investment; the risk in not making the investment or deferring it; the cost and risk in case of failure; and finally, the opportunity cost. Every accounting student is taught these concepts. But before the advent of data-processing capacity, the actual analyses would have taken man-years of clerical toil to complete. Now anyone with a spreadsheet should be able to do them in a few hours.

The availability of this information transforms the capital-investment analysis from opinion into diagnosis, that is, into the rational weighing of alternative assumptions. Then the information transforms the capital-investment decision from an opportunistic, financial decision governed by the numbers into a business decision based on the probability of alternative strategic assumptions. So the decision both presupposes a business strategy and challenges that strategy and its assumptions. What was once a budget exercise becomes an analysis of policy.

The second area that is affected when a company focuses its data-processing capacity on producing information is its organization structure. Almost immediately, it becomes clear that both the number of management levels and the number of managers can be sharply cut. The reason is straightforward: it turns out that whole layers of management neither make decisions nor lead. Instead, their main, if not their only, function is to serve as "relays"—human boosters for the faint, unfocused signals that pass for communication in the traditional pre-information organization.

One of America's largest defense contractors made this discovery when it asked what information its top corporate and operating managers needed to do their jobs. Where did it come from? What form was it in? How did it flow? The search for answers soon revealed that whole layers of management—perhaps as many as 6 out of a total of 14—existed only because these questions had not been asked before. The company had had data galore. But it had always used its copious data for control rather than for information.

Information is data endowed with relevance and purpose. Converting data into information thus requires knowledge. And knowledge, by definition, is specialized. (In fact, truly knowledgeable people tend toward overspecialization, whatever their field, precisely because there is always so much more to know.)

The information-based organization requires far more specialists overall than the command-and-control companies we are accustomed to. Moreover, the specialists are found in operations, not at corporate headquarters. Indeed, the operating organization tends to become an organization of specialists of all kinds.

Information-based organizations need central operating work such as legal counsel, public relations, and labor relations as much as ever. But the need for service staffs—that is, for people without operating responsibilities who only advise, counsel, or coordinate—shrinks drastically. In its *central* management, the information-based organization needs few, if any, specialists.

Because of its flatter structure, the large, information-based organization will more closely resemble the businesses of a century ago than today's big companies. Back then, however, all the knowledge, such as it was, lay with the very top people. The rest were helpers or hands, who mostly did the same work and did as they were told. In the information-based organization, the knowledge will be primarily at the bottom, in the minds of the specialists who do different work and direct themselves. So today's typical organization in which knowledge tends to be concentrated in service staffs, perched rather insecurely between top management and the operating people, will likely be labeled a phase, an attempt to infuse knowledge from the top rather than obtain information from below.

Finally, a good deal of work will be done differently in the information-based organization. Traditional departments will serve as guardians of standards, as centers for training and the assignment of specialists; they won't be where the work gets done. That will happen largely in task-focused teams.

This change is already under way in what used to be the most clearly defined of all departments—research. In pharmaceuticals, in telecommunications, in papermaking, the traditional *sequence* of research, development, manufacturing, and marketing is being replaced by *synchrony*: specialists from all these functions work together as a team, from the inception of research to a product's establishment in the market.

How task forces will develop to tackle other business opportunities and problems remains to be seen. I suspect, however, that the need for a task force, its assignment, its composition, and its leadership will have to be decided on case by case. So the organization that will be developed will go beyond the matrix and may indeed be quite different from it. One thing is clear, though: it will require greater self-discipline and even greater emphasis on individual responsibility for relationships and for communications.

To say that information technology is transforming business enterprises is simple. What this transformation will require of companies and top managements is much harder to decipher. That is why I find it helpful to look for clues in other kinds of information-based organizations, such as the hospital, the symphony orchestra, and the British administration in India.

A fair-sized hospital of about 400 beds will have a staff of several hundred physicians and 1,200 to 1,500 paramedics divided among some 60 medical and paramedical specialties. Each specialty has its own knowledge, its own training, its own language. In each specialty, especially the paramedical ones like the clinical lab and physical therapy, there is a head person who is a working specialist rather than a full-time manager. The head of each specialty reports directly to the top, and there is little middle management. A good deal of the work is done in ad hoc teams as required by an individual patient's diagnosis and condition.

A large symphony orchestra is even more instructive, since for some works there may be a few hundred musicians on stage playing together. According to organization theory then, there should be several group vice president conductors and perhaps a half-dozen division VP conductors. But that's not how it works. There is only the conductor-CEO—and every one of the musicians plays directly to that person without an intermediary. And each is a high-grade specialist, indeed an artist.

But the best example of a large and successful information-based organization, and one without any middle management at all, is the British civil administration in India.[1]

The British ran the Indian subcontinent for 200 years, from the middle of the eighteenth century through World War II, without making any fundamental changes in organization structure or administrative policy. The Indian civil service never had more than 1,000 members to administer the vast and densely populated subcontinent—a tiny fraction (at most 1%) of the legions of Confucian mandarins and palace eunuchs employed next door to administer a not-much-more populous China. Most of the Britishers were quite young; a 30-year-old was a survivor, especially in the early years. Most lived alone in isolated outposts with the nearest countryman a day or two of travel away, and for the first hundred years there was no telegraph or railroad.

The organization structure was totally flat. Each district officer reported directly to the "Coo," the provincial political secretary. And since there were nine provinces, each political secretary had at least 100 people reporting directly to him, many times what the doctrine of the span of control would allow. Nevertheless, the system worked remarkably well, in large part because it was designed to ensure that each of its members had the information he needed to do his job.

Each month the district officer spent a whole day writing a full report to the political secretary in the provincial capital. He discussed each of his principal tasks—there were only four, each clearly delineated. He put down in detail what he had expected would happen with respect to each of them, what actually did happen, and why, if there was a discrepancy, the two differed. Then he wrote down what he expected would happen in the ensuing month with respect to each key task and what he was going to do about it, asked questions about policy, and commented on long-term opportunities, threats, and needs. In turn, the political secretary "minuted" every one of those reports—that is, he wrote back a full comment.

On the basis of these examples, what can we say about the requirements of the information-based organization? And what are its management problems likely to be? Let's look first at the requirements. Several hundred musicians and their CEO, the conductor, can play together because they all have the same score. It tells both flutist and timpanist what to play and when. And it tells the conductor what to expect from each and when. Similarly, all the specialists in the hospital share a common mission: the care and cure of the sick. The diagnosis is their "score"; it dictates specific action for the X-ray lab, the dietitian, the physical therapist, and the rest of the medical team.

Information-based organizations, in other words, require clear, simple, common objectives that translate into particular actions. At the same time, however, as these examples indicate, information-based organizations also need concentration on one objective or, at most, on a few.

Because the "players" in an information-based organization are specialists, they cannot be told how to do their work. There are probably few orchestra conductors who could coax even one note out of a French horn, let alone show the horn player how to do it. But the conductor can focus the horn player's skill and knowledge on the musicians' joint performance. And this focus is what the leaders of an information-based business must be able to achieve.

Yet a business has no "score" to play by except the score it writes as it plays. And whereas neither a first-rate performance of a symphony nor a miserable one will change what the composer wrote, the performance of a business continually creates new and different scores against which its performance is assessed. So an information-based business must be structured around goals that clearly state management's performance expectations for the enterprise and for each part and specialist and around organized feedback that compares results with these performance expectations so that every member can exercise self-control.

The other requirement of an information-based organization is that everyone take information responsibility. The bassoonist in the orchestra does so every time she plays a note. Doctors and paramedics work with an elaborate system of reports and an information center, the nurse's station on the patient's floor. The district officer in India acted on this responsibility every time he filed a report.

The key to such a system is that everyone asks: Who in this organization depends on me for what information? And on whom, in turn, do I depend? Each person's list will always include superiors and subordinates. But the most important names on it will be those of colleagues, people with whom one's primary relationship is coordination. The relationship of the internist, the surgeon, and the anesthesiologist is one example. But the relationship of a biochemist, a pharmacologist, the medical director in charge of clinical testing, and a marketing specialist in a pharmaceutical company is no different. It, too, requires each party to take the fullest information responsibility.

Information responsibility to others is increasingly understood, especially in middle-sized companies. But information responsibility to oneself is still largely neglected. That is, everyone in an organization should constantly be thinking through what information he or she needs to do the job and to make a contribution.

This may well be the most radical break with the way even the most highly computerized businesses are still being run today. There, people either assume the more data, the more information—which was a perfectly valid assumption yesterday when data were scarce, but leads to data overload and information blackout now that they are plentiful. Or they believe that information specialists know what data executives and professionals need in order to have information. But information specialists are tool makers. They can tell us what tool to use to hammer upholstery nails into a chair. We need to decide whether we should be upholstering a chair at all.

Executives and professional specialists need to think through what information is for them, what data they need: first, to know what they are doing; then, to be able to decide what they should be doing; and finally, to appraise how well they are doing. Until this happens MIS departments are likely to remain cost centers rather than become the result centers they could be.

Most large businesses have little in common with the examples we have been looking at. Yet to remain competitive—maybe even to survive—they will have to convert themselves into information-based organizations, and fairly quickly. They will have to change old habits and acquire new ones. And the more successful a company has been, the more difficult and painful this process is apt to be. It will threaten the jobs, status, and opportunities of a good many people in the organization, especially the long-serving, middle-aged people in middle management who tend to be the least mobile and to feel most secure in their work, their positions, their relationships, and their behavior.

The information-based organization will also pose its own special management problems. I see as particularly critical:

1. Developing rewards, recognition, and career opportunities for specialists.
2. Creating unified vision in an organization of specialists.

3. Devising the management structure for an organization of task forces.
4. Ensuring the supply, preparation, and testing of top management people.

Bassoonists presumably neither want nor expect to be anything but bassoonists. Their career opportunities consist of moving from second bassoon to first bassoon and perhaps of moving from a second-rank orchestra to a better, more prestigious one. Similarly, many medical technologists neither expect nor want to be anything but medical technologists. Their career opportunities consist of a fairly good chance of moving up to senior technician, and a very slim chance of becoming lab director. For those who make it to lab director, about 1 out of every 25 or 30 technicians, there is also the opportunity to move to a bigger, richer hospital. The district officer in India had practically no chance for professional growth except possibly to be relocated, after a three-year stint, to a bigger district.

Opportunities for specialists in an information-based business organization should be more plentiful than they are in an orchestra or hospital, let alone in the Indian civil service. But as in these organizations, they will primarily be opportunities for advancement within the specialty, and for limited advancement at that. Advancement into "management" will be the exception, for the simple reason that there will be far fewer middle-management positions to move into. This contrasts sharply with the traditional organization where, except in the research lab, the main line of advancement in rank is out of the specialty and into general management.

More than 30 years ago General Electric tackled this problem by creating "parallel opportunities" for "individual professional contributors." Many companies have followed this example. But professional specialists themselves have largely rejected it as a solution. To them—and to their management colleagues—the only meaningful opportunities are promotions into management. And the prevailing compensation structure in practically all businesses reinforces this attitude because it is heavily biased towards managerial positions and titles.

There are no easy answers to this problem. Some help may come from looking at large law and consulting firms, where even the most senior partners tend to be specialists, and associates who will not make partner are outplaced fairly early on. But whatever scheme is eventually developed will work only if the values and compensation structure of business are drastically changed.

The second challenge that management faces is giving its organization of specialists a common vision, a view of the whole.

In the Indian civil service, the district officer was expected to see the "whole" of his district. But to enable him to concentrate on it, the government services that arose one after the other in the nineteenth century (forestry, irrigation, the archaeological survey, public health and sanitation, roads) were organized outside the administrative structure, and had virtually no contact with the district officer. This meant that the district officer became increasingly isolated from the activities that often had the greatest impact on—and the greatest importance for—his district. In the end, only the provincial government or the central government in Delhi had a view of the "whole," and it was an increasingly abstract one at that.

A business simply cannot function this way. It needs a view of the whole and a focus on the whole to be shared among a great many of its professional specialists, certainly among the senior ones. And yet it will have to accept, indeed will have to foster, the pride and professionalism of its specialists—if only because, in the absence of opportunities to move into middle management, their motivation must come from that pride and professionalism.

One way to foster professionalism, of course, is through assignments to task forces. And the information-based business will use more and more smaller self-governing units, assigning them tasks tidy enough for "a good man to get his arms around," as the old phrase has it. But to what extent should information-based businesses rotate performing specialists out of their specialties and into new ones? And to what extent will top management have to accept as its top priority making and maintaining a common vision across professional specialties?

Heavy reliance on task-force teams assuages one problem. But it aggravates another: the management structure of the information-based organization. Who will the business's managers be? Will they be task-force leaders? Or will there be a two-headed monster—a specialist structure, comparable, perhaps, to the way attending physicians function in a hospital, and an administrative structure of task-force leaders?

The decisions we face on the role and function of the task-force leaders are risky and controversial. Is theirs a permanent assignment, analogous to the job of the supervisory nurse in the hospital? Or is it a function of the task that changes as the task does? Is it an assignment or a position? Does it carry any rank at all? And if it does, will the task-force leaders become in time what the product managers have been at Procter & Gamble: the basic units of management and the company's field officers? Might the task-force leaders eventually replace department heads and vice presidents?

Signs of every one of these developments exist, but there is neither a clear trend nor much understanding as to what each entails. Yet each would give rise to a different organizational structure from any we are familiar with.

Finally, the toughest problem will probably be to ensure the supply, preparation, and testing of top management people. This is, of course, an old and central dilemma as well as a major reason for the general acceptance of decentralization in large businesses in the last 40 years. But the existing business organization has a great many middle-management positions that are supposed to prepare and test a person. As a result, there are usually a good many people to choose from when filling a senior management slot. With the number of middle-management positions sharply cut, where will the information-based organization's top executives come from? What will be their preparation? How will they have been tested?

Decentralization into autonomous units will surely be even more critical than it is now. Perhaps we will even copy the German *Gruppe* in which the decentralized units are set up as separate companies with their own top managements. The Germans use this model precisely because of their tradition of promoting people in their specialties, especially in research and engineering; if they did not have available commands in near-independent subsidiaries to put people in, they would have little opportunity to train and test their most promising professionals. These subsidiaries are thus somewhat like the farm teams of a major-league baseball club.

We may also find that more and more top management jobs in big companies are filled by hiring people away from smaller companies. This is the way that major orchestras get their conductors—a young conductor earns his or her spurs in a small orchestra or opera house, only to be hired away by a larger one. And the heads of a good many large hospitals have had similar careers.

Can business follow the example of the orchestra and hospital where top management has become a separate career? Conductors and hospital administrators come out of courses in conducting or schools of hospital administration respectively. We see something of this sort in France, where large companies are often run by men who have spent their entire previous careers in government service. But in most countries this would be unacceptable to the organization (only France has the *mystique* of the *grandes écoles*). And even in France, businesses, especially large ones, are becoming too demanding to be run by people without firsthand experience and a proven success record.

Thus the entire top management process—preparation, testing, succession—will become even more problematic than it already is. There will be a growing need for experienced businesspeople to go back to school. And business schools will surely need to work out what successful professional specialists must know to prepare themselves for high-level positions as *business* executives and *business* leaders.

Since modern business enterprise first arose, after the Civil War in the United States and the Franco-Prussian War in Europe, there have been two major evolutions in the concept and structure of organizations. The first took place in the ten years between 1895 and 1905. It distinguished management from ownership and established management as work and task in its own right. This happened first in Germany, when Georg Siemens, the founder and head of Germany's premier bank, *Deutsche Bank,* saved the electrical apparatus company his cousin Werner had founded after Werner's sons and heirs had mismanaged it into near collapse. By threatening to cut off the bank's loans, he forced his cousins to turn the company's management over to professionals. A little later, J.P. Morgan, Andrew Carnegie, and John D. Rockefeller, Sr. followed suit in their massive restructurings of U.S. railroads and industries.

The second evolutionary change took place 20 years later. The development of what we still see as the modern corporation began with Pierre S. du Pont's restructuring of his family company in the early twenties and continued with Alfred P. Sloan's redesign of General Motors a few years later. This introduced the command-and-control organization of today, with its emphasis on decentralization, central service staffs, personnel management, the whole apparatus of budgets and controls, and the important distinction between policy and operations. This stage culminated in the massive reorganization of General Electric in the early 1950s, an action that perfected the model most big businesses around the world (including Japanese organizations) still follow.[2]

Now we are entering a third period of change: the shift from the command-and-control organization, the organization of departments and divisions, to the information-based organization, the organization of knowledge specialists. We can perceive, though perhaps only dimly, what this organization will look like. We can identify some of its main characteristics and requirements. We can point to central problems of values, structure, and behavior. But the job of actually building the information-based organization is still ahead of us—it is the managerial challenge of the future.

Notes

1. The standard account is Philip Woodruff, *The Men Who Ruled India,* especially the first volume, *The Founders of Modern India* (New York: St. Martin's, 1954). How the system worked day by day is charmingly told in *Sowing* (New York: Harcourt Brace Jovanovich, 1962), volume one of the autobiography of Leonard Woolf (Virginia Woolf's husband).

2. Alfred D. Chandler, Jr. has masterfully chronicled the process in his two books *Strategy and Structure* (Cambridge: MIT Press, 1962) and *The Visible Hand* (Cambridge: Harvard University Press, 1977)—surely the best studies of the administrative history of any major institution. The process itself and its results were presented and analyzed in two of my books: *The Concept of the Corporation* (New York: John Day, 1946) and *The Practice of Management* (New York: Harper Brothers, 1954).

2
How Networks Reshape Organizations—for Results

Ram Charan

In a world of increasing global competition and unrelenting change, many companies have been strong on crafting vision and strategy and weak on delivering results. As they struggle to improve their capacity to execute, senior managers use words like trust, teamwork, and boundaryless cooperation to describe the organizations they aspire to build.

Recently a new term—networks—has entered the vocabulary of corporate renewal. Yet there remains much confusion over just what networks are and how they operate. In some companies, networks imply a set of external relationships—a global web of alliances and joint ventures. In others, networks mean informal ties among managers—floating teams that work across functions and maneuver through bureaucracy. Still other companies define networks as new ways for executives to share information, using management information systems, video conferencing, and other such tools.

I have spent four years observing and participating in the creation of networks in ten companies based in North America and Europe. (See the Appendix.) These companies are clear about why they are creating networks, what networks are, and how they operate. To them, networks are designed to build the central competitive advantage of the 1990s—superior execution in a volatile environment. No traditional corporate structure, regardless of how decluttered or delayered, can muster the speed, flexibility, and focus that success today

---

Author's note: I wish to acknowledge the collegial support of professors Noel Tichy, Hiro Takeuchi, and Michael Brimm.

demands. Networks are faster, smarter, and more flexible than reorganizations or downsizings—dislocating steps that cause confusion, sap emotional energy, and seldom produce sustainable results.

A network reshapes how and by whom essential business decisions get made. It integrates decisions horizontally at the lowest managerial levels and with superior speed. In effect, a network identifies the "small company inside the large company" and empowers it to make the four-dimensional trade-offs—among functions, business units, geography, and global customers—that determine success in the marketplace. It enables the right people in the organization to converge faster and in a more focused way than the competition on operating priorities determined by the imperatives of meeting customer needs and building concrete advantage.

A network is a recognized group of managers assembled by the CEO and the senior executive team. The number of managers involved almost never exceeds 100 and can be fewer than 25—even in global companies with tens of thousands of employees. The members are drawn from across the company's functions, business units, and geography, and from different levels of the hierarchy. Membership criteria are simple but subtle: What select group of managers, by virtue of their business skills and judgment, personal motivations and drive, control of resources, and positions at the juncture of critical information flows are uniquely qualified to shape and deliver on the corporate strategy? Managers who pass these tests become the core network, hold regular meetings, form subnetworks for critical operating tasks, and use conference calls, electronic mail, and computerized information systems to share information.

Networks really begin to matter when they affect patterns of relationships and change behavior—change driven by the frequency, intensity, and honesty of the dialogue among managers on specific priorities. Networks are designed to empower managers to talk openly, candidly, and emotionally without fear, to enrich the quality of their decisions, to test each other's motives and build trust, and to encourage them to evaluate problems from the perspective of what is right for the customer and the company rather than from narrow functional or departmental interests.

Consider three snapshots of emerging networks:

At Conrail, the freight transportation company based in Philadelphia, 19 middle managers drive the company's key operating decisions. The network, called the operating committee, meets for up to two hours on

Monday mornings to review and make decisions on a wide range of tactical issues—searching for the right mix of price, delivery schedule, and consistency of service that meets the needs of important customers at low cost and that generates competitive returns in a capital-intensive business. The operating committee is also developing a five-year business plan—a first-of-its-kind analysis meant to generate radical new approaches to important segments of the business. Senior executives join in the dialogues of the operating committee and receive briefings on the evolving substance of the strategic plan, but they neither chair the sessions nor dominate the deliberations.

In Montreal, Royal Bank of Canada, one of the largest and most profitable banks in North America, has embraced management reforms that promise to accelerate and sharpen implementation of its retail strategy. The reforms grew out of a six-month study by a network of 12 managers. They conducted a candid and exhaustive review of the most important operational and human resource issues facing the retail bank. The members, called the community banking team, were not senior executives; rather, they were field officers from across Canada—middle managers with titles such as vice president for retail banking in Alberta and area manager for North Winnipeg. They presented the results of their study, including 17 concrete proposals for change, to a major conference of bank executives and other senior officers in May 1990. Since then, senior management has worked with the group's leadership to implement the plan. One goal is to turn all of the bank's area managers into a network—a close-knit group that routinely shares best practices, learns from each other's problems, and works together to understand the business more deeply.

At the United Kingdom headquarters of Dun & Bradstreet Europe, a "development network" evaluates and monitors new business-information products and the customization of existing products. For years, D&B Europe has faced the tensions that afflict so many cross-border and cross-cultural organizations. Its computer databases, technical staff, and marketing group are centralized in the U.K.—a sensible structure given D&B's position as the only pan-European competitor in its business. But centralization has made it harder and more time-consuming to tailor Europewide products to the needs of local customers and to set priorities among competing projects in different countries.

The development network is designed to make these trade-offs more quickly and more skillfully. It is neither a new layer of bureaucracy nor a means to wrest power from the functional organizations. Rather, a core of 12 or so key players meet weekly to monitor the performance of the development process, identify barriers, and devise ways to remove them. One of the network's first steps was to create an investment-management function responsible for specifying which projects get done, in what order, and how quickly—in ways that meet the needs of customers and countries but that also reflect corporate goals and strategies. The network reports to the field through a designated representative in each of the 13 country organizations, thus increasing the speed of communication and reducing confusion. Some members act as business project managers, with complete cross-functional responsibility for the success of major projects.

These three companies, along with the others I have observed, share a common understanding of the urgency and volatility of their competitive environment and the need to break with decision making based purely on hierarchical and functional authority. They are also clear about how networks differ from teams, cross-functional task forces, or other ad hoc innovations designed to break hierarchy. First, networks are not temporary. Most task forces assemble to solve a specific problem and then disband and return to business as usual. They do not sustain change in the behavior of the organization. Members of a network, on the other hand, identify with it and with each other. The frequency and honesty of their dialogues reshape personal relationships. Continuous practice over a sustained period of time builds a shared understanding of the business. Networks even affect how their members move through the company. Managers' performance and promotability is evaluated with respect to their contribution to the network and sometimes by the network itself.

Second, unlike most teams and task forces, networks do not merely solve problems that have been defined for them. Networks are dynamic; they take initiative. They become the vehicle to redirect the flows of information and decisions, the uses of power, and the sources of feedback within the hierarchy. They become a new way of doing business and a new operating mechanism for individual managers to make their presence felt.

Finally, networks make demands on senior management that teams and task forces do not. CEOs and their direct reports no longer define their jobs as making all substantive operating decisions on their own. Rather, their primary job is shaping the processes and personal relationships that allow other managers, the members of the network, to make decisions. To be sure, top managers still set goals and make all kinds of decisions—about personnel, resource levels, acquisitions and divestitures, upgrading technical competences. But they must also become more adept at diagnosing the behavior of their organization, building relationships among key managers, modifying measures and rewards, and linking all of these "soft" changes with the company's economic performance.

This article examines the process of building and sustaining networks in large organizations—a process that begins at the top. Senior managers work as change agents to create a new "social architecture" that becomes the basis of the network. Once the network is in place, they play at least three additional roles. First, they define with clarity and specificity the business outputs they expect of the network and the time frame in which they expect the network to deliver. Second, they guarantee the visibility and free flow of information to all members of the network and promote simultaneous communication (dialogue) among them. Finally, they develop new criteria and processes for performance evaluation and promotion that emphasize horizontal collaboration through networks. They openly share these performance measurements with all members of the network and adjust them in response to changing circumstances. Let us explore these areas one at a time.

Social Architecture and Change

The foundation of a network is its social architecture, which differs in important ways from structure. Organizational structure refers to the systems of vertical power and functional authority through which the routine work of the organization gets done. Social architecture refers to the operating mechanisms through which key managers make trade-offs and to the flow of information, power, and trust among these managers that shapes how those trade-offs get made. Social architecture does not concern itself merely with who is in the loop or the process by which the loop forms. Social architecture concerns *what happens* when the network comes together—the intensity, substance, output, and quality of interactions—as well as the frequency and character of dialogue among members on a day-to-day basis.

A robust social architecture does not imply absolute harmony among peers. Indeed, the single most important role of networks is to surface and resolve conflict—to identify legitimate disagreements between functions, regions, and business units and to make difficult trade-offs quickly and skillfully. A robust social architecture encourages members of the network to become mature and constructive in their approach to conflict, to direct their energies toward the substance of disagreements rather than toward personal clashes and politics, to search for creative solutions rather than to look over each other's shoulders, and to identify new challenges.

Senior management drives the process of building a new social architecture. The first step is design. The CEO must identify the important decision makers in the organization, assemble them into a network, and communicate it throughout the company. This can be a sensitive step since the process of including some managers in a network necessarily means excluding others. And membership seldom relates directly to hierarchy or seniority. Indeed, the criteria are specific to each company, a function of the unique challenges facing the business and the strengths and weaknesses of the managers themselves. The basic objective, though, is to find the right mix of managers whose business skills, personal motivations, and functional expertise allow them to drive the enterprise.

At Conrail, for example, the core network comprises fewer than 50 managers drawn from three layers below the CEO. The operating committee is a subset of this core network. Explains James Hagen, Conrail's CEO: "There are no more than 25 people in this company whose close, horizontal collaboration will have a dramatic impact on the bottom line. There are the seven assistant vice presidents in the marketing department responsible for our lines of business—steel, autos, intermodal, and so on. There are the six general managers responsible for railroad operations in different parts of our service territory. There are some key people at headquarters—the chief mechanical officer and the chief engineer, the head of customer service—as well as the senior management group. On their own, none of these managers can move the business decisively. As a network, they are already making a visible difference."

As the social architecture begins to change, the performance of managers whose behavior hurts the network becomes visible. This raises a second crucial role for senior management—dealing with mismatches by reassigning the problem executives. Networks play to the best instincts of people. Most middle managers don't resist change. They want to cooperate, share information, be open and secure in their interactions with peers. Networks quickly surface people of exceptional competence, informal leaders whose talents have been hidden behind functional or hierarchical walls. They also reveal managers whose business skills or personal style are mismatched with the needs of the network, people who simply can't make the change to a new way of doing business. These managers can have a toxic effect on the rest of the group. At nearly every company I have studied, at least one senior executive (but never more than two) has had to be reassigned or dismissed because of an inhibiting presence and unwillingness to change. With respect to social architecture, one bad apple *can* spoil the whole bunch, especially if that person is in a position of vertical power in the organization.

Third, and most important, building the social architecture requires an intense and sustained focus on the fundamentals of the business rather than abstract appeals to culture, teamwork, or values. Companies do not build networks so that managers will "like" one another or behave like "family." Networks are designed to develop professional trust and empathy and a richer and more widely shared understanding of the specifics of the business. No generic change program imported from the outside can generate such understanding. When network members identify real business problems, diagnose them together, create a broad and common base of specific information, and reach conclusions that reflect the pressures and capabilities of multiple functions and geographic units, they become more skillful at making trade-offs, and more trusting of one another. The keys are immersion, concentration, practice, and the simultaneity of information flows.

The rise of networking at Conrail illustrates the change process associated with building a new social architecture. The operating committee, which officially took shape in late 1990, is the railroad's core network for profitability—the central operating mechanism through which important business trade-offs get made. All told, though, 46 managers from around the company worked for two years to build the trust and confidence necessary to support a departure as radical as the operating committee. The goal was to create a new social architecture among these managers—a real challenge given Conrail's past.

Conrail is an unlikely candidate for management innovation. No industry compares with railroads for its legacy of rigid hierarchy and authoritarian management. And no major railroad compares with Conrail for its commitment to relentless and painful cost cutting and retrenchment. Since 1976, when Conrail was created from the remains of the bankrupt Penn Central and several smaller lines, employment has fallen from roughly 100,000 workers to fewer than 28,000.

These are not ideal circumstances in which to build trust and professional empathy. James Hagen, who became CEO in May 1989, understood that he could not simply assemble a group of middle-level managers into a network and expect them to erase decades of learned behavior. The change process began with the selection of two core groups of managers. Conrail has 450 or so top-line managers, people whose decision-making authority directly or indirectly affects operating income. Top management selected fewer than 50 from this group to serve in the two networks. The senior planning team consisted of 13 executives, essentially the company's top officers, although it did deliberately include two lower level managers. The second network, the strategy managers group (SMG), consisted of about 35 executives from many functions and departments. This is where judgment became important. Top management developed a statement of its selection criteria for the SMG: "The smallest working group whose interlinking can significantly affect both the operation and selling of our basic services." In practice, the criteria meant that SMG membership was weighted toward field managers rather than corporate staff and toward field managers with direct responsibility for pricing service, meeting customer demands, or running the railroad. (Later, as the new social architecture began to evolve, some staff members shifted to line jobs.).

The creation of the network was followed by a series of initiatives designed to change the character of the dialogue and interactions among the members. Some of the techniques were simple, almost quaint. For example, the company published a directory of the SMG members complete with photographs and descriptions of career histories and personal interests. The directory reinforced the SMG as a living network rather than a one-time task force or team. It helped create an identity for a group that had never assembled together before. In fact, several members, despite their complementary roles in the company, had never even met one another.

More substantively, the two groups began a series of meetings, first separately, then together, to diagnose the future of Conrail. At all times, both groups focused tightly on the business itself—there was no wilderness experience, team building, or other generic exercises. For example, the SMG identified nine priority issues and created small teams (or subnetworks) to study them and report back with action-oriented recommendations. The projects included some of the most politically sensitive problems inside the railroad: work force reduction, billing quality, and managerial rewards and evaluation.

These teams became the building blocks of the new social architecture. Small groups of managers, most of whom had barely spoken to each other before the creation of the SMG, devoted hundreds of hours to analyzing real problems and convincing the senior planning team to endorse their recommendations. This investment of time (over and above each member's day-to-day responsibilities) and the total immersion that the subnetworks required created personal bonds of enormous strength.

What's more, the subnetworks embraced rather than avoided conflict—a critical test of the members' good faith and capacity to air differences openly. For example, one group studied customer service at Conrail, specifically, whether and how to consolidate the three separate departments and ten different locations responsible for resolving billing disputes, tracking freight, and otherwise interacting with customers. Customer service had been a sensitive issue for many years; past efforts to consolidate it had been squelched after painful and demoralizing turf battles.

The group faced those turf battles squarely. Each of the six members had a direct or indirect functional stake in customer service: the general manager for information systems, the assistant vice president for customer service, a regional general manager, the assistant vice president for labor relations, the corporate treasurer, and the general manager for stations. Needless to say, a recommendation to consolidate would require compromise among these previously warring factions. But there was more. A move to consolidate would also require two members of the group to eliminate their own jobs; their positions would become redundant. The fact that these two managers took that step and spent several months with unclear prospects about their futures was a powerful statement of the group's capacity to resolve conflict.

The subnetwork also reckoned with conflict vis-à-vis senior management. During the course of their analysis, the group learned that certain senior executives were working behind the scenes to oppose consolidation. At an interim presentation to the SMG, the team members decided to take a stand. They proposed that they dissolve rather than make recommendations destined to fail. The rest of the SMG insisted that the subnetwork stay together and make its presentation to the senior planning team. It did, and after much debate, top management agreed to make the change.

In November 1990, Conrail announced it would consolidate all customer service activities at a new facility near Pittsburgh. To the outside world, this was a reasonable and welcome step to improve service. To the SMG, it was a major victory and a sharp break with the past—the sort of development that builds professional trust, unleashes energy, and, over time, changes behavior.

The Power of Specificity

As the Conrail experience demonstrates, networking represents a decisive break with the past. Although it plays to people's best instincts, it is a demanding journey that requires managers to unlearn attitudes and behaviors reinforced over decades. No amount of general debate over business strategy and vision can build the trust and confidence required for new behaviors to emerge. All too often, managers invest huge amounts of time and energy reaching agreement on vision without investing in the truly hard work—becoming aligned on the nitty-gritty trade-offs and time pressures required to deliver on the vision. Agreement without alignment seldom changes behavior. Instead, it generates frustration, cynicism, and complacency.

That's why senior executives must define with clarity and specificity the business outputs they expect of the network and the time frame (usually less than six months) in which they expect the network to deliver. Such precision forces managers to reckon with the day-to-day realities of the business. Meanwhile, the dialogue and debate required to shape the targets builds commitment and confidence. Specificity allows the members of the network to see that they are making real change and that the change is linked directly to the improved economic performance of the organization. The more visible and persuasive this evidence, the more intense the personal commitments of the members to expanding the initiatives of the network. Over time, making visible progress on economic-priority items generates emotional energy and builds commitment.

The remarkable effectiveness of the Royal Bank of Canada's community banking team is a case in point. In less than one year, a network of 12 managers, most of them middle managers drawn from the field, made a mark on some of the most sensitive management issues in the retail operation: performance measures, spans of control, training and development. How did it succeed? By producing concrete deliverables, developing techniques to measure the organization's support for their proposals, and setting specific dates for implementation. (See "The Power of Specificity—Royal Bank of Canada.")

The Power of Specificity—Royal Bank of Canada

In the spring of 1990, 350 Royal Bank managers gathered in Montreal for a first-of-its-kind (and size) leadership conference. There the community banking team, a 12-member group assembled by chairman Allan Taylor the previous November, unveiled its six-month study. The team's charter was ambitious: to evaluate how well the bank was executing a bold new retail strategy and to recommend without limitations new initiatives to drive execution.

The strategy had been in place for several years. Its main organizational thrust was to increase the authority and prominence of the bank's area managers, senior field officers responsible for the performance of groups of bank branches. Top management was genuinely committed to trans-forming how operating decisions were made. Indeed, the plan could have been a primer on translating the abstract rhetoric of "empowerment" into tangible management principles. It emphasized the importance of personalized leadership by area managers, local market intelligence, inter-active planning driven by the field, and local autonomy to provide area managers with the flexibility they needed.

Precisely because the retail strategy was such a departure and the team's charter so ambitious, there was a risk that the final report would disappoint, especially since no business crisis was evident. Royal Bank is the largest bank in Canada and the third largest in North America. It is also one of the most profitable. Its 1990 net income was nearly $1 billion, more than any U.S. commercial bank, and its return on assets and equity consistently rank it high among North America's leaders. Retail is at the heart of this outstanding performance; Royal Bank has more than 7.5 million customers, 1,600 branches and 3,100 cash machines.

But the report does not disappoint. It is the most candid analysis of Royal Bank's retail operations ever developed. Within a year of its com-pletion, the bank had implemented nearly all of the team's proposals. The work of 12 managers, most of them drawn from the field, it is reshaping some of the most sensitive management issues in the retail operation: performance measures, spans of control, training and development. Why? One reason stands out: by producing specific deliverables, setting precise dates for implementation, and developing ways to measure progress, the community banking team embraced the power of specificity and used it to advantage.

The team's written report ran less than 100 pages, and its presen-tation to the spring conference (along with group processing of the presentation) lasted three hours. Packed into this limited space and time was a penetrating analysis filled with evaluations of particular incidents, documents, and success stories. There were no abstract calls for greater empowerment, more resources, of a deeper commitment to customer service.

Each of the team's proposals (there were 17 in all) included numbers, targets, or specific language that left no room for ambiguity or misinterpretation. For example:

- Limit the number of branches under the control of an area manager to between 7 and 12.
- Create formal mechanisms (conferences, newsletters, computer systems) to allow area managers to share expertise and competitor intelligence more systematically.
- Guarantee 15 days of training per year for existing area managers and launch Area Manager University, an intensive series of courses and training modules. Provide resources so that all new area managers would be graduates of the university by the spring of 1991.
- Institute standard, minimum autonomies for all area managers, including the right to hire, transfer, and evaluate employees below a certain pay grade, and the right to freely substitute between certain expense categories within the overall budget constraints. Negotiate even greater autonomies with high-performing area managers.

Of course, the very specificity of these recommendations meant they were likely to be controversial. So the community banking team, working with the top managers who designed the leadership conference, created special group-processing techniques for immediate feedback from the group of 350. For example, the group was divided into sets of ten, each set reflecting a mix of hierarchy, function, and geography. These sets debated the report and were invited to offer feedback.

Here too clarity played a role. The team did not merely ask for general reactions. Rather, personal computers allowed the 350 attendees to "vote" on a series of questions designed to measure their enthusiasm about, confidence in, and commitment to the proposals. The voting was confidential, but the results could be tabulated by function, geography, or hierarchical position. The community banking team (and the entire leadership conference) could see immediately whether managers in Western Canada reacted differently from those in Montreal or whether headquarters executives were more strongly in favor of a proposal than field managers.

This detailed feedback was a vital source of information for the community banking team. It also energized and built the commitment of the audience. Never before had such a large group of executives been privy to such candid, detailed analyses and proposals.

The final step was implementation. The day after the leadership conference, the community banking team held an all-day session with Royal Bank's top 50 executives. This group of 50 had been meeting on a regular basis for several years, working to build their own horizontal collaboration and trust. By securing the collective commitment of these executives, the community banking team acquired powerful allies. Moreover, for each of the 17 proposals, at least two managers—one from the community banking group and one from the group of 50—accepted deadlines and personal responsibilities for implementation. Successful implementation also became part of the annual objectives by which the senior executives were evaluated.

The results have been encouraging. By the middle of 1991, all geographic areas had been broken down into units small enough that an area manager can visit every branch at least once a week. Area Manager University is up and running, and the first graduates have completed their course work. The retail bank has implemented standard "key result areas" so that all area managers know the criteria on which they will be measured. Nearly two-thirds of the area managers have negotiated extended autonomies with senior management, and negotiations continue with the remaining area managers.

The work of the community banking team is just a beginning. The ultimate goal is for area managers across Canada to function as a horizontal network: sharing expertise, transferring best practices, learning from mistakes. In fact, all 175 area managers will come together in November 1991 for their first-ever meeting. The concrete, measurable, and substantive achievements of the community banking team will serve as an encouraging and energizing backdrop.

The Conrail operating committee is another example. After only six months, the network can point to concrete achievements. For example, the introduction of a computer-based simulation model is helping to redesign the company's huge intermodal (truck-to-train) business. But all 19 members of the network are clear about their ultimate goal—to move the railroad's operating ratio to 80% from the 1990 level of more than 87%. This is not an arbitrary target. The ratio, which measures operating expenses as a percentage of revenues, is the company's central indicator of profitability. Conrail needs a ratio of 80% for earnings to exceed its cost of capital and thus for the railroad to remain self-sustaining as a financial enterprise.

Every member of the operating committee (and the broader group of 46) understands the logic behind this target and the urgency of hitting it. The group monitors the ratio as a way to track its progress, and senior management uses specially designed feedback instruments to monitor the network's confidence that it will achieve the target. The fact that the ratio has begun to move even under adverse economic circumstances (most recently the ratio was at 84%) has been an enormous source of emotional energy and confidence—evidence that the network has begun to shape the company's economic performance.

Richard Archer, president of Dun & Bradstreet Europe, has chosen to personalize the D&B network's commitment to clear performance targets. The company's development subnetwork is one of several that Archer has assembled to meet the new cross-border competition in Europe. The challenges facing D&B are similar to those facing all companies struggling to globalize their operations: How does the organization strike the right balance between the power of centralization and the responsiveness of decentralization? How do managers balance the demands of cross-border customers, who expect uniform service at the same price everywhere, with the demands of national customers in what remain very different markets? What makes D&B Europe noteworthy is the clarity with which Archer and the network are addressing these issues.

The network-building process began in January 1989 and, at the time, involved 45 continental managers. Through a series of meetings, this group refined the company's strategic direction and business priorities. Each session strove to develop greater clarity than the one before it, and by late that year, Archer was able to develop a mission statement for D&B Europe. In early 1990, at a three-day workshop, he shared the statement with 98 top managers across all countries and functions, and revised the statement based on their feedback. At the end of that session, he assembled three cross-border project teams (not unlike Conrail's SMG subnetworks) to attack the highest priority issues facing the organization. Finally, drawing on the project reports and the revised mission statement, Archer worked with ten senior managers to craft a document that communicates the tangible and measurable results the network is expected to produce. He insisted that the final document run no more than one page—a discipline that forced even greater clarity and precision—and then published it as his *personal* goals for 1991.

Again, the development subnetwork is a case in point. The network is clear about its goals: reduce lead times by 50%; eliminate 80% of the old system's "process loss"; respond to all development requests (usually modifying existing products) within ten days. The results have been equally clear. Overall lead times for new products have been reduced from one year to six months. The D&B technical center has cleared a backlog of 100 requests from the country organizations; a country manager who puts in a development request can now expect a response in less than three weeks. In 1991, for the first time, D&B Europe agreed to a detailed schedule for the implementation of new products. To date, all important deadlines have been met.

To be sure, the process of settling on meaningful specificity in time-based goals and outcomes is tedious and emotionally demanding. Many managers, especially senior managers, find it intellectually un-appealing—less exhilarating, say, than crafting a stirring vision statement or a bold corporate strategy. (As one CEO noted, "There is a fine line between vision and hallucination.") Specificity requires dialogue, repetition, negotiation, candor, practice. Over time, though, these are the investments that generate alignment on and commitment to the details of execution. And it is precisely the speed and quality of exe-cution—the trade-offs among functions, business units, geography, and customers—that the network is designed to change.

Information—Visible and Simultaneous

No organization of two or more people can function without infor-mation. Indeed, in any organization, the character of information flows is one of the most critical variables determining the speed and accuracy with which decisions get made—and thus the quality of execution. Two companies with identical structures will behave very differently based on the answer to a simple question: Who receives what information when, and why do these people (as opposed to others) receive it? In most large companies, the flow of information remains incomplete and sequential and thus prone to distortion and manipulation.

In a network, especially a global network that extends across bor-ders, information must be visible and simultaneous. When members of the network receive the *same* information at the *same* time, and receive it quickly, business decisions take on a different character. Disagreement over substance no longer generates damaging personal conflicts or organizational politics; personal conflicts arise when infor-mation flows are selective or secret. More to the point, disagreements themselves are reduced. Most members of a network, when faced with an impartial set of facts, tend to arrive at roughly the same business options for a given set of goals. The visibility and simultaneity of information improves the quality of decisions.

Some of what I mean by information is hard data on performance, the operating and financial indicators that capture the pulse of the company. At Conrail, for example, all 46 members of the network are connected through a management information system called Commander. They receive daily reports on critical business indicators: traffic levels, carloads, revenues per ton, and many others. Sharing this data openly and immediately and using electronic messages to allow people to evaluate the information enriches the business perspectives of network members, keeps them updated and focused on the company's performance, and allows managers from different parts of the company to offer their unique perspectives on specific business developments.

But data is in many respects the least important dimension of information. The network must also share openly and simultaneously each member's experiences, successes, and problems, soft information that can't be captured in databases and spreadsheets and that remains hidden for as long as possible in most traditional organizations. This is the kind of sharing that builds trust, empathy, and secure relationships. It also broadens the participants. They begin to see the organization through multiple viewpoints and understand more instinctively the pressures, challenges, and capabilities of functions and business units outside their own traditional boundaries.

Consider the case of Armstrong World Industries. In late 1989, Armstrong created five cross-border, cross-functional networks to begin the process of globalizing its businesses. Armstrong is one of the few companies with a strong international presence in many of its product lines, but it can hardly be considered a model global organization. It is a product of its conservative roots in the Pennsylvania Dutch country. Most decision-making power resides in its Lancaster headquarters, and virtually all R&D is still conducted there.

These "global teams"—one each for flooring, building products, insulation, gaskets, and textiles—have been working for more than a year to increase cross-border collaboration and to make more effective decisions on global-local trade-offs. They have held meetings outside the United States, identified business priorities, and begun to solve real problems.

In the last 18 months, the building-products network has visited all of the group's factories in Europe, developed sourcing plans to redesign the flow of products between Europe and the United States, and encouraged Lancaster R&D to tailor new products for the Asian market. (The new R&D responsiveness has increased Armstrong's share of the Korean building-products market from virtually zero to 15%.) The network has also encouraged lower ranking managers to emulate network interactions. Plant managers in the building-products group have already held two global conferences—intensive sessions in which they share technical information and operational insights.

Still, network members understand that much work remains to be done and that their work requires frequent contact and dialogue. Yet these managers are based thousands of miles from each other, travel widely, and find it almost impossible to gather physically more than three or four times each year. So they have devised a simple technique to share and react to hard and soft information—regular conference calls in which all members of the network participate all the time. This may seem a modest technique, and, technically speaking, it is. But it works because the members have learned to trust each other—and because sharing and reacting to new information fully and frequently enhances that trust.

For example, the ten-member building-products network includes managers from Pennsylvania, Europe, and the Pacific. At least every other Monday at 7:00 A.M. Lancaster time (which turns out to be a convenient time for all ten managers worldwide), the network participates for at least an hour in a global conference call. Henry Bradshaw, an Armstrong group vice president and the leader of the building-products network, describes the substance of the calls: "We talk about business conditions. We talk about competitors. We talk about service, which is especially important in the Pacific. We talk about particular orders. We talk about new products. Europe wants to know where the labs are with a new kind of ceiling board that they think will be a big hit in their market. Simple as they sound, these conference calls have been very effective. Before we created the global network, I didn't know most of the guys on it. And we had complicated communication channels; important information got lost. Today we're on a first-name basis. The more we talk, the more we want to talk. The more information we share, the more natural it becomes to share it."

Armstrong also shares openly and simultaneously a third critical kind of information—how the network evaluates its own performance. Recently, senior management polled each member of the network with a specially crafted survey designed to measure how behavior is changing and whether the group is producing tangible results. The surveys had four core themes: progress on global business projects, the quality and frequency of global communication, changes in individual mind-sets, and the global team process. The questions were direct: How often do you communicate with your team members? To what extent has your ability to see a broader global picture of the business grown? To what extent has your behavior been inhibited because of the reward system? What is the nature of conflict resolution during team meetings? What steps have you taken personally to build the social architecture? The answers almost always involve numerical rankings or choices among specific alternatives—a way to keep the information concrete and comparable over time as management repeats the exercise.

This kind of detailed evaluation often allows top management to act more quickly or more decisively than it otherwise might. For example, Armstrong recently announced a corporate streamlining that simplifies global reporting relationships. This streamlining was a direct outgrowth of the networks' self-evaluations. The more the global networks worked on concrete problems, the more convinced they became that the hierarchy needed simplification. The feedback surveys documented wide agreement and a need for urgency, so top management took action. In effect, the networks helped reshape Armstrong's corporate structure.

Armstrong executive vice president Allen Deaver, emphasizes this spillover effect: "The creation of the global teams and the measuring and sharing of members' perspectives on their work and the company helped us make better decisions about people and organization. This change is designed to facilitate the work of the teams. It is natural, logical, and evolutionary—and perceived as such. So we expect it to generate energy rather than confusion. It is perfectly in line with policies the teams themselves endorsed."

Sharing information openly, visibly, and simultaneously is one of the most important dimensions of sustaining a network. Over time, the free flow of information allows networks to become self-correcting. New information inspires debate, triggers action, generates offers of assistance from network members—without instructions from above. Networks cannot altogether abolish personal and departmental rivalries. But sharing information openly makes them visible and encourages people to redirect their energies in constructive directions. It eliminates the need for checks and checkers and becomes a central building block in improving managerial productivity.

Measuring Performance: New Criteria, New Systems

The single most important lever for reinforcing behavior in networks is evaluation. Every manager, regardless of position or seniority, responds to the criteria by which he or she is evaluated, who conducts the review, and how it is conducted. In most organizations, even those committed to cross-functional collaboration, reviews are still based on performance against departmental budgets or functional goals and are still conducted vertically.

These traditional reviews are sharply at odds with networks. Vertical reviews encourage turf mentalities. Functional reviews promote narrow vision of the business and discourage horizontal collaboration. For a network to thrive, top management must focus on behavior and horizontal leadership: Does a manager share information willingly and openly? Does he or she ask for and offer help? Is he or she emotionally committed to the business? Does the manager exercise informal leadership to energize the work of subnetworks?

Admittedly, these are difficult criteria to quantify, which is why they seldom figure into performance reviews. But in a network, they become the central measures of performance, the vital criteria for assigning increasing general management responsibility. Senior management must find ways to make these criteria precise, to demonstrate that they are the basis for rewards and promotion within the organization, and to share them among all members of the network. In so doing, management reduces the old-boy-network style of vertical promotion politics.

Royal Bank of Canada has taken the lead in devising new performance metrics that reflect the behavioral imperatives of networks. Top management has developed a one-page statement that specifies the five new criteria by which the bank's top 300 executives will be evaluated. These criteria are crucial ingredients in succession planning and career development. And they are noteworthy precisely because they emphasize behavior and mind-set rather than functional expertise. Although the document itself must remain confidential, these excerpts suggest the qualities it emphasizes.

A strong business-profit orientation: instinctively thinks customer needs, customer service; understands the anatomy of the economic structure of the business; strong innate instincts for making money.

Demonstrated ability to accept accountability, assume leadership and initiative: raises standards constantly as the environment changes; by personality and chemistry, is open and secure in assuming the initiative in building leadership, without horizontal power or authority; believes in sharing information and engendering trust; less control mentality, more empowering mentality; team builder.

Demonstrated record for making a "qualitative shift" and impact on the bank: has shown the vision and courage to change things, not just run things; willingness to experiment.

Astute in the selection of people: demonstrated evidence that this person has the judgment and the security to select and build a team of superior people; willing to cut losses.

Intellectual curiosity and global mind-set: has the mental makeup for learning continuously about global developments, technology, etc., from the outside world.

Royal Bank has also devised an ambitious evaluation program called the "leadership review process" to put these criteria into practice. The new process is a sharp break with the past. Under the old system, a committee of senior executives (the chairman, the president, four other top executives, and the director of personnel) convened twice a year to review the performance of the bank's top 200 or so managers. Each was assigned to one of three lists—the "A" list, the "B" list, and the "C" list—that reflected their perceived career potential at that point in time. "A" list members were high performers capable of moving into top management; "B" list people were promotable but not outstanding; and "C" list members were not promotable.

This process had the virtues of simplicity and efficiency, and top management was largely satisfied with the outcomes. But there were at least two serious weaknesses, especially for an organization committed to collaboration through networks. First, knowledge of a manager's leadership and personal styles (as opposed to quantifiable business results) was limited to the handful of top executives in the room, few of whom had worked directly with the managers under review. Also, the standards of evaluation, especially with respect to behavior, were more intuitive than explicit. The review team could see in black and white whether a manager's department was running ahead of or behind budget and by what percentage. But how could it evaluate with any clarity how managers shared information, how eagerly they worked to solve problems outside their domains, how effectively they led without authority?

The new system uses a four-step process to overcome both weaknesses. Here is an abbreviated description. First, the manager under review writes a statement of career aspirations and a self-appraisal against the performance criteria. Next, the manager submits a list of colleagues to be interviewed by a trusted executive about his or her performance. (Top management's selection of the interviewer is uniquely important; he or she must be widely regarded as honest, apolitical, and seasoned in business judgment.) The list must include at least 7 names (3 peers, 3 subordinates, and 1 boss) but can go as high as 15. The interviews run for an average of one hour and, like the criteria themselves, are meant to be subjective and to focus on behavior. These are not mere note-taking sessions by a human-resource staffer or scripted conversations to rank-order executives along a few obvious dimensions. The interviewer is a savvy, senior-level player with keen insights into other executives. He probes to elicit each individual's opinions and thoughts, always in the context of the business.

Next, the interviewer prepares a one-page profile of the executive's leadership capabilities. This profile, along with the self-assessment, goes for final review to the president and the chairman. In "feedback sessions," the interviewer discusses the review with the executive and allows him or her to express reservations and reactions.

The leadership review process represents an enormous commitment of time and resources. Indeed, after two years, the bank has still not completed its evaluations of all 200 top executives. But think of its powerful impact on behavior and motivation—even beyond the 200 executives. The dialogue through which top managers devised the performance criteria was itself a valuable learning exercise for them and for everyone who sees the criteria. For the first time, standards of effective behavior have been made visible and concrete. Moreover, the new evaluation system influences the values and behavior of managers interviewed about the performance of their peers and superiors. These managers (many of whom get interviewed about more than one executive) listen to the questions, formulate judgments about individual leadership, decisiveness, and accountability, and become more aware of their own values and behavior in the process. Finally, the promotion of executives based in part on the review—people who might not have been promoted under the old system—sends a visible and powerful message throughout the bank about how management values horizontal leadership and behaviors that sustain the network.

Networks offer a promising alternative to the two-dimensional lens of strategy and structure through which most senior managers evaluate their organizations. By addressing the character of the interactions among a select group of managers, rather than the formal relationships among hundreds or thousands of managers, networks begin to give substance to the values that CEOs so often invoke—trust, teamwork, empowerment—but so seldom deliver. Over time, the members of the network influence values and behavior both above and below them in the larger organization. In this way, networks become an essential building block in the creation of boundaryless organizations.

The companies I have observed understand that their networks remain in the early stages of development. But their success thus far—at Conrail, Dun & Bradstreet Europe, Royal Bank of Canada, Armstrong World Industries, and the other companies I researched— offers evidence of the power of this approach and its impact on real economic value. The performance of networks should also go a long way to overturning the fashionable (and all-too-convenient) perception of middle managers as obstacles to corporate change. Middle managers are not born defensive and narrow-minded. They learn their behaviors from those above and around them. Most people want to cooperate and collaborate. They would prefer to innovate than to block. By forging a strong set of relationships and values, networks reinforce managers' best instincts—and unleash emotional energy and the joy of work.

Appendix

A NOTE ON RESEARCH

For the last four years, I have observed and participated in the creation of networks in ten companies based in North America and Europe: Armstrong World Industries, Blue Cross/Blue Shield of Georgia, CIGNA, Conrail, Consolidated Natural Gas, Dun & Bradstreet, Du Pont, General Electric (certain business units), MasterCard International, and Royal Bank of Canada.

Unlike most academic research, my research has been conducted *as events took place.* I worked with management to improve group-processing techniques, to design feedback surveys to measure progress, and to encourage openness and candor in all discussions. By participating in critical meetings and remaining in close touch with the participants, I was able to observe developments "on-line" and test reactions with all participants. This on-line dimension is important. After-the-fact surveys and interviews, the traditional academic research tools, seldom provide the range of perspectives required to understand individual and group behavior in large organizations. As with networks themselves, research benefits from the power of specificity.

3
From Value Chain to Value Constellation: Designing Interactive Strategy

Richard Normann and Rafael Ramírez

Strategy is the art of creating value. It provides the intellectual frameworks, conceptual models, and governing ideas that allow a company's managers to identify opportunities for bringing value to customers and for delivering that value at a profit. In this respect, strategy is the way a company defines its business and links together the only two resources that really matter in today's economy: knowledge and relationships or an organization's competencies and customers.

But in a fast-changing competitive environment, the fundamental logic of value creation is also changing and in a way that makes clear strategic thinking simultaneously more important and more difficult. Our traditional thinking about value is grounded in the assumptions and the models of an industrial economy. According to this view, every company occupies a position on a value chain. Upstream, suppliers provide inputs. The company then adds value to these inputs, before passing them downstream to the next actor in the chain, the customer (whether another business or the final consumer). Seen from this perspective, strategy is primarily the art of positioning a company in the right place on the value chain—the right business, the right products and market segments, the right value-adding activities.

Today, however, this understanding of value is as outmoded as the old assembly line that it resembles and so is the view of strategy that goes with it. Global competition, changing markets, and new technologies are opening up qualitatively new ways of creating value. The options available to companies, customers, and suppliers are proliferating in ways Henry Ford never dreamed of.

Of course, more opportunities also mean more uncertainty and greater risk. Forecasts based on projections from the past become unreliable. Factors that have always seemed peripheral turn out to be key drivers of change in a company's key markets. Invaders from previously unrelated sectors change the rules of the game overnight.

In so volatile a competitive environment, strategy is no longer a matter of positioning a fixed set of activities along a value chain. Increasingly, successful companies do not just *add* value, they *reinvent* it. Their focus of strategic analysis is not the company or even the industry but the *value-creating system* itself, within which different economic actors—suppliers, business partners, allies, customers—work together to *co-produce* value. Their key strategic task is the *reconfiguration* of roles and relationships among this constellation of actors in order to mobilize the creation of value in new forms and by new players. And their underlying strategic goal is to create an ever-improving fit between competencies and customers.

To put it another way, successful companies conceive of strategy as systematic social innovation: the continuous design and redesign of complex business systems.

IKEA: The Wealth of Realizing New Ideas

For an example of what this means, consider the story of IKEA's transformation from a small Swedish mail-order furniture operation into the world's largest retailer of home furnishings. In an industry where few companies move beyond their home-country base, IKEA has created a global network of more than 100 stores. In 1992, these stores were visited by 96 *million* people and generated revenues of $4.3 billion. They have made IKEA into a growth and profit engine with an average annual growth rate of 15% over the past 5 years and profit margins that outside observers estimate at 8% to 10%, high enough to allow the company to expand without going to the stock exchange for funding.

By now, the key elements of IKEA's winning business formula are well-known: simple, high-quality, Scandinavian design; global sourcing of components; knock-down furniture kits that customers transport and assemble themselves; huge suburban stores with plenty of parking and amenities like coffee shops, restaurants, even day-care facilities. A portion of what IKEA saves on low-cost components, efficient warehousing, and customer self-service it passes on to customers in the form of lower prices, anywhere from 25% to 50% below those of its competitors.

But to focus on IKEA's low costs and low prices is to miss the true significance of the company's business innovation. IKEA is able to keep costs and prices down because it has systematically redefined the roles, relationships, and organizational practices of the furniture business. The result is an integrated business system that invents value by matching the various capabilities of participants more efficiently and effectively than was ever the case in the past.

Start with IKEA's relationship to its customers. The company offers customers something more than just low prices. It offers a brand new division of labor that looks something like this: if customers agree to take on certain key tasks traditionally done by manufacturers and retailers—the assembly of products and their delivery to customers' homes— then IKEA promises to deliver well-designed products at substantially lower prices.

Every aspect of the IKEA business system is carefully designed to make it easy for customers to take on this new role. For example, IKEA prints more than 45 million catalogues every year in 10 different languages. Though each catalogue features only 30% to 40% of the company's roughly 10,000 products, every copy becomes a "script," explaining the roles each actor performs in the company's business system.

So too with the company's stores. Free strollers, supervised child care, and playgrounds are available for children, as well as wheelchairs for the disabled and elderly. There are cafés and restaurants so customers can get a quick bite to eat. The goal is to make IKEA not just a furniture store but a family-outing destination.

At the front door, customers are supplied with catalogues, tape measures, pens, and notepaper to help customers make choices without the aid of salespeople. Products are grouped together to offer not just chairs and tables but designs for living. In addition, each item carries simple readable labels with the name and price of the product; the dimensions, materials, and colors in which it is available; instructions for care; and the location in the shop where it can be ordered and picked up. After payment, customers place their packages in carts to take them to their cars. If the package won't fit, IKEA will even lend or sell at cost an automobile roof rack.

IKEA wants its customers to understand that their role is not to *consume* value but to *create* it. IKEA offers families more than co-produced furniture, it offers co-produced improvements in family living—

everything from interior design to safety information and equipment, insurance, and shopping as a form of entertainment.

To call these services amenities is to underestimate their central significance to IKEA's strategic intent: to understand how customers can create their own value and to create a business system that allows them to do it better. IKEA's goal is not to *relieve* customers of doing certain tasks but to *mobilize* them to do easily certain things they have never done before. Put another way, IKEA invents value by enabling customers' own value-creating activities. As one company brochure puts it, "Wealth is [the ability to] realize your ideas."

To mobilize its customers to create value, IKEA must similarly mobilize its 1,800 suppliers, located in more than 50 countries around the world. In order to keep its side of the work-sharing bargain, IKEA must find suppliers that can offer both low costs and good quality. It takes enormous care to find and evaluate potential suppliers and to prepare them to play their role in the IKEA business system. Thirty buying offices around the world seek out candidates. Then designers in the centralized design office at IKEA's operational headquarters in Älmhult, Sweden, who work two to three years ahead of current product, decide which suppliers will provide which parts.

Once part of the IKEA system, long-term suppliers not only gain access to global markets but also receive technical assistance, leased equipment, and advice on bringing production up to world quality standards. This effort got started in the early 1960s, when IKEA began to purchase components from Polish manufacturers. Today IKEA works with some 500 suppliers in Eastern Europe. There, as elsewhere, the company plays a major role in improving the business infrastructure and manufacturing standards of its partners.

For example, the company employs about a dozen technicians in a unit called IKEA Engineering to provide suppliers with technical assistance. The company's Vienna-based Business Service Department runs a computer database that helps suppliers find raw materials and introduces them to new business partners.

Finally, what is true for IKEA's relationships with customers and suppliers is also true for its internal business processes, which it designed to mirror and support the logic of the whole value-creating system. A good example is IKEA's highly efficient logistics system.

The company's insistence on low costs from its suppliers has two important implications. First, the sourcing of components is widely dispersed. The back and seat of a chair may be made in Poland, the legs in France, and the screws that hold it all together in Spain.

Second, the company must order parts in high volumes. Both factors make it imperative for IKEA to have an efficient system for ordering parts, integrating them into products, and delivering them to stores—all the while minimizing the costs of inventory.

The centerpiece of this system is IKEA's world network of 14 warehouses. The largest, 135,000 square meters in Älmhult, holds enough items to furnish 30,000 three-bedroom apartments. Most ordering is done electronically. Cash registers at IKEA stores around the world relay sales information to the nearest warehouse as well as to operational headquarters in Älmhult, where information systems oversee and analyze sales and shipping patterns worldwide.

Big as they are, these warehouses are much more than simple storage facilities. Instead, they operate as logistical control points, consolidation centers, and transit hubs. They play a proactive role in the integration of supply and demand, reducing the need to store production runs for long periods, holding unit costs down, and helping retail stores to anticipate needs and eliminate shortages.

The image of a value chain fails to capture the complexity of roles and relationships in the IKEA business system. IKEA did *not* position itself to add value at any one point in a predetermined sequence of activities. Rather, IKEA set out systematically to reinvent value and the business system that delivers it for an entire cast of economic actors. The work-sharing, co-productive arrangements the company offers to customers and suppliers alike force both to think about value in a new way—one in which customers are also suppliers (of time, labor, information, and transportation), suppliers are also customers (of IKEA's business and technical services), and IKEA itself is not so much a retailer as the central star in a constellation of services, goods, design, management, support, and even entertainment. The result: IKEA has succeeded, arguably, in creating more value per person (customer, supplier, and employee) and in securing greater total profit from and for its financial and human resources than all but a handful of other companies in any consumer industry.

The New Logic of Value

IKEA's extraordinary business innovation is made possible by a fundamental transformation in the way that value is created. But what is this new logic of value, and what are its strategic implications for today's managers?

To answer these questions, begin with the simple observation that any product or service is really the result of a complicated set of activities: myriad economic transactions and institutional arrangements among suppliers and customers, employees and managers, teams of technical and organizational specialists. In fact, what we usually think of as products or services are really frozen activities, concrete manifestations of the relationships among actors in a value-creating system. To emphasize the way all products and services are grounded in activity, we prefer to call them offerings.

Every economic revolution redefines the roles and relationships on which offerings are based. This was true during the industrial revolution when technological breakthroughs in the application of energy to useful work made possible the factory system with its highly specialized division of labor. Today, under the impact of information technology and the resulting globalization of markets and production, new methods of combining activities into offerings are producing new opportunities for creating value.

One implication of this phenomenon is that the very distinction between physical products and intangible services is currently breaking down. Does IKEA offer a product or a service? The answer is neither—and both. Very few offerings can be clearly defined as one or the other anymore. Increasingly, they involve some complex combination of the two roles.

Take the simple example of an economic transaction familiar to everyone: a cash withdrawal from one's bank account. Not so long ago, this transaction was clearly a service, a personal exchange between a customer, who went to his or her local bank, and a teller, who fulfilled the customer's request for cash. But in the last decade, this traditional service has been completely transformed by the application of information technology.

Today the vast majority of cash withdrawals take place by means of automatic teller machines (ATMs). This change has reconfigured the transaction in two directions. First, the customer engages in a self-service activity not so different from the role of the buyer of IKEA furniture. Second, a great deal of attention, expertise, and activity is now devoted to the design, building, and maintenance of self-service support tools: the cash machines themselves, the plastic cards used by customers to access the machines, the computer networks connecting the machines to the bank's information and accounting systems.

This is not merely a change in technology or even in the transaction itself. It is a change in the entire value-creating system. The scene, the script, the roles of the relevant actors have all been transformed. When ATMs were first introduced, some observers questioned whether customers would play their assigned part. Critics even speculated that customers would resist this attempt by banks to burden them with extra work, that customers would insist on retaining the personal interaction with the teller.

Such criticisms missed the point and for a simple reason. The reconfiguration of the cash-withdrawal transaction offered customers a qualitatively new kind of value. In particular, it eliminated traditional constraints of space and time. No longer do customers have to go to their local bank branch during business hours. They can get cash at any time and, with the proliferation of ATM networks, pretty much anywhere. Thus the vast majority of customers flocked to ATMs and adapted to them quickly and easily. So much so that, today, few remember the long lines that used to form at banks on Friday afternoons as depositors rushed to cash their payroll checks or get money for the weekend.

What is so different about this new kind of value? One useful way to describe it is that value has become more *dense*. Think of density as a measure of the amount of information, knowledge, and other resources that an economic actor has at hand at any moment in time to leverage his or her own value creation. Value has become more dense in that more and more opportunities for value creation are packed into any particular offering. A visit to an IKEA shop is not just shopping but entertainment. ATMs allow people not just to get cash but to get it anytime and nearly anywhere. A Swatch watch allows its owner not only to tell time but also to make a fashion statement.

The new logic of value presents companies with three strategic implications:

> First, in a world where value occurs not in sequential chains but in complex constellations, the goal of business is not so much to make or do something of value for customers as it is to mobilize customers to take advantage of proffered density and create value *for themselves.* That is why ATMs are so popular despite the critics. And that is why IKEA has become the world's largest furniture retailer. To put it another way, companies do not really compete with one another anymore. Rather, it is offerings that compete for the time and attention and money of customers.
>
> Second, what is true for individual offerings is also true for entire value-creating systems. As potential offerings become more complex

and varied, so do the relationships necessary to produce them. A single company rarely provides everything anymore. Instead, the most attractive offerings involve customers and suppliers, allies and business partners, in new combinations. As a result, a company's principal strategic task is the reconfiguration of its relationships and business systems.

Third, if the key to creating value is to co-produce offerings that mobilize customers, then the only true source of competitive advantage is the ability to conceive the entire value-creating system and make it work. IKEA creates more value because it mobilizes more activities—of customers and suppliers. It reshuffles activities among actors so that actor and activity are better matched. To win, a company must write the script, mobilize and train the players, and make the customer the final arbiter of success or failure. To go *on* winning, a company must create a dialogue with its customers in order to repeat this performance over and over again and keep its offerings competitive.

Companies create value when they make not only their offerings more intelligent but their customers (and suppliers) more intelligent as well. To do this, companies must continuously reassess and redesign their competencies and relationships in order to keep their value-creating systems malleable, fresh, and responsive. In the new logic of value, this dialogue between competencies and customers explains the survival and success of some companies and the decline and failure of others.

Danish Pharmacies: Reconfiguring Business Systems

The new logic of value, and the dialogue between competencies and customers that it creates, presents every company with a stark choice: either reconfigure its business system to take advantage of these trends or be reconfigured by more dynamic competitors.

To exploit these trends, managers must take a number of steps. To begin with, they must reconsider the business potential of their chief assets:the company's knowledge base and its customer base. Then they must reposition or reinvent the company's offerings to create a better fit between the company's competencies and the value-creating activities of its customers. Finally, they need to make new business arrangements and, sometimes, new social and political alliances to make these offerings feasible and efficient.

Consider the example of a business that at first glance may seem anything but a promising candidate for business-system redesign: Denmark's network of 300 privately owned pharmacies. Just over ten years ago, Denmark, like many other European countries, began to reform and deregulate its state-funded health care system in an effort to put a brake on rising costs.

Danish pharmacies are privately owned but nonetheless heavily regulated. For centuries, they have enjoyed a legal monopoly on the sale of both over-the-counter and prescription drugs. In addition, the pharmacies have had the right to manufacture generic drugs and thus the means to compete with their suppliers on everything except patented pharmaceuticals.

The other side of the coin is that the Danish state sets pharmaceutical prices and that it does so in a negotiation that looks at drug margins in the context of overall pharmacy profits. Until recently, this negotiation was annual, which meant that if pharmacy profits suddenly rose, then the state would cut drug prices the following year to bring profits back into line and share this "windfall" with the taxpayers. In practice, pharmacy profits *never* rose or fell very much in the old days, because, while the system guaranteed a high degree of security, it did nothing at all to encourage efficiency, innovation, or gains in productivity.

Decades of this system also left the pharmacies highly vulnerable to competition if they ever lost their monopoly. Worse yet, the movement to control health care costs had prompted a call in several quarters for outright nationalization of the pharmacies in order to make regulation complete.

So when the political system began to focus on health care, the pharmacies and their professional organization, the Danish Pharmaceutical Association, thought they saw the handwriting on the wall—an altered industry, new competitors, new dangers—and decided to take a hard look at their assets to see if they could find new opportunities as well. They concluded that their network of local pharmacies had two potential but so-far under-utilized strengths.

The first was the corps of local pharmacists themselves, who were well-educated health care professionals. (Of course in Denmark, as elsewhere in the West, most critical decisions about patient health care were made by other actors in the system: primarily the physicians who wrote prescriptions and the pharmaceutical companies that developed new drugs.)

The second strength was the fact that the network of 300 pharmacies and 1,600 subsidiary outlets throughout the country represented a highly effective access channel to the Danish population. People respected and trusted their local pharmacists. What's more, as the general public became better informed, people began to see that good health was not something they could delegate to the government or the health care industry. Health depended on personal behavior and individual lifestyle choices. The public was hungry for information and advice on how to live a healthier life.

These two strengths gave the pharmacists an opportunity to reposition their offerings and redefine their business. A pharmacy could be more than a place to buy prescription drugs and other pharmaceutical products. It could become a comprehensive source of health care information and services.

This redefinition of its business led the Association to adopt three interconnected goals: to develop pharmacies into a more advanced knowledge and service business; to establish a solid, productive relationship with government health care agencies; and to reorganize the Association along lines that would help to achieve goals one and two.

Alongside these articulated aims, the Association had several tacit goals. For one thing, it meant to do everything possible to preserve its monopoly in pharmaceuticals retailing and its strong position in wholesaling. For another, it wanted to lower operating costs and increase pharmacy productivity—and to get legislation enacted that would give pharmacies some incentive to work more efficiently.

Efficiency had had a low priority for Danish pharmacies ever since the advent of strict state regulation. In setting prices, the state had always allowed for a modest profit. There had never been any reason to streamline operations. That now changed. If deregulation was coming, the Association would need to compete more effectively on every front, and it now sought a new legal environment that would allow it to benefit from its own efforts to improve efficiency and expand services.

In 1984, the Danish parliament changed the law. The state would set prices for two years at a time; if pharmacies could generate higher margins than predicted, they could keep the difference, at least until the next negotiation. Immediately, the pharmacies began to rationalize operations and cut staff. Net profits rose dramatically, with periodic setbacks as the Ministry of Health lowered prices.

At about this same time, the Association took two other steps to strengthen its position. First, in an effort to undercut attacks on its monopoly in drug retailing, the Association tried to downplay its direct competition with the pharmaceutical industry by setting up a subsidiary to do its drug manufacturing. Second, it managed to emerge from a series of mergers in pharmaceuticals wholesaling with a 25% controlling interest in a wholesaling giant that had 70% of the market.

Meanwhile, the pharmacists went to work on their retailing operation. In essence, the pharmacies wanted to broaden their traditional approach, delivery of conventional pharmaceutical "hardware" (in other words, selling drugs), into a concept they called Pharmaceutical Care, which would emphasize the "software" portion of health care delivery. They saw Pharmaceutical Care as a way of carving out and legitimizing a strong position within the health care system and, at the same time, of gaining access to the core of their customers' value-creating activities in health maintenance.

Beginning in 1982 and continuing into the 1990s, the pharmacies and their national association devised and carried out a series of strategies that sought to involve private customers and health care institutions in new relationships and offerings.

They expanded their range of products to include health and diet foods, high-quality herbal medicines, skin-care and other items, and they worked with suppliers to develop new quality-control measures and informational labeling.

They upgraded their customer-information services, installed computers to access health information, and published and distributed self-help books and preventive health care pamphlets.

They initiated their own antitobacco campaign and started selling literature and antismoking chewing gum. In 1986, they began offering stop-smoking courses that combined education and group therapy.

They developed a computer database on pharmaceutical interactions and side effects and installed a computer prescription service and an electronic pharmaceutical ordering system.

They developed home health care packages for newly discharged hospital patients, self-care packages for routine health problems such as measuring blood-pressure, support packages for health care institutions, and preventive-care packages for customers with special nutritional or dietary needs.

These strategies met with limited success, at least in the beginning.

In fact, the pharmacies had set themselves a difficult task. They were trying to protect their monopoly in pharmaceutical retailing; improve their position in wholesaling; take on a more central role in drug training, education, and quality control; and greatly enlarge their activities in health counseling, preventive medicine, and the sale of herbals, health food, and diet products. The other players in the health care industry tended to see these latter goals in particular as encroach-ments on their own exclusive preserves. It did not help that, in the midst of this seemingly predatory expansionism, the pharmacists were making bigger net profits than ever before in their history.

The Association saw all this in quite a different light, of course. After decades of strategic hibernation, the pharmacists were rising to the business and social challenges of fundamental health care reform. Indeed, given their history, they showed themselves surprisingly ready and able to modernize their operations, update their expertise, re-define their customer base, rethink their business, and tailor a fresh fit between competencies and customers both new and old.

It was just that neither the state nor the customers themselves were quite up to so much sudden change. The state moved so slowly in deregulating and reforming Danish health care (84% of health care is still in the public sector) that the Association's innovations kept run-ning into regulatory barriers and political pitfalls. And the customers that the Association had thought to mobilize around its new concept of holistic, preventive health maintenance—doctors, hospitals, long-term care facilities, even patients—tended to greet proposed innova-tion with suspicion and resistance almost regardless of the circum-stances.

The antismoking campaign, for example, amounted to a test of physician response to the notion of pharmacies operating in a coun-seling role. To the Association's disappointment, though to no one's great surprise, the doctors viewed the program as an incursion on their own professional territory. They applied pressure and got the courses taken off the market.

Similarly, the pharmacists found little demand for their home health care packages for newly discharged patients, partly because hospitals and the public health-insurance agency viewed the pharmacies as competitors and declined to recommend the service.

Self-care packages also fared poorly. True, on Blood Pressure Day in 1991, thousands of Danes came to pharmacies all over the country for blood pressure and cholesterol readings, but as a general rule, people wanted their physicians to go on conducting even simple tests and recommending even basic treatments free of charge, the way they had always done in the past.

Clearly, the pharmacies were doing something wrong, and it wasn't hard to figure out what. The new strategy itself was a good one as far as it went—reinvention of a centuries-old business to fit new social and commercial realities, development of denser offerings, more interaction with suppliers and customers to co-produce value. The problem was credibility.

Rethinking Business Alliances

Denmark's individual pharmacies had always been private businesses, and their professional Association had always been a nonprofit organization. But in recent years, the Association had strayed further and further into outright commercial competition. With their customers, the pharmacists still had a reputation for professionalism and excellence. Within its industry, the Association was developing a reputation for sharp elbows.

The Association urgently needed to improve its relations with the political system and other stakeholders in the health care sector. To achieve this end, it had to behave a little less like a competitor and think more seriously and consistently about the co-productive constellations in which it wished to operate. It needed to rethink its concept of reconfiguration and push its new strategy further.

The Association is a purely voluntary organization of independent pharmacists. It has long had the authority to negotiate drug prices with the government, but it has never had the power to force its strategic thinking on individual member pharmacies. Yet the process of business reconfiguration is in great part a process of building new competencies. The government may have moved slowly on deregulation, but the pharmacies had also moved slowly in learning to understand their new roles in the health care complex.

In 1969, the Association had established an educational center outside Copenhagen to centralize the training of licensed pharmacy technicians and to offer its pharmacist members continuing, post-graduate education in new pharmaceutical developments. In the 1980s, as the Association's new direction began to take hold, the school broadened its program to include courses in marketing, service management, customer orientation, and business skills. Now the old center also became a tool for promoting ideas and disseminating the Association's new understanding of its business.

In 1990, to eliminate once and for all its direct competition with the drug companies, the Association sold its drug manufacturing subsidiary and withdrew from pharmaceutical production for the first time in its history.

In 1991, the Association further redesigned its organization and divided its activities in two. It assembled its business assets—computer operations, wholesaling, and the profits from the sale of its drug-production subsidiary—into a separate company that operated according to normal business principles. Strategic planning and coordination of educational, informational, and social services remained not-for-profit activities and stayed in the hands of the Association itself, strongly backed by profits from business activities.

The Association also increased its past efforts to build alliances with Denmark's national organizations for the elderly and disabled, as well as those for heart disease, epilepsy, asthma, and diabetes, among others. The Association now also works closely with the Danish Consumer Council in areas such as drug information and labeling.

The Association's progressive efforts at health care-sector redesign won it international acclaim, and this exposure helped it to forge alliances with sister organizations across Europe and around the world. In 1985, the Association urged the World Health Organization to work more closely with pharmacists, and this led to the establishment of the Europharm Forum, linking pharmaceutical organizations in WHO's European region. In 1988, WHO issued guidelines recommending that pharmacists assume a central role in health care systems as drug advisors par excellence to patients, physicians, and other professionals.

Perhaps most important of all, the Association is now taking part in an international, multicenter study of the pharmacist's role in drug therapies. In Denmark, the research project is working with 300 asthma patients in a double-blind study of pharmacist-assisted asthma therapies. Because the study incorporates a new division of responsibility among patient, physician, and pharmacist, the Association has named two doctors—a professor of medicine and a clinical pharmacologist—to the project's steering committee.

The result of these efforts has been striking. In 1992, the Association reintroduced its antismoking courses in a joint venture with Europharm Forum and WHO. This time, thanks to the Association's alliances and its international standing, Danish physicians found themselves in de facto recognition of the pharmacies' counseling activities. The program was a box-office success, and WHO wants to export it to other parts of Europe.

Also in 1992, the Association's business subsidiary acquired 10% of Denmark's only ambulance operator, creating a co-productive alliance between two businesses with the same set of customers. Among other things, this alliance has revived the home-care concept with a system for dependable delivery of drug, support, and security services to the elderly and to patients recently discharged from the hospital.

Overall, greater efficiency has allowed the pharmacies to increase their net profits steadily while reducing gross profits substantially, a strong argument for preserving their retail monopoly. Moreover, the Association, while one of the world's smallest, is economically one of the world's strongest, with more than $200 million in assets, not, of course, counting the value of the independent pharmacies themselves. In 1992, the Association developed a plan that pushes reconfiguration and co-production into the twenty-first century with new initiatives that saved Danish taxpayers more than $16 million the first year.

The pharmacies' struggles are no doubt far from over. Their business environment is also a political environment, a fact that has complicated their efforts to work with other health care players to produce new offerings and enlarge the opportunities for value creation available to the average citizen-customer. Yet what the pharmacies discovered was that reconfiguration made more than political sense. It also made business sense. The reinvention of any business constellation is at least partly a matter of thinking through the social implications of change. In the end, new offerings have gradually allowed the pharmacies to get a far higher return on their knowledge base and their customer base than they ever enjoyed in the past.

Increasingly, the companies that survive and thrive are those that look beyond their immediate boundaries to the social and business systems in which they are enmeshed and discover new ways to reconfigure those systems in order to reinvent value for their customers.

French Concessions: Of Customers and Competencies

In an economy founded on the new logic of value, only two assets really matter: knowledge and relationships or a company's competencies and its customers. Competencies are the technologies, specialized expertise, business processes and techniques that a company has accumulated over time and packaged in its offerings. But knowledge alone is not enough. Obviously, a company's competencies are worthless without customers willing to pay for them. Thus the other key asset for any company is its established customer base.

A company's relationship with a customer is really an access channel to the customer's ongoing value-creating activities. Any customer, whether another business or an individual, uses a wide range of inputs in order to create value. A company's offerings have value to the degree that customers can use them as inputs to leverage their own value creation. In this respect, then, companies don't profit from customers. They profit from customers' value-creating activities.

One of the chief strategic challenges of the new economy is to integrate knowledge and relationships—devise a good fit between competencies and customers and keep that fit current. In order to exploit established relationships, in other words, a company needs to enlarge its knowledge base continuously. It must invest in an ever-broadening range of knowledge resources and combine ever-expanding kinds of knowledge into its offerings.

What is more, these investments in new knowledge can become so large that a company's own offerings to its existing customer base are no longer adequate to recoup its investment. So the new knowledge tends to propel companies into new businesses in search of new relationships with new customers. And the cycle repeats.

For an example of how this dialogue between competencies and customers, knowledge and relationships, is shaping the nature of business competition, consider the recent evolution of two French corporations: Compagnie Générale des Eaux and Lyonnaise des Eaux Dumez. With 1992 revenues of $27 billion and $18 billion respectively, Générale and Lyonnaise rank 6th and 11th among France's largest companies. They are also among that country's most technologically dynamic and successful global competitors.

As their names suggest, Générale des Eaux and Lyonnaise des Eaux Dumez got their start by providing water to French cities and towns, and they are still very much in the water business. Between them, Générale and Lyonnaise provide drinking water to about 37 million French residents. In addition, Lyonnaise is now the biggest private water company in the world, with some 35 or 40 million consumers on 6 continents. Générale is the next largest. But to think of either as a water company entirely fails to capture the complexity and dynamism of their business or, for that matter, its fundamental logic.

In addition to water, Générale and Lyonnaise and their numerous subsidiaries provide cities and towns with everything from heating systems, sewers, and utilities to hazardous waste treatment, municipal construction, nursing homes, golf courses, and even funeral services. In Toulouse, for example, Générale not only manages the city's water distribution but has also developed a local recreation center known as Aqualand and is an investor in the city's cable television network. In

Avignon, Lyonnaise manages the city's historical monuments, art museum, public gardens, and parks. And a Lyonnaise subsidiary, Pompes Funébres Générales, is the world's largest undertaker, handling almost 40% of all funerals in France. Some of these businesses seem to follow logically from the business of water delivery, others seem to represent an aggressive effort at diversification. But, in fact, all these activities grow organically from a particularly French understanding of the business that Générale and Lyonnaise are in and of the special skills that they possess.

In most Western countries, public infrastructure is a public responsibility. City (or state or county) governments put out tenders for public-works projects to be built according to designs and specifications supplied by the city or its consultants and paid for using its authority to issue bonds and assume debt. Construction is carried out under contract with the city; operation and maintenance of the completed system is done by the city or contracted out, often piecemeal and for brief periods. From beginning to end, the brains controlling the project are on the city payroll or work for the city as consultants. This tender system is nearly universal in the Anglo-Saxon world and is standard practice in most of Europe as well.

But the French handle these matters differently. Since the nineteenth century, France has actively encouraged a separation between the political responsibility and the production responsibility for public services. While elected officials must answer to the voters for the provision of roads, utilities, and other amenities, and while water assets, for example, are publicly owned, private companies act as *concessionaires*, designing the projects and specifications, raising the capital, building the infrastructure, managing the assets, bearing the risks, pocketing the profits, and assuming a large part of the local government's relevant authority and responsibility in order to do so. In effect, the government—local or national—delegates virtually all its public-service duties and prerogatives to a private company, retaining only the political responsibility for governance. The social reasoning behind this separation of responsibilities is essentially twofold.

First, concessions have allowed an activist French state to finance extensive infrastructure development without using the public purse. Government simply delegated the obligation to build and paid for it with the right to operate. The first such concessions were granted by France's strong central government in the nineteenth century for the construction of canals. (See "French Concessions," for a brief account of their history.) Later, the state gave concessions for aqueducts, water distribution systems, market halls, and railways. Later still, concessions were used to construct gas and electrical networks and tramways. The concessionaire designed, built, and paid for these systems. The government owned them and granted a concession on their profitable operation for periods of 30 years or more.

French Concessions

From the beginning, concessionaires took a broad view of their business. Napoleon III created Compagnie Générale des Eaux by imperial decree in 1853, and the Rothschilds bought 5,000 of its 80,000 shares, becoming the company's banker. Générale won a 99-year water-distribution concession from Lyons that same year, added Nantes in 1854, expanded steadily into smaller communities, entered a complex agreement with the city of Paris in the early 1860s, began introducing new technologies in the 1890s aimed at the improvement of water quality as well as quantity, and eventually moved into heating, construction, and other services.

It was Crédit Lyonnaise that founded Lyonnaise des Eaux in 1880 to operate water and lighting systems in Cannes. In 1891, Lyonnaise created its first subsidiary to build and operate a sewer system in Marseilles. Throughout the remainder of the nineteenth century and through the first half of the twentieth, Lyonnaise engaged heavily in various types of infrastructure construction and operation, all of it by concession. By the late 1930s, Lyonnaise was preeminent in the operation of gas and electrical networks throughout France.

Although privately owned concessionaires provided the vast majority of public services in France by 1900, the concession system suffered a series of setbacks in the first half of the twentieth century. The first blow came in 1916, when municipalities were made liable for the unpaid debts of their concessionaires, and the second in 1926, when cities and towns were finally granted the right to own and operate their own public-service companies. As municipal companies began to replace local concessionaires, the great national concessions also began to vanish: the airlines in 1933, the railways in 1937. By 1939, concessionaires operated less than half of French public services, and in 1946, a wave of nationalizations stripped them of much of what remained, including most of the French electrical grid.

Then in 1951, public-service policy did another about face as the need to rebuild infrastructure, neglected during and after the war, once again far outstripped the taxpayers' capacity to foot the bill. The law was altered, concessions made a wholesale comeback, and concessionaires like Générale and Lyonnaise regained their raison d'être and their former expansive energy.

Today concessionaires—some of them partly controlled by state-owned institutional investors—operate not only the majority of public utilities in France but also toll motorways, bridges, marinas, ports, parking lots, hospitals, housing developments, and soon, perhaps, prisons.

Second, concessions have kept governments out of the commercial, industrial sphere and helped to protect them from spiraling debt and operational waste. Moreover, by tying profit to the efficient operation of the assets once installed, the concession system also made good use of the capitalist interests that sought to profit from public infrastructure construction. Until well into the twentieth century, French courts typically disallowed the efforts of cities to create municipal companies and operate public services for themselves.

But perhaps the concession system's most profound effect has been on the concessionaires themselves: on the way they developed and how they now view their competencies and their business strategies. There is a French term that managers at both Générale and Lyonnaise use to describe their distinctive expertise: *aménageur des villes,* roughly translated "urban-systems designer and outfitter." Put simply, the business of Générale and Lyonnaise is not any one service so much as the production of entire systems of services, and their core competence is not water or even utilities but rather the financial, social, legal, managerial, and technical engineering that ensures the smooth operation of public service infrastructures.

Developing Knowledge for Relationships

For French concessionaires, the principal business risk has never been the ordinary hazards of the marketplace: day-to-day competition, fluctuating demand, changing fashion. The great challenge (in addition to getting the concession renewed for another 30 or 40 years) has always been to find new services to offer an existing customer base and so to exploit further the concessionaire's own investment in knowledge and knowledge workers. Générale and Lyonnaise have addressed this problem by developing a higher order interorganizational competence: their expertise is precisely that of developing, acquiring, and integrating a broad cross-section of technologies and knowledge and focusing them on their customers' continuously evolving value creation.

Générale has some 2,000 subsidiaries and Lyonnaise about 720, ranging in size from very small to very large and grouped according to specialization or *métier*. Both Générale and Lyonnaise see themselves as necessarily multilocal companies, and their subsidiaries enjoy considerable autonomy. At the same time, both companies concentrate intently on the possibilities for synergy and on the management of integration. Générale's 60 *métiers*, for example, are richly interconnected at every level and within every jurisdiction in order to help services build on each other and to open the door to new services as soon as, and sometimes before, the client sees a need for them. This continuous, ad hoc flowering of co-productive relationships among subsidiaries and between subsidiaries and clients represents an ongoing reinvention of the parent company. As one Générale executive told us, "Our people have no a priori right to say no to a client request. If one of the companies in our group cannot produce what the client wants, then we will create a company that can."

Générale and Lyonnaise have put France on the cutting edge of R&D on water purification, transport, and waste-water treatment. In Méry-sur-Oise, Générale has established the first chlorine-free water-treatment system in the world. In Tokyo, Lyonnaise researchers are working with the Japanese to develop compact water-purification plants using biological systems.

The companies have also become leaders in emerging markets for "green" industrial services, such as waste management, a market estimated at $34.5 billion in Europe alone in 1991 and expected to double by the year 2000. A Générale subsidiary runs Europe's largest hazardous-waste-treatment facility in Limay, outside Paris.

Finally, the two companies have also emphasized the technological synergies that integration can provide. In Paris, for example, they use the garbage and trash their street-cleaning subsidiaries collect to fuel cogeneration plants. Ten percent of Parisians heat their homes with electricity produced by garbage incineration.

As Générale and Lyonnaise invest in a broader and broader range of technologies and expertise, they seek out new customers in order to defray the costs of the investments. One way is to provide similar services to customers in the private sector. Both companies are now managing outsourced services for private companies, for example, hazardous waste disposal.

Even more important, as city services around the world become privatized, both companies are moving aggressively to compete on a global scale. Lyonnaise has built and managed water distribution networks in more than 50 cities on 6 continents. Over the last four years, Générale has developed a $60 million business managing waste-water-treatment plants and drinking-water-production facilities for small towns in the United States.

What's more, the companies' integrated solutions are proving to be a strong competitive advantage. In contrast to companies that specialize in only one aspect of public-infrastructure provision—such as Bechtel in engineering, Veba in energy systems, or Browning-Ferris Industries in waste management—Générale and Lyonnaise can provide cities and towns with an integrated package of offerings. The advantage for the client is that some activities—for example, cable television or hazardous-waste management—can take years to become profitable. The city cannot afford to take on the development expense itself, and a tender for this kind of infrastructure must take into account several years of operating losses. But long-term investments of precisely this kind are the stock-in-trade of concessionaires like Générale and Lyonnaise, which see such investments in the larger context of competence and customer development.

Public service packages that expand from one expertise to another have thus become not only a strong source of profit growth but also a powerful negotiating card in dealing with local governments. In the city of Macao, for example, Lyonnaise first won a contract for water distribution and waste-water treatment from the Portuguese colonial authorities. Then the company used its presence in the local market to acquire a concession for the generation and distribution of electricity. This in turn led to construction of a new electric power station, while the water concession led to the establishment in Macao of the largest water-analysis laboratory in Asia.

So far, Générale and Lyonnaise have tried to manage the interplay of competencies and customers under a single corporate umbrella: by creating new companies or acquiring existing ones and integrating them into the group. A complementary tactic, of course, is to form partnerships with outside companies that have developed different sets of resources. Such alliances permit the concessionaire to provide its traditional customer base with appropriately denser offerings without the expense of developing new expertise of its own. Moreover, alliances also provide conduits to new customer bases and allow companies to capitalize on their core knowledge by selling it to the customers of their allies.

Trends appear to be pushing Générale and Lyonnaise in this direction. Générale, for example, has formed alliances with several other European companies that are, in the words of one Générale executive, "clients as well as suppliers." For that matter, Générale and Lyonnaise themselves, while relentless competitors at home, have in a few cases bid jointly on contracts to provide drinking water and waste-water treatment in other parts of the world.

However it takes place, the integration of different disciplines into viable global offerings is a skill that Générale and Lyonnaise have raised to the level of a virtual *metacompetence*. They have not merely learned to combine expertise in construction, engineering, finance, operational management, project management, risk management, infrastructure development, contractual law, social policy, and much more, they have made consistent use of the logic of public responsibility—their clients' logic—to leverage this bundle of value-creating activities.

The concession system is still unique to France, where it is regarded as unexportable, perhaps even untranslatable. Yet its obvious benefits to the taxpayer and its clear advantages for the quality of infrastructure construction and operation have made it an object of study around the world, and new jurisdictions are adapting it to fit new circumstances. The regulatory bodies of the EEC are giving the concession system particular scrutiny.

Regardless of its future, however, the concession system has already made hugely creative demands on concessionaires by requiring strategic skill on three levels: Concessionaires have learned to master the design and management of interconnected, co-productive offerings. They have learned how to mobilize value creation in their customers and partners by reconfiguring roles, relationships, and structures. And they have learned the art of perpetually reinventing value in a dialogue between competencies and customers. These are the skills that have kept concessionaires alive and profitable for more than one hundred years. And these are the skills that winning corporations will have to acquire in the post-assembly-line economy that is now emerging.

4

The Logic of Global Business: An Interview with ABB's Percy Barnevik

William Taylor

Percy Barnevik, president and CEO of ABB Asea Brown Boveri, is a corporate pioneer. He is moving more aggressively than any CEO in Europe, perhaps in the world, to build the new model of competitive enterprise—an organization that combines global scale and world-class technology with deep roots in local markets. He is working to give substance to the endlessly invoked corporate mantra, "Think global, act local."

Headquartered in Zurich, ABB is a young company forged through the merger of two venerable European companies. Asea, created in 1883, has been a flagship of Swedish industry for a century. Brown Boveri, which took shape in 1891, holds a comparable industrial status in Switzerland. In August 1987, Barnevik altered the course of both companies when he announced that Asea, where he was managing director, would merge with Brown Boveri to create a potent new force in the European market for electrical systems and equipment.

The creation of ABB became a metaphor for the changing economic map of Europe. Barnevik initiated a wrenching process of consolidation and rationalization—layoffs, plant closings, product exchanges between countries—that observers agreed will one day come to European industries from steel to telecommunications to automobiles. And soon more than a metaphor, Barnevik's bold moves triggered a wholesale restructuring of the Continent's electrical power industry.

The creation of ABB also turned out to be the first step in a trans-Atlantic journey of acquisition, restructuring, and growth. ABB has acquired or taken minority positions in 60 companies representing investments worth $3.6 billion—including two major acquisitions in

North America. In 1989, ABB acquired Westinghouse's transmission and distribution operation in a transaction involving 25 factories and businesses with revenues of $1 billion. That same year, it spent $1.6 billion to acquire Combustion Engineering, the manufacturer of power-generation and process-automation equipment.

Today ABB generates annual revenues of more than $25 billion and employs 215,000 people around the world. It is well balanced on both sides of the Atlantic. Europe accounts for more than 60% of its total revenues, and its business is split roughly equally between the European Community countries and the non-EC European trading bloc. Germany, ABB's largest national market, accounts for 15% of total revenues. The company also generates annual revenues of $7 billion in North America, with 40,000 employees. Although ABB remains underrepresented in Asia, which accounts for only 15% of total revenues, it is an important target for expansion and investment. And ABB's business activities are not limited to the industrialized world. The company has 10,000 employees in India, 10,000 in South America, and is one of the most active Western investors in Eastern Europe.

In this interview, Percy Barnevik, 49, offers a detailed guide to the theory and practice of building a "multidomestic" enterprise. He explains ABB's matrix system, a structure designed to leverage core technologies and global economies of scale without eroding local market presence and responsiveness. (See "The Organizing Logic of ABB.") He describes a new breed of "global managers" and explains how their skills differ from those of traditional managers. He reckons candidly with the political implications of companies such as ABB.

The interview was conducted at ABB's Zurich headquarters by HBR associate editor William Taylor.

HBR: *Companies everywhere are trying to become global, and everyone agrees that ABB is more global than most companies. What does that mean?*

Percy Barnevik: ABB is a company with no geographic center, no national ax to grind. We are a federation of national companies with a global coordination center. Are we a Swiss company? Our headquarters is in Zurich, but only 100 professionals work at headquarters and we will not increase that number. Are we a Swedish company? I'm the CEO, and I was born and educated in Sweden. But our headquarters is not in Sweden, and only two of the eight members of our board of directors are Swedes. Perhaps we are an American company. We report our financial results in U.S. dollars, and English is ABB's official language. We conduct all high-level meetings in English.

My point is that ABB is none of those things—and all of those things. We are not homeless. We are a company with many homes.

The Organizing Logic of ABB

ABB Asea Brown Boveri is a global organization of staggering business diversity. Yet its organizing principles are stark in their simplicity. Along one dimension, the company is a distributed global network. Executives around the world make decisions on product strategy and performance without regard for national borders. Along a second dimension, it is a collection of traditionally organized national companies, each serving its home market as effectively as possible. ABB's global matrix holds the two dimensions together.

At the top of the company sit CEO Percy Barnevik and 12 colleagues on the executive committee. The group, which meets every three weeks, is responsible for ABB's global-strategy and performance. The executive committee consists of Swedes, Swiss, Germans, and Americans. Several members of the executive committee are based outside Zurich, and their meetings are held around the world.

Reporting to the executive committee are leaders of the 50 or so business areas (BAs), located worldwide, into which the company's products and services are divided. The BAs are grouped into 8 business segments, for which different members of the executive committee are responsible. For example, the "industry" segment, which sells components, systems, and software to automate industrial processes, has 5 BAs, including metallurgy, drives, and process engineering. The BA leaders report to Gerhard Schulmeyer, a German member of the executive committee who works out of Stamford, Connecticut.

Each BA has a leader responsible for optimizing the business on a global basis. The BA leader devises and champions a global strategy, holds factories around the world to cost and quality standards, allocates export markets to each factory, and shares expertise by rotating people across borders, creating mixed-nationality teams to solve problems, and building a culture of trust and communication. The BA leader for power transformers, who is responsible for 25 factories in 16 countries, is a Swede who works out of Mannheim, Germany. The BA leader for instrumentation is British. The BA leader for electric metering is an American based in North Carolina.

Alongside the BA structure sits a country structure. ABB's operations in the developed world are organized as national enterprises with presidents, balance sheets, income statements, and career ladders. In Germany, for example, Asea Brown Boveri Aktiengesellschaft, ABB's national company, employs 36,000 people and generates annual revenues of more than $4 billion. The managing director of ABB Germany, Eberhard von Koerber, plays a role comparable with that of a traditional German CEO. He reports to a supervisory board whose members include German bank representatives and trade union officials. His company produces financial statements comparable with those from any other German company and participates fully in the German apprenticeship program.

The BA structure meets the national structure at the level of ABB's member companies. Percy Barnevik advocates strict decentralization. Wherever possible, ABB creates separate companies to do the work of the 50 business areas in different countries. For example, ABB does not merely sell industrial robots in Norway. Norway has an ABB robotics company charged with manufacturing robots, selling to and servicing domestic customers, and exporting to markets allocated by the BA leader.

There are 1,100 such local companies around the world. Their presidents report to two bosses—the BA leader, who is usually located outside the country, and the president of the national company of which the local company is a subsidiary. At this intersection, ABB's "multidomestic" structure becomes a reality.

Are all businesses becoming global?

No, and this is a big source of misunderstanding. We are in the process of building this federation of national companies, a multidomestic organization, as I prefer to call it. That does not mean all of our businesses are global. We do a very good business in electrical installation and service in many countries. That business is superlocal. The geographic scope of our installation business in, say, Stuttgart does not extend beyond a ten-mile radius of downtown Stuttgart.

We also have businesses that are superglobal. There are not more than 15 combined-cycle power plants or more than 3 or 4 high-voltage DC stations sold in any one year around the world. Our competitors fight for nearly every contract—they battle us on technology, price, financing—and national borders are virtually meaningless.

Every project requires our best people and best technology from around the world.

The vast majority of our businesses—and of most businesses—fall somewhere between the superlocal and the superglobal. These are the businesses in which building a multidomestic organization offers powerful advantages. You want to be able to optimize a business globally—to specialize in the production of components, to drive economies of scale as far as you can, to rotate managers and technologists around the world to share expertise and solve problems. But you also want to have deep local roots everywhere you operate—building products in the countries where you sell them, recruiting the best local talent from the universities, working with the local government to increase exports. If you build such an organization, you create a business advantage that's damn difficult to copy.

What is a business that demonstrates that advantage?

Transportation is a good one. This is a vibrant business for us, and we consider ourselves number one in the world. We generate $2 billion a year in revenues when you include all of our activities: locomotives, subway cars, suburban trains, trolleys, and the electrical and signaling systems that support them. We are strong because we are the only multidomestic player in the world.

First, we know what core technologies we have to master, and we draw on research from labs across Europe and the world. Being a technology leader in locomotives means being a leader in power electronics, mechanical design, even communications software. Ten years ago, Asea beat General Electric on a big Amtrak order for locomotives on the Metro-liner between New York and Washington. That win caused quite a stir; it was the first time in one hundred years that an American railroad bought locomotives from outside the United States. We won because we could run that track from Washington to New York, crooked and bad as it was, at 125 miles an hour. Asea had been pushing high-speed design concepts for more than a decade, and Brown Boveri pioneered the AC technology. That's why our X2 tilting trains are running in Sweden and why ABB will play a big role in the high-speed rail network scheduled to run throughout Europe.

Second, we structure our operations to push cross-border economies of scale. This is an especially big advantage in Europe, where the locomotive industry is hopelessly fragmented. There are two companies headquartered in the United States building locomotives for the

U.S. market. There are three companies in Japan. There are 24 companies in Western Europe, and the industry runs at less than 75% of capacity. There are European companies still making only 10 or 20 locomotives a year! How can they compete with us, when we have factories doing ten times their volume and specializing in components for locomotives across the Continent? For example, one of our new plants makes power electronics for many of the locomotives we sell in Europe. That specialization creates huge cost and quality advantages. We work to rationalize and specialize as much as we can across borders.

Third, we recognize the limits to specialization. We can't ignore borders altogether. We recently won a $420-million order from the Swiss Federal Railways—we call it the "order of the century"—to build locomotives that will move freight through the Alps. If we expect to win those orders, we had *better* be a Swiss company. We had better understand the depth of the Swiss concern for the environment, which explains the willingness to invest so heavily to get freight moving on trains through the mountains to Italy or Germany and off polluting trucks. We had better understand the Alpine terrain and what it takes to build engines powerful enough to haul heavy loads. We had better understand the effects of drastic temperature changes on sensitive electronics and build locomotives robust enough to keep working when they go from the frigid, dry outdoors to extreme heat and humidity inside the tunnels.

There are other advantages to a multidomestic presence. India needs locomotives—thousands of locomotives—and the government expects its suppliers to manufacture most of them inside India. But the Indians also need soft credit to pay for what is imported. Who has more soft credit than the Germans and the Italians? So we have to be a German and an Italian company, we have to be able to build locomotive components there as well as in Switzerland, Sweden, and Austria, since our presence may persuade Bonn and Rome to assist with financing.

We test the borderlines all the time: How far can we push cross-border specialization and scale economies? How effectively can we translate our multidomestic presence into competitive advantages in third markets?

Is there such a thing as a global manager?

Yes, but we don't have many. One of ABB's biggest priorities is to create more of them; it is a crucial bottleneck for us. On the other hand, a global company does not need thousands of global managers. We need maybe 500 or so out of 15,000 managers to make ABB work well—not more. I have no interest in making managers more "global" than they have to be. We can't have people abdicating their nationalities, saying "I am no longer German, I am international." The world doesn't work like that. If you are selling products and services in Germany, you better be German!

That said, we do need a core group of global managers at the top: on our executive committee, on the teams running our business areas (BAs), in other key positions. How are they different? Global managers have exceptionally open minds. They respect how different countries do things, and they have the imagination to appreciate why they do them that way. But they are also incisive, they push the limits of the culture. Global managers don't passively accept it when someone says, "You can't do that in Italy or Spain because of the unions," or "You can't do that in Japan because of the Ministry of Finance." They sort through the debris of cultural excuses and find opportunities to innovate.

Global managers are also generous and patient. They can handle the frustrations of language barriers. As I mentioned earlier, English is the official language of ABB. Every manager with a global role *must* be fluent in English, and anyone with regional general management responsibilities must be competent in English. When I write letters to ABB colleagues in Sweden, I write them in English. It may seem silly for one Swede to write to another in English, but who knows who will need to see that letter a year from now?

We are adamant about the language requirement—and it creates problems. Only 30% of our managers speak English as their first language, so there is great potential for misunderstanding, for misjudging people, for mistaking facility with English for intelligence or knowledge. I'm as guilty as anyone. I was rushing through an airport last year and had to return a phone call from one of our managers in Germany. His English wasn't good, and he was speaking slowly and tentatively. I was in a hurry, and finally I insisted, "Can't you speak any faster?" There was complete silence. It was a dumb thing for me to say. Things like that happen every day in this company. Global managers minimize those problems and work to eliminate them.

Where do these new managers come from?

Global managers are made, not born. This is not a natural process. We are herd animals. We like people who are like us. But there are many things you can do. Obviously, you rotate people around the world. There is no substitute for line experience in three or four countries to create a global perspective. You also encourage people to work in mixed-nationality teams. You *force* them to create personal alliances across borders, which means that sometimes you interfere in hiring decisions.

This is why we put so much emphasis on teams in the business areas. If you have 50 business areas and five managers on each BA team, that's 250 people from different parts of the world—people who meet regularly in different places, bring their national perspectives to bear on tough problems, and begin to understand how things are done elsewhere. I experience this every three weeks in our executive committee. When we sit together as Germans, Swiss, Americans, and Swedes, with many of us living, working, and traveling in different places, the insights can be remarkable. But you have to force people into these situations. Mixing nationalities doesn't just happen.

You also have to acknowledge cultural differences without becoming paralyzed by them. We've done some surveys, as have lots of other companies, and we find interesting differences in perception. For example, a Swede may think a Swiss is not completely frank and open, that he doesn't know exactly where he stands. That is a cultural phenomenon. Swiss culture shuns disagreement. A Swiss might say, "Let's come back to that point later, let me review it with my colleagues." A Swede would prefer to confront the issue directly. How do we undo hundreds of years of upbringing and education? We don't, and we shouldn't try to. But we do need to broaden understanding.

Is your goal to develop an "ABB way" of managing that cuts across cultural differences?

Yes and no. Naturally, as CEO, I set the tone for the company's management style. With my Anglo-Saxon education and Swedish upbringing, I have a certain way of doing things. Someone recently asked if my ultimate goal is to create 5,000 little Percy Barneviks, one for each of our profit centers. I laughed for a moment when I thought of the horror of sitting on top of such an organization, then I realized it wasn't a silly question. And the answer is no. We can't have managers who are "un-French" managing in France because 95% of them are dealing every day with French customers, French colleagues, French suppliers. That's why global managers also need humility. A global manager respects a formal German manager—Herr Doktor and all that—because that manager may be an outstanding performer in the German context.

Let's talk about the structures of global business. How do you organize a multidomestic enterprise?

ABB is an organization with three internal contradictions. We want to be global and local, big and small, radically decentralized with centralized reporting and control. If we resolve those contradictions, we create real organizational advantage.

That's where the matrix comes in. The matrix is the framework through which we organize our activities. It allows us to optimize our businesses globally *and* maximize performance in every country in which we operate. Some people resist it. They say the matrix is too rigid, too simplistic. But what choice do you have? To say you don't like a matrix is like saying you don't like factories or you don't like breathing. It's a fact of life. If you deny the formal matrix, you wind up with an informal one—and that's much harder to reckon with. As we learn to master the matrix, we get a truly multidomestic organization.

Can you walk us through how the matrix works?

Look at it first from the point of view of one business area, say, power transformers. The BA manager for power transformers happens to sit in Mannheim, Germany. His charter, however, is worldwide. He runs a business with 25 factories in 16 countries and global revenues of more than $1 billion. He has a small team around him of mixed nationalities—we don't expect superheroes to run our 50 BAs. Together with his colleagues, the BA manager establishes and monitors the trajectory of the business.

The BA leader is a business strategist and global optimizer. He decides which factories are going to make what products, what export markets each factory will serve, how the factories should pool their expertise and research funds for the benefit of the business worldwide. He also tracks talent—the 60 or 70 real standouts around the world. Say we need a plant manager for a new company in Thailand. The BA head should know of three or four people—maybe there's one at our plant in Muncie, Indiana, maybe there's one in Finland—who could help in Thailand. (See "Power Transformers—The Dynamics of Global Coordination.")

Power Transformers—The Dynamics of Global Coordination

ABB is the world's leading manufacturer of power transformers, expensive products used in the transmission of electricity over long distances. The business generates annual revenues of $1 billion, nearly four times the revenues of its nearest competitor. More to the point, ABB's business is consistently and increasingly profitable—a real achievement in an industry that has experienced 15 years of moderate growth and intense price competition.

Power transformers are a case study in Percy Barnevik's approach to global management. Sune Karlsson, a vice president of ABB with a long record in the power transformer field, runs the business area (BA) from Mannheim, Germany. Production takes place in 25 factories in 16 countries. Each of these operations is organized as an independent company with its own president, budget, and balance sheet. Karlsson's job is to optimize the group's strategy and performance independent of national borders—to set the global rules of the game for ABB—while allowing local companies freedom to drive execution.

"We are not a global business," Karlsson says. "We are a collection of local businesses with intense global coordination. This makes us unique. We want our local companies to think small, to worry about their home market and a handful of export markets, and to learn to make money on smaller volumes."

Indeed, ABB has used its global production web to bring a new model of competition to the power transformer industry. Most of ABB's 25 factories are remarkably small by industry standards, with annual sales ranging from as little as $10 million to not more than $150 million, and 70% of their output serves their local markets. ABB transformer factories concentrate on slashing throughput times, maximizing design and production flexibility, and focusing tightly on the needs of domestic customers. In short, the company deploys the classic tools of flexible, time-based management in an industry that has traditionally competed on cost and volume.

As with many of its business areas, ABB built its worldwide presence in power transformers through a series of acquisitions. Thus one of Karlsson's jobs is to spread the new model of competition to the local companies ABB acquires.

"Most of the companies we acquired had volume problems, cost problems, quality problems," he says. "We have to convince local managers that they can run smaller operations more efficiently, meet customer needs more flexibly—and make money. Once you've done this 10 or 15 times, in several countries, you become confident of the merits of the model."

Karlsson's approach to change is in keeping with the ABB philosophy: show local managers what's been achieved elsewhere, let them drive the change process, make available ABB expertise from around the world, and demand quick results. A turnaround for power transformers takes about 18 months.

In Germany, for example, one of the company's transformer plants had generated red ink for years. It is now a growing, profitable operation, albeit smaller and more focused than before. The work force has been slashed from 520 to 180, throughput time has been cut by one-third, work-in-process inventories have decreased by 80%. Annual revenues have fallen $70 million per year to a mere $50 million—but profits are up substantially. Today the German manager who championed this company's changes is in Muncie, Indiana, helping managers of a former Westinghouse plant acquired by ABB to reform their operation.

ABB's global scale also gives it clout with suppliers. The company buys up to $500 million of materials each year—an enormous presence that gives it leverage on price, quality, and delivery schedules. Karlsson has made strategic purchasing a priority. ABB expects zero-defect suppliers, just-in-time deliveries, and price increases lower than 75% of inflation—major advantages that it is in a position to win with intelligent coordination.

Sune Karlsson believes these and other "hard" advantages may be less significant, however, than the "soft" advantages of global coordination. "Our most important strength is that we have 25 factories around the world, each with its own president, design manager, marketing manager, and production manager," he says. "These people are working on the same problems and opportunities day after day, year after year, and learning a tremendous amount. We want to create a process of continuous expertise transfer. If we do, that's a source of advantage none of our rivals can match."

Creating these soft advantages requires internal competition and coordination. Every month, the Mannheim headquarters distributes detailed information on how each of the 25 factories is performing on critical parameters, such as failure rates, throughput times, inventories as a percentage of revenues, and receivables as a percentage of revenues. These reports generate competition for outstanding performance within the ABB network—more intense pressure, Karlsson believes, than external competition in the marketplace.

The key, of course, is that this internal competition be constructive, not destructive. Since the creation of ABB, one of Sune Karlsson's most important jobs has been to build a culture of trust and exchange among ABB's power transformer operations around the world and to create forums that facilitate the process of exchange. At least three such forums exist today:

- The BA's management board resembles the executive committee of an independent company. Karlsson chairs the group, and its members include the presidents of the largest power transformer companies—people from the United States, Canada, Sweden, Norway, Germany, and Brazil. The board meets four to six times a year and shapes the BA's global strategy, monitors performance, and resolves big problems.

- Karlsson's BA staff in Mannheim is not "staff" in the traditional sense—young professionals rotating through headquarters on their way to a line job. Rather, it is made up of five veteran managers each with worldwide responsibility for activities in critical areas such as purchasing and R&D. They travel constantly, meet with the presidents and top managers of the local companies, and drive the coordination agenda forward.

- Functional coordination teams meet once or twice a year to exchange information on the details of implementation in production, quality, marketing, and other areas. The teams include managers with functional responsibilities in all the local companies, so they come from around the world. These formal gatherings are important, Karlsson argues, but the real value comes in creating informal exchange throughout the year. The system works when the quality manager in Sweden feels compelled to telephone or fax the quality manager in Brazil with a problem or an idea.

"Sharing expertise does not happen automatically," Karlsson emphasizes. "It takes trust, it takes familiarity. People need to spend time together, to get to know and understand each other. People must also see a payoff for themselves. I never expect our operations to coordinate unless all sides get real benefits. We have to demonstrate that sharing pays—that contributing one idea gets you 24 in return."

It is possible to leave the organization right there, to optimize every business area without regard for ABB's broad collection of activities in specific countries. But think about what we lose. We have a power transformer company in Norway that employs 400 people. It builds transformers for the Norwegian market and exports to markets allocated by the BA. But ABB Norway has more than 10,000 other employees in the country. There are tremendous benefits if power transformers coordinates its Norwegian operation with our operations in power generation, switchgear, and process automation: recruiting top people from the universities, building an efficient distribution and service network across product lines, circulating good people among the local companies, maintaining productive relations with top government officials.

So we have a Norwegian company, ABB Norway, with a Norwegian CEO and a headquarters in Oslo, to make these connections. The CEO has the same responsibilities as the CEO of a local Norwegian company for labor negotiations, bank relationships, and high-level contacts with customers. This is no label or gimmick. We *must* be a Norwegian company to work effectively in many businesses. Norway's oil operations in the North Sea are a matter of great national importance and intense national pride. The government wouldn't—and shouldn't—trust some faraway foreign company as a key supplier to those operations.

The opportunities for synergy are clear. So is the potential for tension between the business area structure and the country structure. Can't the matrix pull itself apart?

BA managers, country managers, and presidents of the local companies have very different jobs. They must understand their roles and appreciate that they are *complementing* each other, not competing.

The BA managers are crucial people. They need a strong hand in crafting strategy, evaluating performance around the world, and working with teams made up of different nationalities. We've had to replace some of them—people who lacked vision or cultural sensitivity or the ability to lead without being dictators. You see, BA managers don't own the people working in any business area around the world. They can't order the president of a local company to fire someone or to use a particular strategy in union negotiations. On the other hand, BA managers can't let their role degrade into a statistical coordinator or scorekeeper. There's a natural tendency for this to happen. BA managers don't have a constituency of thousands of direct reports in the same way that country managers do. So it's a difficult balancing act.

Country managers play a different role. They are regional line managers, the equivalent of the CEO of a local company. But country managers must also respect ABB's global objectives. The president of, say, ABB Portugal can't tell the BA manager for low-voltage switchgear or drives to stay out of his hair. He has to cooperate with the BA managers to evaluate and improve what's happening in Portugal in those businesses. He should be able to tell a BA manager, "You may think the plant in Portugal is up to standards, but you're being too loose. Turnover and absenteeism is twice the Portugese average. There are problems with the union, and it's the managers' fault."

Now, the presidents of our local companies—ABB Transformers in Denmark, say, or ABB Drives in Greece—need a different set of skills. They must be excellent profit center managers. But they must also be able to answer to two bosses effectively. After all, they have two sets of responsibilities. They have a global boss, the BA manager, who creates the rules of the game by which they run their businesses. They also have their country boss, to whom they report in the local setting. I don't want to make too much of this. In all of Germany, where we have 36,000 people, only 50 or so managers have two bosses. But these managers have to handle that ambiguity. They must have the self-confidence not to become paralyzed if they receive conflicting signals and the integrity not to play one boss off against the other.

Isn't all this much easier said than done?

It does require a huge mental change, especially for country managers. Remember, we've built ABB through acquisitions and restructurings. Thirty of the companies we've bought had been around for more than 100 years. Many of them were industry leaders in their countries, national monuments. Now they've got BA managers playing a big role in the direction of their operations. We have to convince country managers that they benefit by being part of this federation, that they gain more than they lose when they give up some autonomy.

What's an example?

Finland has been one of our most spectacular success stories, precisely because the Finns understood how much they could gain. In 1986, Asea acquired Strömberg, the Finnish power and electrical products company. At the time, Strömberg made an unbelievable assortment of products, probably half of what ABB makes today. It built generators, transformers, drives, circuit breakers—all of them for the Finnish market, many of them for export. It was a classic example of a big company in a small country that survived because of a protected market. Not surprisingly, much of what it made was not up to world-class standards, and the company was not very profitable. How can you expect a country with half the population of New Jersey to be profitable in everything from hydropower to circuit breakers?

Strömberg is no longer a stand-alone company. It is part of ABB's global matrix. The company still exists—there is a president of ABB Strömberg—but its charter is different. It is no longer the center of the world for every product it sells. It still manufactures and services many products for the Finnish market. It also sells certain products to allocated markets outside Finland. And it is ABB's worldwide center of excellence for one important group of products, electric drives, in which it had a long history of technology leadership and effective manufacturing.

Strömberg is a hell of a lot stronger because of this. Its total exports from Finland have increased more than 50% in three years. ABB Strömberg has become one of the most profitable companies in the whole ABB group, with a return on capital employed of around 30%. It is a recognized world leader in drives. Strömberg produces more than 35% of all the drives ABB sells, and drives are a billion-dollar business. In four years, Strömberg's exports to Germany and France have increased ten times. Why? Because the company has access to a distribution network it never could have built itself.

This sounds enormously complicated, almost unmanageable. How does the organization avoid getting lost in the complexity?

The only way to structure a complex, global organization is to make it as simple and local as possible. ABB is complicated from where I sit. But on the ground, where the real work gets done, all of our operations must function as closely as possible to stand-alone operations. Our managers need well-defined sets of responsibilities, clear accountability, and maximum degrees of freedom to execute. I don't expect most of our people to have "global mind-sets," to do things that hurt their business but are "good for ABB." That's not natural.

Take Strömberg and drives in France. I don't want the drive company president in Finland to think about what's good for France. I want him to think about Finland, about how to sell the hell out of the export markets he has been allocated. Likewise, I don't expect our profit center manager in France to think about Finland. I expect him to do what makes sense for his French customers. If our French salespeople find higher quality drives or more cost-effective drives outside ABB, they are free to sell them in France so long as ABB gets a right of first refusal. Finland has increased its shipments to France because it makes economic sense for both sides. That's the only way to operate.

But how can an organization with 240,000 people all over the world be simple and local?

ABB *is* a huge enterprise. But the work of most of our people is organized in small units with P&L responsibility and meaningful autonomy. Our operations are divided into nearly 1,200 companies with an average of 200 employees. These companies are divided into 4,500 profit centers with an average of 50 employees.

We are fervent believers in decentralization. When we structure local operations, we always push to create separate legal entities. Separate companies allow you to create *real* balance sheets with *real* responsibility for cash flow and dividends. With real balance sheets, managers inherit results from year to year through changes in equity. Separate companies also create more effective tools to recruit and motivate managers. People can aspire to meaningful career ladders in companies small enough to understand and be committed to.

What does that mean for the role of headquarters?

We operate as lean as humanly possible. It's no accident that there are only 100 people at ABB headquarters in Zurich. The closer we get to top management, the tougher we have to be with head count. I believe you can go into any traditionally centralized corporation and cut its headquarters staff by 90% in one year. You spin off 30% of the staff into free-standing service centers that perform real work—treasury functions, legal services—and charge for it. You decentralize 30% of the staff—human resources, for example—by pushing them into the line organization. Then 30% disappears through head count reductions.

These are not hypothetical calculations. We bought Combustion Engineering in late 1989. I told the Americans that they had to go from 600 people to 100 in their Stamford, Connecticut headquarters. They didn't believe it was possible. So I told them to go to Finland and take a look. When we bought Strömberg, there were 880 people in headquarters. Today there are 25. I told them to go to Mannheim and take a look at the German operation. In 1988, right after the creation of ABB, there were 1,600 people in headquarters. Today there are 100.

Doesn't such radical decentralization threaten the very advantages that ABB's size creates?

Those are the contradictions again—being simultaneously big and small, decentralized and centralized. To do that, you need a structure at the top that facilitates quick decision making and carefully monitors developments around the world. That's the role of our executive committee. The 13 members of the executive committee are collectively responsible for ABB. But each of us also has responsibility for a business segment, a region, some administrative functions, or more than one of these. Eberhard von Koerber, who is a member of the executive committee located in Mannheim, is responsible for Germany, Austria, Italy, and Eastern Europe. He is also responsible for a worldwide business area, installation materials, and some corporate staff functions. Gerhard Schulmeyer sits in the United States and is responsible for North America. He is also responsible for our global "industry" segment.

Naturally, these 13 executives are busy, stretched people. But think about what happens when we meet every three weeks, which we do for a full day. Sitting in one room are the senior managers collectively responsible for ABB's global strategy and performance. These same managers individually monitor business segments, countries, and staff functions. So when we make a decision—snap, it's covered. The members of the executive committee communicate to their direct reports, the BA managers and the country managers, and the implementation process is under way.

We also have the glue of transparent, centralized reporting through a management information system called Abacus. Every month, Abacus collects performance data on our 4,500 profit centers and compares performance with budgets and forecasts. The data are collected in local currencies but translated into U.S. dollars to allow for analysis across borders. The system also allows you to work with the data. You can aggregate and disaggregate results by business segments, countries, and companies within countries.

What kind of information does the executive committee use to support the fast decision making you need?

We look for early signs that businesses are becoming more or less healthy. On the tenth of every month, for example, I get a binder with information on about 500 different operations—the 50 business areas, all the major countries, and the key companies in key countries. I look at several parameters—new orders, invoicing, margins, cash flows—around the world and in various business segments. Then I stop to study trends that catch my eye.

Let's say the industry segment is behind budget. I look to see which of the five BAs in the segment are behind. I see that process automation is way off. So I look by country and learn that the problem is in the United States and that it's poor margins, not weak revenues. So the answer is obvious—a price war has broken out. That doesn't mean I start giving orders. But I want to have informed dialogues with the appropriate executives.

Let's go back to basics. How do you begin building this kind of global organization?

ABB has grown largely through mergers and strategic investments. For most companies in Europe, this is the right way to cross borders. There is such massive overcapacity in so many European industries and so few companies with the critical mass to hold their own against Japanese and U.S. competitors. My former company, Asea, did fine in the 1980s. Revenues in 1987 were 4 times greater than in 1980, profits were 10 times greater, and our market value was 20 times greater. But the handwriting was on the wall. The European electrical industry was crowded with 20 national competitors. There was up to 50% overcapacity, high costs, and little cross-border trade. Half the companies were losing money. The creation of ABB started a painful—but long overdue—process of restructuring.

That same restructuring process will come to other industries: automobiles, telecommunications, steel. But it will come slowly. There have been plenty of articles in the last few years about all the cross-border mergers in Europe. In fact, the more interesting issue is why there have been so *few*. There should be *hundreds* of them, involving *tens of billions* of dollars, in industry after industry. But we're not seeing it. What we're seeing instead are strategic alliances and minority investments. Companies buy 15% of each other's shares. Or two rivals agree to cooperate in third markets but not merge their home-market organizations. I worry that many European alliances are poor substitutes for doing what we try to do—complete mergers and cross-border rationalization.

What are the obstacles to such cross-border restructuring?

One obstacle is political. When we decided on the merger between Asea and Brown Boveri, we had no choice but to do it secretly and to do it quickly, with our eyes open about discovering skeletons in the closet. There were no lawyers, no auditors, no environmental investigations, and no due diligence. Sure, we tried to value assets as best we could. But then we had to make the move, with an extremely thin legal document, because we were absolutely convinced of the strategic merits. In fact, the documents from the premerger negotiations are locked away in a Swiss bank and won't be released for 20 years.

Why the secrecy? Think of Sweden. Its industrial jewel, Asea—a 100 year-old company that had built much of the country's infrastructure—was moving its headquarters out of Sweden. The unions were angry: "Decisions will be made in Zurich, we have no influence in Zurich, there is no codetermination in Switzerland."

I remember when we called the press conference in Stockholm on August 10. The news came as a complete surprise. Some journalists didn't even bother to attend; they figured it was an announcement about a new plant in Norway or something. Then came the shock, the fait accompli. That started a communications war of a few weeks where we had to win over shareholders, the public, governments, and unions. But strict confidentiality was our only choice.

Are there obstacles besides politics?

Absolutely. The more powerful the strategic logic behind a merger—the greater the cross-border synergies—the more powerful the human and organizational obstacles. It's hard to tell a competent country manager in Athens or Amsterdam, "You've done a good job for 15 years, but unfortunately this other manager has done a better job and our only choice is to appoint your colleague to run the operation." If you have two plants in the same country running well but you need only one after the merger, it's tough to explain that to employees in the plant to be closed. Restructuring operations creates lots of pain and heartache, so many companies choose not to begin the process, to avoid the pain.

Germany is a case in point. Brown Boveri had operated in Germany for almost 90 years. Its German operation was so big—it had more than 35,000 employees—that there were rivalries with the Swiss parent. BBC Germany was a technology-driven, low-profit organization—a real underperformer. The formation of ABB created the opportunity to tackle problems that had festered for decades.

So what did you do?

We sent in Eberhard von Koerber to lead the effort. He made no secret of our plans. We had to reduce the work force by 10%, or 4,000 employees. We had to break up the headquarters, which had grown so big because of all the tensions with Switzerland. We had to rationalize the production overlaps, especially between Switzerland and Germany. We needed lots of new managers, eager people who wanted to be leaders and grow in the business.

The reaction was intense. Von Koerber faced strikes, demonstrations, barricades—real confrontation with the unions. He would turn on the television set and see protesters chanting, "Von Koerber out! Von Koerber out!" After a while, once the unions understood the game plan, the loud protests disappeared and our relationship became very constructive. The silent resistance from managers was more formidable. In fact, much of the union resistance was fed by management. Once the unions got on board, they became allies in our effort to reform management and rationalize operations.

Three years later, the results are in. ABB Germany is a well-structured, dynamic, market-oriented company. Profits are increasing steeply, in line with ABB targets. In 1987, BBC Germany generated revenues of $4 billion. ABB Germany will generate twice that by the end of next year. Three years ago, the management structure in Mannheim was centralized and functional, with few clear responsibilities or accountability. Today there are 30 German companies, each with its own president, manufacturing director, and so on. We can see who the outstanding performers are and apply their talents elsewhere. If we need someone to sort out a problem with circuit breakers in Spain, we know who from Germany can help.

What lessons can other companies learn from the German experience?

To make real change in cross-border mergers, you have to be factual, quick, and neutral. And you have to move boldly. You must avoid the "investigation trap"—you can't postpone tough decisions by studying them to death. You can't permit a "honeymoon" of small changes over a year or two. A long series of small changes just prolongs the pain. Finally, you have to accept a fair share of mistakes. I tell my people that if we make 100 decisions and 70 turn out to be right, that's good enough. I'd rather be roughly right and fast than exactly right and slow. We apply these principles everywhere we go, including in Eastern Europe, where we now have several change programs under way. (See "Change Comes to Poland—The Case of ABB Zamech.")

Change Comes to Poland—The Case of ABB Zamech

Last May, Zamech, Poland's leading manufacturer of steam turbines, transmission gears, marine equipment and metal castings began a new life as ABB Zamech—a joint venture of ABB (76% ownership), the Polish government (19% ownership), and the company's employees (5% ownership). ABB Zamech employees 4,300 people in the town of Elblag, outside Gdańsk. In September, two more Polish joint ventures became official— ABB Dolmel and Dolmel Drives. These companies manufacture a wide range of generating equipment and electric drives and employ some 2,400 workers.

The joint ventures are noteworthy for their size alone. ABB has become the largest Western investor in Poland. But they are perhaps more significant for their managerial implications, in particular, how ABB is revitalizing these deeply troubled operations. The company intends to demonstrate that the philosophy of business and managerial reform it has applied in places like Mannheim, Germany and Muncie, Indiana can also work in the troubled economies of Eastern Europe. That philosophy has at least four core principles:

1. Immediately reorganize operations into profit centers with well-defined budgets, strict performance targets, and clear lines of authority and accountability.

2. Identify a core group of change agents from local management, give small teams responsibility for championing high-priority programs, and closely monitor results.

3. Transfer ABB expertise from around the world to support the change process without interfering with it or running it directly.

4. Keep standards high and demand quick results.

Barbara Kux, president of ABB Power Ventures negotiated the Polish joint ventures and plays a lead role in the turnaround process. "Our goal is to make these companies as productive and profitable as ABB's operations worldwide," she says. "We don't make a 'discount' for Eastern Europe, and we don't expect the change process to take forever. We provide more technical and managerial support than we might to a company in the United States, but we are just as demanding in terms of results."

ABB Zamech has come the furthest to date. The change program began immediately after the creation of the joint venture. For decades, the company had been organized along functional lines, a structure that blurred managerial authority, confused product-line profitability, and slowed decision making. Within four weeks, ABB Zamech was reorganized into discrete profit centers. There are now three business areas (BAs)—the casting foundry turbines and gears, and marine equipment—as well as a finance and administration department and an in-house service department. Each area has a leadership team that generates the business plans, budgets, and performance targets by which their operations are judged. These teams made final decisions on which employees would stay, which would go, what equipment they would need—tough-minded business choices made for the first time so as to maximize productivity (employee and capital) and business area profitability.

The reorganization was a crucial first step. The second big step was installing ABB's standard finance and control system. For decades, Zamech had been run as a giant overhead machine. Roughly 80% of the company's total costs were allocated by central staff accountants rather than traced directly to specific products and services. Managers had no clear idea what their products cost to make and thus no idea which ones made money. Tight financial controls and maximum capital productivity are critical in an economy with interest rates of 40%.

Formal reorganization and new control systems no matter how radical, won't have much of an effect without big changes in who is in charge, however. ABB made two important decisions. First, there would be no "rescue team" from Western Europe. All managerial positions, from the CEO down, would be held by Polish managers from the former Zamech. Second, managers would be selected without regard to rank or seniority; indeed, there would be a premium on young, creative talent. ABB was looking for "hungry wolves"—smart, ambitious change agents who would receive intense training and be the core engine of Zamech's revival.

Most of the new leaders came from the ranks of middle management. The company's top executive, general manager Pawel Olechnowicz, ran the steel castings department prior to the joint venture's creation—a position that put him several layers below the top of the 15-layer management hierarchy. Employees had already elected him general manager shortly before the creation of ABB Zamech, so he looked like a good choice. The marine BA leader had been a production manager in the old Zamech, another low-level position, and the turbines and gears BA manager had been a technical director.

"We put in place a management team that lacked the standard business tools," Kux explains. "They didn't know what cash flow was, they didn't understand much about marketing. But their ambition was incredible. You could feel their hunger to excel. When we began the talent search, we told our Zamech contacts that we wanted to see the 30 people they would take along tomorrow if they were going to open their own business."

Next came the process of developing a detailed agenda for reform. The leadership team settled on 11 priority issues, from reorganizing and retraining the sales force to slashing total cycle times and redesigning the factory layout. Each project was led by a champion—some from top management ranks, some from the other "hungry wolves." A steering committee made up of the general manager, the deputy general manager, the business area managers, and Kux meets monthly to review these critical projects.

To support the change initiatives, ABB created a team of high-level experts from around the world—authorities in functional areas like finance and control and quality, as well as technology specialists and managers with heavy restructuring experience. Team members do not live in Poland. Kux says it is unrealistic to expect top people to spend a year or two in the conditions they would find in Elblag. But they visit frequently and stay updated on progress and problems.

The logistics of expertise transfer are more complicated than they sound. For example, most of the Polish managers spoke little or no English—a serious barrier to effective dialogue. So ABB began intensive language training. "If Polish managers want to draw from the worldwide ABB resource pool, they *must* speak English," Kux emphasizes. "Most communication doesn't happen face-to-face where you can have an interpreter. Last May, I couldn't simply pick up the phone and talk to the general manager. Today we speak in English on the phone almost every day."

Of course, speaking on the telephone in English assumes a working telephone system—a dangerous assumption in the case of Poland. Thus another prerequisite for effective expertise transfer was creating the infrastructure to make it possible. ABB has linked Zamech and Dolmel by satellite to its Zurich headquarters for reliable telephone and fax communications. (It is now easier to communicate between Zamech and

Zurich and Dolmel and Zurich than it is between Zamech and Dolmel.) In January, ABB Zamech began electronically transferring three monthly performance reports to Zurich—another big step to make communications more intensive and effective.

Once it created the communications infrastructure, however, ABB had to reckon with a second language barrier—the language of business. To introduce ABB Zamech's "hungry wolves" to basic business concepts and to enable them to transfer these concepts into the ranks, ABB created a "mini MBA program" in Warsaw. The program began in September, covers five key modules (business strategy, marketing, finance, manufacturing, human resources) and is taught by faculty members of INSEAD, the French business school. Sessions run from Thursday evening through Saturday noon, use translated copies of Western business school cases, and closely resemble what goes on in MBA classes everywhere else.

The change program at ABB Zamech has been under way for less than a year, and much remains to be done. But it is already generating results. The company is issuing monthly financial reports that conform to ABB standards—a major achievement in light of the simple systems in place before the joint venture. Cycle times for the production of steam turbines have been cut in half and now meet the ABB worldwide average. A task force is implementing a plan to reduce factory space by 20%—an important step in streamlining the operation. ABB will draw on the Zamech experience as it begins the reform process at Dolmel and Dolmel Drives.

"You *can* change these companies," Kux says. "You *can* make them more competitive and profitable. I can't believe the quality of the reports and presentations these people do today, how at ease they are discussing their strategy and targets. I have worked with many corporate restructurings, but never have I seen so much change so quickly. The energy is incredible. These people really want to learn; they are very ambitious. Basically, ABB Zamech is their business now."

Why emphasize speed at the expense of precision? Because the costs of delay are vastly greater than the costs of an occasional mistake. I won't deny that it was absolutely crazy around here for the first few months after the merger. We *had* to get the matrix in place—we couldn't debate it—and we *had* to figure out which plants would close and which would stay open. We took ten of our best people, the superstars, and gave them six weeks to design the restructuring. We called it the Manhattan Project. I personally interviewed 400 people, virtually day and night, to help select and motivate the people to run our local companies.

Once you've put the global pieces together and have the matrix concept working, what other problems do you have to wrestle with?

Communications. I have no illusions about how hard it is to communicate clearly and quickly to tens of thousands of people around the world. ABB has about 15,000 middle managers prowling around markets all over the world. If we in the executive committee could connect with all of them or even half of them and get them moving in roughly the same direction, we would be unstoppable.

But it's enormously difficult. Last year, for example, we made a big push to squeeze our accounts receivable and free up working capital. We called it the Cash Race. There are 2,000 people around the world with some role in accounts receivable, so we had to mobilize them to make the program work. Three or four months after the program started—and we made it very visible when it started—I visited an accounts receivable office where 20 people were working. These people hadn't even *heard* of the program, and it should have been their top priority. When you come face-to-face with this lack of communication, this massive inertia, you can get horrified, depressed, almost desperate. Or you can concede that this is the way things are, this is how the world works, and commit to doing something about it.

So what do you do?

You don't inform, you *overinform*. That means breaking taboos. There is a strong tendency among European managers to be selective about sharing information.

We faced a huge communications challenge right after the merger. In January 1988, just days after the birth of ABB, we had a management meeting in Cannes with the top 300 people in the company. At that meeting, we presented our policy bible, a 21-page book that communicates the essential principles by which we run the company. It's no glossy brochure. It's got tough, direct language on the role of BA managers, the role of country managers, the approach to change we just discussed, our commitment to decentralization and strict accountability. I told this group of 300 that they had to reach 30,000 ABB people around the world within 60 days—and that didn't mean just sending out the document. It meant translating it into the local languages, sitting with people for a full day and hashing it out.

Cannes and its aftermath was a small step. Real communication takes time, and top managers must be willing to make the investment.

We are the "overhead company." I personally have 2,000 overhead slides and interact with 5,000 people a year in big and small groups. This afternoon, I'll fly up to Lake Constance in Germany, where we have collected 35 managers from around the world. They've been there for three days, and I'll spend three hours with them to end their session. Half the executive committee has already been up there. These are active, working sessions. We talk about how we work in the matrix, how we develop people, about our programs around the world to cut cycle times and raise quality.

I'll give a talk at Lake Constance, but then we'll focus on problems. The manager running high-voltage switchgear in some country may be unhappy about the BA's research priorities. Someone may think we're paying too much attention to Poland. There are lots of tough questions, and my job is to answer on the spot. We'll have 14 such sessions during the course of the year—one every three weeks. That means 400 top managers from all over the world living in close quarters, really communicating about the business and their problems, and meeting with the CEO in an open, honest dialogue.

Let's discuss the politics of global business. For senior executives, the world becomes smaller every day. For most production workers, though, the world is not much different from the way it was 20 years ago, except now their families and communities may depend for jobs on companies with headquarters thousands of miles away. Why shouldn't these workers worry about the loss of local and national control?

It's inevitable that a global business will have global decision centers and that for many workers these decision centers will not be located in their community or even their country. The question is, does the company making decisions have a national ax to grind? In our case the answer is no. We have global coordination, but we have no national bias. The 100 professionals who happen to sit in Zurich could just as easily sit in Chicago or Frankfurt. We're not here very much anyway. So what does it mean to have a headquarters in Zurich? It's where my mail arrives before the important letters are faxed to wherever I happen to be. It's where Abacus collects our performance data. Beyond that, I'm not sure if it means much at all.

Of course, saying we have no national ax to grind does not mean there are any guarantees. Workers will often ask if I can can guarantee their jobs in Norway or Finland or Portugal. I don't sit like a godfather, allocating jobs. ABB has a global game plan, and the game plan creates opportunities for employment, research, exports. What I guarantee is that every member of the federation has a fair shot at the opportunities.

Let's say you're a production worker at ABB Combustion Engineering in Windsor, Connecticut. Two years ago, you worked for a company that you knew was an "American" company. Today you are part of a "federation" of ABB companies around the world. Should you be happy about that?

You should be happy as hell about it. A production worker in Windsor is probably in the boiler field. He or she doesn't much care what ABB is doing with process automation in Columbus, Ohio, let alone what we're doing with turbines outside Gdańsk, Poland. And that's fair. Here's what I would tell that worker: we acquired Combustion Engineering because we believe ABB is a world leader in power plant technology, and we want to extend our lead. We believe that the United States has a great future in power plants both domestically and on an export basis. Combustion represents 80 years of excellence in this technology. Unfortunately, the company sank quite a bit during the 1980s, like many of its U.S. rivals, because of the steep downturn in the industry. It had become a severely weakened organization.

Today, however, the business is coming back, and we have a game plan for the United States. We plan to beef up the Windsor research center to three or four times its current size. We want to tie Windsor's work in new materials, emissions reduction, and pollution control technology with new technologies from our European labs. That will let us respond more effectively to the environmental concerns here. Then we want to combine Combustion's strengths in boilers with ABB's strengths in turbines and generators and Westinghouse's strengths in transmission and distribution to become a broad and unique supplier to the U.S. utility industry. We also have an ambition for Combustion to be much more active in world markets, not with sales agents but through the ABB multidomestic network.

What counts to this production worker is that we deliver, that we are increasing our market share in the United States, raising exports, doing more R&D. That's what makes an American worker's life more secure, not whether the company has its headquarters in the United States.

Don't companies like ABB represent the beginning of a power shift, a transfer of power away from national government to supranational companies?

Are we above governments? No. We answer to governments. We obey the laws in every country in which we operate, and we don't make the laws. However, we do change relations *between* countries. We function as a lubricant for worldwide economic integration.

Think back 15 years ago, when Asea was a Swedish electrical company with 95% of its engineers in Sweden. We could complain about high taxes, about how the high cost of living made it difficult to recruit Germans or Americans to come to Sweden. But what could Asea do about it? Not much. Today I can tell the Swedish authorities that they must create a more competitive environment for R&D or our research there will decline.

That adjustment process would happen regardless of the creation of ABB. Global companies speed up the adjustment. We don't create the process, but we push it. We make visible the invisible hand of global competition.

PART

II

The Process of Change

1
Leading Change: Why Transformation Efforts Fail

John P. Kotter

Over the past decade, I have watched more than 100 companies try to remake themselves into significantly better competitors. They have included large organizations (Ford) and small ones (Landmark Communications), companies based in the United States (General Motors) and elsewhere (British Airways), corporations that were on their knees (Eastern Airlines), and companies that were earning good money (Bristol-Myers Squibb). These efforts have gone under many banners: total quality management, reengineering, right sizing, restructuring, cultural change, and turnaround. But, in almost every case, the basic goal has been the same: to make fundamental changes in how business is conducted in order to help cope with a new, more challenging market environment.

A few of these corporate change efforts have been very successful. A few have been utter failures. Most fall somewhere in between, with a distinct tilt toward the lower end of the scale. The lessons that can be drawn are interesting and will probably be relevant to even more organizations in the increasingly competitive business environment of the coming decade.

The most general lesson to be learned from the more successful cases is that the change process goes through a series of phases that, in total, usually require a considerable length of time (see the exhibit). Skipping steps creates only the illusion of speed and never produces a satisfying result. A second very general lesson is that critical mistakes in any of the phases can have a devastating impact, slowing momentum and negating hard-won gains. Perhaps because we have relatively little experience in renewing organizations, even very capable people often make at least one big error.

Error #1: Not Establishing a Great Enough Sense of Urgency

Most successful change efforts begin when some individuals or some groups start to look hard at a company's competitive situation, market position, technological trends, and financial performance. They focus on the potential revenue drop when an important patent expires, the five-year trend in declining margins in a core business, or an emerging market that everyone seems to be ignoring. They then find ways to communicate this information broadly and dramatically, especially with respect to crises, potential crises, or great opportunities that are very timely. This first step is essential because just getting a transformation program started requires the aggressive cooperation of many individuals. Without motivation, people won't help and the effort goes nowhere.

Compared with other steps in the change process, phase one can sound easy. It is not. Well over 50% of the companies I have watched fail in this first phase. What are the reasons for that failure? Sometimes executives underestimate how hard it can be to drive people out of their comfort zones. Sometimes they grossly overestimate how successful they have already been in increasing urgency. Sometimes they lack patience: "Enough with the preliminaries; let's get on with it." In many cases, executives become paralyzed by the downside possibilities. They worry that employees with seniority will become defensive, that morale will drop, that events will spin out of control, that short-term business results will be jeopardized, that the stock will sink, and that they will be blamed for creating a crisis.

A paralyzed senior management often comes from having too many managers and not enough leaders. Management's mandate is to minimize risk and to keep the current system operating. Change, by definition, requires creating a new system, which in turn always demands leadership. Phase one in a renewal process typically goes nowhere until enough real leaders are promoted or hired into senior-level jobs.

Transformations often begin, and begin well, when an organization has a new head who is a good leader and who sees the need for a major change. If the renewal target is the entire company, the CEO is

Eight Steps to Transforming Your Organization

I Establishing a Sense of Urgency
- Examining market and competitive realities
- Identifying and discussing crises, potential crises, or major opportunities

2 Forming a Powerful Guiding Coalition
- Assembling a group with enough power to lead the charge effort
- Encouraging the group to work together as a team

3 Creating a Vision
- Creating a vision to help direct the change effort
- Developing strategies for achieving that vision

4 Communicating the Vision
- Using every vehicle possible to communicate the new vision and strategies
- Teaching new behaviors by the example of the guiding coalition

5 Empowering Others to Act on the Vision
- Getting rid of obstacles to change
- Changing systems or structures that seriously undermine the vision
- Encouraging risk taking and nontraditional ideas, activities, and actions

6 Planning for and Creating Short-Term Wins
- Planning for visible performance improvements
- Creating those improvements
- Recognizing and rewarding employees involved in the improvement

7 Consolidating Improvements and Producing Still More Change
- Using increased credibility to change systems, structures, and policies that don't fit the vision
- Hiring, promoting, and developing employees who can implement the vision
- Reinvigorating the process with new projects, themes, and change agents

8 Institutionalizing New Approaches
- Articulating the connections between the new behaviors and corporate success
- Developing the means to ensure leadership development and succession

key. If change is needed in a division, the division general manager is key. When these individuals are not new leaders, great leaders, or change champions, phase one can be a huge challenge.

Bad business results are both a blessing and a curse in the first phase. On the positive side, losing money does catch people's attention. But it also gives less maneuvering room. With good business results, the opposite is true: convincing people of the need for change is much harder, but you have more resources to help make changes.

But whether the starting point is good performance or bad, in the more successful cases I have witnessed, an individual or a group always facilitates a frank discussion of potentially unpleasant facts: about new competition, shrinking margins, decreasing market share, flat earnings, a lack of revenue growth, or other relevant indices of a declining competitive position. Because there seems to be an almost universal human tendency to shoot the bearer of bad news, especially if the head of the organization is not a change champion, executives in these companies often rely on outsiders to bring unwanted information. Wall Street analysts, customers, and consultants can all be helpful in this regard. The purpose of all this activity, in the words of one former CEO of a large European company, is "to make the status quo seem more dangerous than launching into the unknown."

In a few of the most successful cases, a group has manufactured a crisis. One CEO deliberately engineered the largest accounting loss in the company's history, creating huge pressures from Wall Street in the process. One division president commissioned first-ever customer-satisfaction surveys, knowing full well that the results would be terrible. He then made these findings public. On the surface, such moves can look unduly risky. But there is also risk in playing it too safe: when the urgency rate is not pumped up enough, the transformation process cannot succeed and the long-term future of the organization is put in jeopardy.

When is the urgency rate high enough? From what I have seen, the answer is when about 75% of a company's management is honestly convinced that business-as-usual is totally unacceptable. Anything less can produce very serious problems later on in the process.

Error #2: Not Creating a Powerful Enough Guiding Coalition

Major renewal programs often start with just one or two people. In cases of successful transformation efforts, the leadership coalition grows and grows over time. But whenever some minimum mass is not achieved early in the effort, nothing much worthwhile happens.

It is often said that major change is impossible unless the head of the organization is an active supporter. What I am talking about goes far beyond that. In successful transformations, the chairman or president or division general manager, plus another 5 or 15 or 50 people, come together and develop a shared commitment to excellent performance through renewal. In my experience, this group never includes all of the company's most senior executives because some people just won't buy in, at least not at first. But in the most successful cases, the coalition is always pretty powerful—in terms of titles, information and expertise, reputations and relationships.

In both small and large organizations, a successful guiding team may consist of only three to five people during the first year of a renewal effort. But in big companies, the coalition needs to grow to the 20 to 50 range before much progress can be made in phase three and beyond. Senior managers always form the core of the group. But sometimes you find board members, a representative from a key customer, or even a powerful union leader.

Because the guiding coalition includes members who are not part of senior management, it tends to operate outside of the normal hierarchy by definition. This can be awkward, but it is clearly necessary. If the existing hierarchy were working well, there would be no need for a major transformation. But since the current system is not working, reform generally demands activity outside of formal boundaries, expectations, and protocol.

A high sense of urgency within the managerial ranks helps enormously in putting a guiding coalition together. But more is usually required. Someone needs to get these people together, help them develop a shared assessment of their company's problems and opportunities, and create a minimum level of trust and communication. Off-site retreats, for two or three days, are one popular vehicle for accomplishing this task. I have seen many groups of 5 to 35 executives attend a series of these retreats over a period of months.

Companies that fail in phase two usually underestimate the difficulties of producing change and thus the importance of a powerful guiding coalition. Sometimes they have no history of teamwork at the top and therefore undervalue the importance of this type of coalition. Sometimes they expect the team to be led by a staff executive from human resources, quality, or strategic planning instead of a key line manager. No matter how capable or dedicated the staff head, groups without strong line leadership never achieve the power that is required.

Efforts that don't have a powerful enough guiding coalition can make apparent progress for a while. But, sooner or later, the opposition gathers itself together and stops the change.

Error #3: Lacking a Vision

In every successful transformation effort that I have seen, the guiding coalition develops a picture of the future that is relatively easy to communicate and appeals to customers, stockholders, and employees. A vision always goes beyond the numbers that are typically found in five-year plans. A vision says something that helps clarify the direction in which an organization needs to move. Sometimes the first draft comes mostly from a single individual. It is usually a bit blurry, at least initially. But after the coalition works at it for 3 or 5 or even 12 months, something much better emerges through their tough analytical thinking and a little dreaming. Eventually, a strategy for achieving that vision is also developed.

In one midsize European company, the first pass at a vision contained two-thirds of the basic ideas that were in the final product. The concept of global reach was in the initial version from the beginning. So was the idea of becoming preeminent in certain businesses. But one central idea in the final version—getting out of low value-added activities—came only after a series of discussions over a period of several months.

Without a sensible vision, a transformation effort can easily dissolve into a list of confusing and incompatible projects that can take the organization in the wrong direction or nowhere at all. Without a sound vision, the reengineering project in the accounting department, the new 360-degree performance appraisal from the human resources department, the plant's quality program, the cultural change project in the sales force will not add up in a meaningful way.

In failed transformations, you often find plenty of plans and directives and programs, but no vision. In one case, a company gave out four-inch-thick notebooks describing its change effort. In mind-numbing detail, the books spelled out procedures, goals, methods, and deadlines. But nowhere was there a clear and compelling statement of where all this was leading. Not surprisingly, most of the employees with whom I talked were either confused or alienated. The big, thick books did not rally them together or inspire change. In fact, they probably had just the opposite effect.

In a few of the less successful cases that I have seen, management had a sense of direction, but it was too complicated or blurry to be useful. Recently, I asked an executive in a midsize company to describe his vision and received in return a barely comprehensible 30-minute lecture. Buried in his answer were the basic elements of a sound vision. But they were buried—deeply.

A useful rule of thumb: if you can't communicate the vision to someone in five minutes or less and get a reaction that signifies both understanding and interest, you are not yet done with this phase of the transformation process.

Error #4: Undercommunicating the Vision by a Factor of Ten

I've seen three patterns with respect to communication, all very common. In the first, a group actually does develop a pretty good transformation vision and then proceeds to communicate it by holding a single meeting or sending out a single communication. Having used about .0001% of the yearly intracompany communication, the group is startled that few people seem to understand the new approach. In the second pattern, the head of the organization spends a considerable amount of time making speeches to employee groups, but most people still don't get it (not surprising, since vision captures only .0005% of the total yearly communication). In the third pattern, much more effort goes into newsletters and speeches, but some very visible senior executives still behave in ways that are antithetical to the vision. The net result is that cynicism among the troops goes up, while belief in the communication goes down.

Transformation is impossible unless hundreds or thousands of people are willing to help, often to the point of making short-term sacrifices. Employees will not make sacrifices, even if they are unhappy with the status quo, unless they believe that useful change is possible. Without credible communication, and a lot of it, the hearts and minds of the troops are never captured.

This fourth phase is particularly challenging if the short-term sacrifices include job losses. Gaining understanding and support is tough when downsizing is a part of the vision. For this reason, successful visions usually include new growth possibilities and the commitment to treat fairly anyone who is laid off.

Executives who communicate well incorporate messages into their hour-by-hour activities. In a routine discussion about a business problem, they talk about how proposed solutions fit (or don't fit) into the bigger picture. In a regular performance appraisal, they talk about how the employee's behavior helps or undermines the vision. In a review of a division's quarterly performance, they talk not only about the numbers but also about how the division's executives are contributing to the transformation. In a routine Q&A with employees at a company facility, they tie their answers back to renewal goals.

In more successful transformation efforts, executives use all existing communication channels to broadcast the vision. They turn boring and unread company newsletters into lively articles about the vision. They take ritualistic and tedious quarterly management meetings and turn them into exciting discussions of the transformation. They throw out much of the company's generic management education and replace it with courses that focus on business problems and the new vision. The guiding principle is simple: use every possible channel, especially those that are being wasted on nonessential information.

Perhaps even more important, most of the executives I have known in successful cases of major change learn to "walk the talk." They consciously attempt to become a living symbol of the new corporate culture. This is often not easy. A 60-year-old plant manager who has spent precious little time over 40 years thinking about customers will not suddenly behave in a customer-oriented way. But I have witnessed just such a person change, and change a great deal. In that case, a high level of urgency helped. The fact that the man was a part of the guiding coalition and the vision-creation team also helped. So did all the communication, which kept reminding him of the desired behavior, and all the feedback from his peers and subordinates, which helped him see when he was not engaging in that behavior.

Communication comes in both words and deeds, and the latter are often the most powerful form. Nothing undermines change more than behavior by important individuals that is inconsistent with their words.

Error #5: Not Removing Obstacles to the New Vision

Successful transformations begin to involve large numbers of people as the process progresses. Employees are emboldened to try new approaches, to develop new ideas, and to provide leadership. The only constraint is that the actions fit within the broad parameters of the overall vision. The more people involved, the better the outcome.

To some degree, a guiding coalition empowers others to take action simply by successfully communicating the new direction. But communication is never sufficient by itself. Renewal also requires the removal of obstacles. Too often, an employee understands the new vision and wants to help make it happen. But an elephant appears to be blocking the path. In some cases, the elephant is in the person's head, and the challenge is to convince the individual that no external obstacle exists. But in most cases, the blockers are very real.

Sometimes the obstacle is the organizational structure: narrow job categories can seriously undermine efforts to increase productivity or make it very difficult even to think about customers. Sometimes compensation or performance-appraisal systems make people choose between the new vision and their own self-interest. Perhaps worst of all are bosses who refuse to change and who make demands that are inconsistent with the overall effort.

One company began its transformation process with much publicity and actually made good progress through the fourth phase. Then the change effort ground to a halt because the officer in charge of the company's largest division was allowed to undermine most of the new initiatives. He paid lip service to the process but did not change his behavior or encourage his managers to change. He did not reward the unconventional ideas called for in the vision. He allowed human resource systems to remain intact even when they were clearly inconsistent with the new ideals. I think the officer's motives were complex. To some degree, he did not believe the company needed major change. To some degree, he felt personally threatened by all the change. To some degree, he was afraid that he could not produce both change and the expected operating profit. But despite the fact that they backed the renewal effort, the other officers did virtually nothing to stop the one blocker. Again, the reasons were complex. The company had no history of confronting problems like this. Some people were afraid of the officer. The CEO was concerned that he might lose a talented executive. The net result was disastrous. Lower level managers concluded that senior management had lied to them about their commitment to renewal, cynicism grew, and the whole effort collapsed.

In the first half of a transformation, no organization has the momentum, power, or time to get rid of all obstacles. But the big ones must be confronted and removed. If the blocker is a person, it is important that he or she be treated fairly and in a way that is consistent with the new vision. But action is essential, both to empower others and to maintain the credibility of the change effort as a whole.

Error #6: Not Systematically Planning For and Creating Short-Term Wins

Real transformation takes time, and a renewal effort risks losing momentum if there are no short-term goals to meet and celebrate. Most people won't go on the long march unless they see compelling evidence within 12 to 24 months that the journey is producing expected results. Without short-term wins, too many people give up or actively join the ranks of those people who have been resisting change.

One to two years into a successful transformation effort, you find quality beginning to go up on certain indices or the decline in net income stopping. You find some successful new product introductions or an upward shift in market share. You find an impressive productivity improvement or a statistically higher customer-satisfaction rating. But whatever the case, the win is unambiguous. The result is not just a judgment call that can be discounted by those opposing change.

Creating short-term wins is different from hoping for short-term wins. The latter is passive, the former active. In a successful transformation, managers actively look for ways to obtain clear performance improvements, establish goals in the yearly planning system, achieve the objectives, and reward the people involved with recognition, promotions, and even money. For example, the guiding coalition at a U.S. manufacturing company produced a highly visible and successful new product introduction about 20 months after the start of its renewal effort. The new product was selected about six months into the effort because it met multiple criteria: it could be designed and launched in a relatively short period; it could be handled by a small team of people who were devoted to the new vision; it had upside potential; and the new product-development team could operate outside the established departmental structure without practical problems. Little was left to chance, and the win boosted the credibility of the renewal process.

Managers often complain about being forced to produce short-term wins, but I've found that pressure can be a useful element in a change effort. When it becomes clear to people that major change will take a long time, urgency levels can drop. Commitments to produce short-term wins help keep the urgency level up and force detailed analytical thinking that can clarify or revise visions.

Error #7: Declaring Victory Too Soon

After a few years of hard work, managers may be tempted to declare victory with the first clear performance improvement. While celebrating a win is fine, declaring the war won can be catastrophic. Until changes sink deeply into a company's culture, a process that can take five to ten years, new approaches are fragile and subject to regression.

In the recent past, I have watched a dozen change efforts operate under the reengineering theme. In all but two cases, victory was declared and the expensive consultants were paid and thanked when the first major project was completed after two to three years. Within two more years, the useful changes that had been introduced slowly disappeared. In two of the ten cases, it's hard to find any trace of the reengineering work today.

Over the past 20 years, I've seen the same sort of thing happen to huge quality projects, organizational development efforts, and more. Typically, the problems start early in the process: the urgency level is not intense enough, the guiding coalition is not powerful enough, and the vision is not clear enough. But it is the premature victory celebration that kills momentum. And then the powerful forces associated with tradition take over.

Ironically, it is often a combination of change initiators and change resistors that creates the premature victory celebration. In their enthusiasm over a clear sign of progress, the initiators go overboard. They are then joined by resistors, who are quick to spot any opportunity to stop change. After the celebration is over, the resistors point to the victory as a sign that the war has been won and the troops should be sent home. Weary troops allow themselves to be convinced that they won. Once home, the foot soldiers are reluctant to climb back on the ships. Soon thereafter, change comes to a halt, and tradition creeps back in.

Instead of declaring victory, leaders of successful efforts use the credibility afforded by short-term wins to tackle even bigger problems. They go after systems and structures that are not consistent with the transformation vision and have not been confronted before. They pay great attention to who is promoted, who is hired, and how people are developed. They include new reengineering projects that are even bigger in scope than the initial ones. They understand that renewal efforts take not months but years. In fact, in one of the most successful transformations that I have ever seen, we quantified the amount of change that occurred each year over a seven-year period. On a scale of one (low) to ten (high), year one received a two, year two a four, year three a three, year four a seven, year five an eight, year six a four, and year seven a two. The peak came in year five, fully 36 months after the first set of visible wins.

Error #8: Not Anchoring Changes in the Corporation's Culture

In the final analysis, change sticks when it becomes "the way we do things around here," when it seeps into the bloodstream of the corporate body. Until new behaviors are rooted in social norms and shared values, they are subject to degradation as soon as the pressure for change is removed.

Two factors are particularly important in institutionalizing change in corporate culture. The first is a conscious attempt to show people how the new approaches, behaviors, and attitudes have helped improve performance. When people are left on their own to make the connections, they sometimes create very inaccurate links. For example, because results improved while charismatic Harry was boss, the troops link his mostly idiosyncratic style with those results instead of seeing how their own improved customer service and productivity were instrumental. Helping people see the right connections requires communication. Indeed, one company was relentless, and it paid off enormously. Time was spent at every major management meeting to discuss why performance was increasing. The company newspaper ran article after article showing how changes had boosted earnings.

The second factor is taking sufficient time to make sure that the next generation of top management really does personify the new approach. If the requirements for promotion don't change, renewal rarely lasts. One bad succession decision at the top of an organization can undermine a decade of hard work. Poor succession decisions are possible when boards of directors are not an integral part of the renewal effort. In at least three instances I have seen, the champion for change was the retiring executive, and although his successor was not a resistor, he was not a change champion. Because the boards did not understand the transformations in any detail, they could not see that their choices were not good fits. The retiring executive in one case tried unsuccessfully to talk his board into a less seasoned candidate who better personified the transformation. In the other two cases, the CEOs did not resist the boards' choices, because they felt the transformation could not be undone by their successors. They were wrong. Within two years, signs of renewal began to disappear at both companies.

There are still more mistakes that people make, but these eight are the big ones. I realize that in a short article everything is made to sound a bit too simplistic. In reality, even successful change efforts are messy and full of surprises. But just as a relatively simple vision is needed to guide people through a major change, so a vision of the change process can reduce the error rate. And fewer errors can spell the difference between success and failure.

2
Reengineering Work: Don't Automate, Obliterate

Michael Hammer

Despite a decade or more of restructuring and downsizing, many U.S. companies are still unprepared to operate in the 1990s. In a time of rapidly changing technologies and ever-shorter product life cycles, product development often proceeds at a glacial pace. In an age of the customer, order fulfillment has high error rates and customer inquiries go unanswered for weeks. In a period when asset utilization is critical, inventory levels exceed many months of demand.

The usual methods for boosting performance—process rationalization and automation—haven't yielded the dramatic improvements companies need. In particular, heavy investments in information technology have delivered disappointing results—largely because companies tend to use technology to mechanize old ways of doing business. They leave the existing processes intact and use computers simply to speed them up.

But speeding up those processes cannot address their fundamental performance deficiencies. Many of our job designs, work flows, control mechanisms, and organizational structures came of age in a different competitive environment and before the advent of the computer. They are geared toward efficiency and control. Yet the watchwords of the new decade are innovation and speed, service and quality.

It is time to stop paving the cow paths. Instead of embedding outdated processes in silicon and software, we should obliterate them and start over. We should "reengineer" our businesses: use the power of modern information technology to radically redesign our business processes in order to achieve dramatic improvements in their performance.

Every company operates according to a great many unarticulated rules. "Credit decisions are made by the credit department." "Local inventory is needed for good customer service." "Forms must be filled in completely and in order." Reengineering strives to break away from the old rules about how we organize and conduct business. (See "Why Did We Design Inefficient Processes?") It involves recognizing and rejecting some of them and then finding imaginative new ways to accomplish work. From our redesigned processes, new rules will emerge that fit the times. Only then can we hope to achieve quantum leaps in performance.

Why Did We Design Inefficient Processes?

In a way, we didn't. Many of our procedures were not designed at all; they just happened. The company founder one day recognized that he didn't have time to handle a chore, so he delegated it to Smith. Smith improvised. Time passed, the business grew, and Smith hired his entire clan to help him cope with the work volume. They all improvised. Each day brought new challenges and special cases, and the staff adjusted its work accordingly. The hodgepodge of special cases and quick fixes was passed from one generation of workers to the next.

We have institutionalized the ad hoc and enshrined the temporary. Why do we send foreign accounts to the corner desk? Because 20 years ago, Mary spoke French and Mary had the corner desk. Today Mary is long gone, and we no longer do business in France, but we still send foreign accounts to the corner desk. Why does an electronics company spend $10 million a year to manage a field inventory worth $20 million? Once upon a time the inventory was worth $200 million, and managing it cost $5 million. Since then, warehousing costs have escalated, components have become less expensive, and better forecasting techniques have minimized units in inventory. But the inventory procedures, alas, are the same as always.

Of the business processes that *were* designed, most took their present forms in the 1950s. The goal then was to check overambitious growth— much as the typewriter keyboard was designed to slow typists who would otherwise jam the keys. It is no accident that organizations stifle innovation and creativity. That's what they were *designed* to do.

Nearly all of our processes originated before the advent of modern computer and communications technology. They are replete with mechanisms designed to compensate for "information poverty." Although we are now information affluent, we still use those mechanisms, which are now deeply embedded in automated systems.

Reengineering cannot be planned meticulously and accomplished in small and cautious steps. It's an all-or-nothing proposition with an uncertain result. Still, most companies have no choice but to muster the courage to do it. For many, reengineering is the only hope for breaking away from the antiquated processes that threaten to drag them down. Fortunately, managers are not without help. Enough businesses have successfully reengineered their processes to provide some rules of thumb for others.

What Ford and MBL Did

Japanese competitors and young entrepreneurial ventures prove every day that drastically better levels of process performance are possible. They develop products twice as fast, utilize assets eight times more productively, respond to customers ten times faster. Some large, established companies also show what can be done. Businesses like Ford Motor Company and Mutual Benefit Life Insurance have reengineered their processes and achieved competitive leadership as a result. Ford has reengineered its accounts payable processes, and Mutual Benefit Life, its processing of applications for insurance.

In the early 1980s, when the American automotive industry was in a depression, Ford's top management put accounts payable—along with many other departments—under the microscope in search of ways to cut costs. Accounts payable in North America alone employed more than 500 people. Management thought that by rationalizing processes and installing new computer systems, it could reduce the head count by some 20%.

Ford was enthusiastic about its plan to tighten accounts payable—until it looked at Mazda. While Ford was aspiring to a 400-person department, Mazda's accounts payable organization consisted of a total of 5 people. The difference in absolute numbers was astounding, and even after adjusting for Mazda's smaller size, Ford figured that its accounts payable organization was five times the size it should be. The Ford team knew better than to attribute the discrepancy to calisthenics, company songs, or low interest rates.

Ford managers ratcheted up their goal: accounts payable would perform with not just a hundred but many hundreds fewer clerks. It then set out to achieve it. First, managers analyzed the existing system. When Ford's purchasing department wrote a purchase order, it sent a copy to accounts payable. Later, when material control received the goods, it sent a copy of the receiving document to accounts payable. Meanwhile, the vendor sent an invoice to accounts payable. It was up to accounts payable, then, to match the purchase order against the receiving document and the invoice. If they matched, the department issued payment.

The department spent most of its time on mismatches, instances where the purchase order, receiving document, and invoice disagreed. In these cases, an accounts payable clerk would investigate the discrepancy, hold up payment, generate documents, and all in all gum up the works.

One way to improve things might have been to help the accounts payable clerk investigate more efficiently, but a better choice was to prevent the mismatches in the first place. To this end, Ford instituted "invoiceless processing." Now when the purchasing department initiates an order, it enters the information into an on-line database. It doesn't send a copy of the purchase order to anyone. When the goods arrive at the receiving dock, the receiving clerk checks the database to see if they correspond to an outstanding purchase order. If so, he or she accepts them and enters the transaction into the computer system. (If receiving can't find a database entry for the received goods, it simply returns the order.)

Under the old procedures, the accounting department had to match 14 data items between the receipt record, the purchase order, and the invoice before it could issue payment to the vendor. The new approach requires matching only three items—part number, unit of measure, and supplier code—between the purchase order and the receipt record. The matching is done automatically, and the computer prepares the check, which accounts payable sends to the vendor. There are no invoices to worry about since Ford has asked its vendors not to send them.

Ford didn't settle for the modest increases it first envisioned. It opted for radical change—and achieved dramatic improvement. Where it has instituted this new process, Ford has achieved a 75% reduction in head count, not the 20% it would have gotten with a conventional program. And since there are no discrepancies between the financial record and the physical record, material control is simpler and financial information is more accurate.

Mutual Benefit Life, the country's eighteenth largest life carrier, has reengineered its processing of insurance applications. Prior to this, MBL handled customers' applications much as its competitors did. The long, multistep process involved credit checking, quoting, rating, underwriting, and so on. An application would have to go through as many as 30 discrete steps, spanning 5 departments and involving 19 people. At the very best, MBL could process an application in 24 hours, but more typical turnarounds ranged from 5 to 25 days—most of the time spent passing information from one department to the next. (Another insurer estimated that while an application spent 22 days in process, it was actually worked on for just 17 minutes.)

MBL's rigid, sequential process led to many complications. For instance, when a customer wanted to cash in an existing policy and purchase a new one, the old business department first had to authorize the treasury department to issue a check made payable to MBL. The check would then accompany the paperwork to the new business department.

The president of MBL, intent on improving customer service, decided that this nonsense had to stop and demanded a 60% improvement in productivity. It was clear that such an ambitious goal would require more than tinkering with the existing process. Strong measures were in order, and the management team assigned to the task looked to technology as a means of achieving them. The team realized that shared databases and computer networks could make many different kinds of information available to a single person, while expert systems could help people with limited experience make sound decisions. Applying these insights led to a new approach to the application-handling process, one with wide organizational implications and little resemblance to the old way of doing business.

MBL swept away existing job definitions and departmental boundaries and created a new position called a case manager. Case managers have total responsibility for an application from the time it is received to the time a policy is issued. Unlike clerks, who performed a fixed task repeatedly under the watchful gaze of a supervisor, case managers work autonomously. No more handoffs of files and responsibility, no more shuffling of customer inquiries.

Case managers are able to perform all the tasks associated with an insurance application because they are supported by powerful PC-based workstations that run an expert system and connect to a range of automated systems on a mainframe. In particularly tough cases, the case manager calls for assistance from a senior underwriter or physician, but these specialists work only as consultants and advisers to the case manager, who never relinquishes control.

Empowering individuals to process entire applications has had a tremendous impact on operations. MBL can now complete an application in as little as four hours, and average turnaround takes only two to five days. The company has eliminated 100 field office positions, and case managers can handle more than twice the volume of new applications the company previously could process.

The Essence of Reengineering

At the heart of reengineering is the notion of discontinuous thinking—of recognizing and breaking away from the outdated rules and fundamental assumptions that underlie operations. Unless we change these rules, we are merely rearranging the deck chairs on the Titanic. We cannot achieve breakthroughs in performance by cutting fat or automating existing processes. Rather, we must challenge old assumptions and shed the old rules that made the business underperform in the first place.

Every business is replete with implicit rules left over from earlier decades. "Customers don't repair their own equipment." "Local warehouses are necessary for good service." "Merchandising decisions are made at headquarters." These rules of work design are based on assumptions about technology, people, and organizational goals that no longer hold. The contemporary repertoire of available information technologies is vast and quickly expanding. Quality, innovation, and service are now more important than cost, growth, and control. A large portion of the population is educated and capable of assuming responsibility, and workers cherish their autonomy and expect to have a say in how the business is run.

It should come as no surprise that our business processes and structures are outmoded and obsolete: our work structures and processes have not kept pace with the changes in technology, demographics, and business objectives. For the most part, we have organized work as a sequence of separate tasks and employed complex mechanisms to track its progress. This arrangement can be traced to the Industrial Revolution, when specialization of labor and economies of scale promised to overcome the inefficiencies of cottage industries. Businesses disaggregated work into narrowly defined tasks, reaggregated the people performing those tasks into departments, and installed managers to administer them.

Our elaborate systems for imposing control and discipline on those who actually do the work stem from the postwar period. In that halcyon period of expansion, the main concern was growing fast without going broke, so businesses focused on cost, growth, and control. And since literate, entry-level people were abundant but well-educated professionals hard to come by, the control systems funneled information up the hierarchy to the few who presumably knew what to do with it.

These patterns of organizing work have become so ingrained that, despite their serious drawbacks, it's hard to conceive of work being accomplished any other way. Conventional process structures are fragmented and piecemeal, and they lack the integration necessary to maintain quality and service. They are breeding grounds for tunnel vision, as people tend to substitute the narrow goals of their particular department for the larger goals of the process as a whole. When work is handed off from person to person and unit to unit, delays and errors are inevitable. Accountability blurs, and critical issues fall between the cracks. Moreover, no one sees enough of the big picture to be able to respond quickly to new situations. Managers desperately try, like all the king's horses and all the king's men, to piece together the fragmented pieces of business processes.

Managers have tried to adapt their processes to new circumstances, but usually in ways that just create more problems. If, say, customer service is poor, they create a mechanism to deliver service but overlay it on the existing organization. Bureaucracy thickens, costs rise, and enterprising competitors gain market share.

In reengineering, managers break loose from outmoded business processes and the design principles underlying them and create new ones. Ford had operated under the old rule that "We pay when we receive the invoice." While no one had ever articulated or recorded it, that rule determined how the accounts payable process was organized. Ford's reengineering effort challenged and ultimately replaced the rule with a new one: "We pay when we receive the *goods.*"

Reengineering requires looking at the fundamental processes of the business from a cross-functional perspective. Ford discovered that reengineering only the accounts payable department was futile. The appropriate focus of the effort was what might be called the goods acquisition process, which included purchasing and receiving as well as accounts payable.

One way to ensure that reengineering has a cross-functional perspective is to assemble a team that represents the functional units involved in the process being reengineered and all the units that depend on it. The team must analyze and scrutinize the existing process until it really understands what the process is trying to accomplish. The point is not to learn what happens to form 73B in its peregrinations through the company but to understand the purpose of having form 73B in the first place. Rather than looking for opportunities to improve the current process, the team should determine which of its steps really add value and search for new ways to achieve the result.

The reengineering team must keep asking Why? and What if? Why do we need to get a manager's signature on a requisition? Is it a control mechanism or a decision point? What if the manager reviews only requisitions above $500? What if he or she doesn't see them at all? Raising and resolving heretical questions can separate what is fundamental to the process from what is superficial. The regional offices of an East Coast insurance company had long produced a series of reports that they regularly sent to the home office. No one in the field realized that these reports were simply filed and never used. The process outlasted the circumstances that had created the need for it. The reengineering study team should push to discover situations like this.

In short, a reengineering effort strives for dramatic levels of improvement. It must break away from conventional wisdom and the constraints of organizational boundaries and should be broad and cross-functional in scope. It should use information technology not to automate an existing process but to enable a new one.

Principles of Reengineering

Creating new rules tailored to the modern environment ultimately requires a new conceptualization of the business process—which comes down to someone having a great idea. But reengineering need not be haphazard. In fact, some of the principles that companies have already discovered while reengineering their business processes can help jump start the effort for others.

ORGANIZE AROUND OUTCOMES, NOT TASKS

This principle says to have one person perform all the steps in a process. Design that person's job around an objective or outcome instead of a single task. The redesign at Mutual Benefit Life, where individual case managers perform the entire application approval process, is the quintessential example of this.

The redesign of an electronics company is another example. It had separate organizations performing each of the five steps between selling and installing the equipment. One group determined customer requirements, another translated those requirements into internal product codes, a third conveyed that information to various plants and warehouses, a fourth received and assembled the components, and a fifth delivered and installed the equipment. The process was based on the centuries-old notion of specialized labor and on the limitations inherent in paper files. The departments each possessed a specific set of skills, and only one department at a time could do its work.

The customer order moved systematically from step to step. But this sequential processing caused problems. The people getting the information from the customer in step one had to get all the data anyone would need throughout the process, even if it wasn't needed until step five. In addition, the many handoffs were responsible for numerous errors and misunderstandings. Finally, any questions about customer requirements that arose late in the process had to be referred back to the people doing step one, resulting in delay and rework.

When the company reengineered, it eliminated the assembly-line approach. It compressed responsibility for the various steps and assigned it to one person, the "customer service representative." That person now oversees the whole process—taking the order, translating it into product codes, getting the components assembled, and seeing the product delivered and installed. The customer service rep expedites and coordinates the process, much like a general contractor. And the customer has just one contact, who always knows the status of the order.

HAVE THOSE WHO USE THE OUTPUT OF THE PROCESS PERFORM THE PROCESS

In an effort to capitalize on the benefits of specialization and scale, many organizations established specialized departments to handle specialized processes. Each department does only one type of work and is a "customer" of other groups' processes. Accounting does only accounting. If it needs new pencils, it goes to the purchasing department, the group specially equipped with the information and expertise to perform that role. Purchasing finds vendors, negotiates price, places the order, inspects the goods, and pays the invoice—and eventually the accountants get their pencils. The process works (after a fashion), but it's slow and bureaucratic.

Now that computer-based data and expertise are more readily available, departments, units, and individuals can do more for themselves. Opportunities exist to reengineer processes so that the individuals who need the result of a process can do it themselves. For example, by using expert systems and databases, departments can make their own purchases without sacrificing the benefits of specialized purchasers. One manufacturer has reengineered its purchasing process along just these lines. The company's old system, whereby the operating departments submitted requisitions and let purchasing do the rest, worked well for controlling expensive and important items like raw materials and capital equipment. But for inexpensive and nonstrategic purchases, which constituted some 35% of total orders, the system was slow and cumbersome; it was not uncommon for the cost of the purchasing process to exceed the cost of the goods being purchased.

The new process compresses the purchase of sundry items and pushes it on to the customers of the process. Using a database of approved vendors, an operating unit can directly place an order with a vendor and charge it on a bank credit card. At the end of the month, the bank gives the manufacturer a tape of all credit card transactions, which the company runs against its internal accounting system.

When an electronics equipment manufacturer reengineered its field service process, it pushed some of the steps of the process on to its customers. The manufacturer's field service had been plagued by the usual problems: technicians were often unable to do a particular repair because the right part wasn't on the van, response to customer calls was slow, and spare-parts inventory was excessive.

Now customers make simple repairs themselves. Spare parts are stored at each customer's site and managed through a computerized inventory-management system. When a problem arises, the customer calls the manufacturer's field-service hot line and describes the symptoms to a diagnostician, who accesses a diagnosis support system. If the problem appears to be something the customer can fix, the diagnostician tells the customer what part to replace and how to install it. The old part is picked up and a new part left in its place at a later time. Only for complex problems is a service technician dispatched to the site, this time without having to make a stop at the warehouse to pick up parts.

When the people closest to the process perform it, there is little need for the overhead associated with managing it. Interfaces and liaisons can be eliminated, as can the mechanisms used to coordinate those who perform the process with those who use it. Moreover, the problem of capacity planning for the process performers is greatly reduced.

SUBSUME INFORMATION-PROCESSING WORK INTO THE REAL WORK THAT PRODUCES THE INFORMATION

The previous two principles say to compress linear processes. This principle suggests moving work from one person or department to another. Why doesn't an organization that produces information also process it? In the past, people didn't have the time or weren't trusted to do both. Most companies established units to do nothing but collect and process information that other departments created. This arrangement reflects the old rule about specialized labor and the belief that people at lower organizational levels are incapable of acting on information they generate. An accounts payable department collects information from purchasing and receiving and reconciles it with data that the vendor provides. Quality assurance gathers and analyzes information it gets from production.

Ford's redesigned accounts payable process embodies the new rule. With the new system, receiving, which produces the information about the goods received, processes this information instead of sending it to accounts payable. The new computer system can easily compare the delivery with the order and trigger the appropriate action.

TREAT GEOGRAPHICALLY DISPERSED RESOURCES AS THOUGH THEY WERE CENTRALIZED

The conflict between centralization and decentralization is a classic one. Decentralizing a resource (whether people, equipment, or inventory) gives better service to those who use it, but at the cost of redundancy, bureaucracy, and missed economies of scale. Companies no longer have to make such trade-offs. They can use databases, telecommunications networks, and standardized processing systems to get the benefits of scale and coordination while maintaining the benefits of flexibility and service.

At Hewlett-Packard, for instance, each of the more than 50 manufacturing units had its own separate purchasing department. While this arrangement provided excellent responsiveness and service to the plants, it prevented HP from realizing the benefits of its scale, particularly with regard to quantity discounts. HP's solution is to maintain the divisional purchasing organizations and to introduce a corporate unit to coordinate them. Each purchasing unit has access to a shared database on vendors and their performance and issues its own purchase orders. Corporate purchasing maintains this database and uses it to negotiate contracts for the corporation and to monitor the units. The payoffs have come in a 150% improvement in on-time deliveries, 50% reduction in lead times, 75% reduction in failure rates, and a significantly lower cost of goods purchased.

LINK PARALLEL ACTIVITIES INSTEAD OF INTEGRATING THEIR RESULTS

HP's decentralized purchasing operations represent one kind of parallel processing in which separate units perform the same function. Another common kind of parallel processing is when separate units perform different activities that must eventually come together. Product development typically operates this way. In the development of a photocopier, for example, independent units develop the various subsystems of the copier. One group works on the optics, another on the mechanical paper-handling device, another on the power supply, and so on. Having people do development work simultaneously saves time, but at the dreaded integration and testing phase, the pieces often fail to work together. Then the costly redesign begins.

Or consider a bank that sells different kinds of credit—loans, letters of credit, asset-based financing—through separate units. These groups may have no way of knowing whether another group has already extended credit to a particular customer. Each unit could extend the full $10 million credit limit.

The new principle says to forge links between parallel functions and to coordinate them while their activities are in process rather than after they are completed. Communications networks, shared databases, and teleconferencing can bring the independent groups together so that coordination is ongoing. One large electronics company has cut its product development cycle by more than 50% by implementing this principle.

PUT THE DECISION POINT WHERE THE WORK IS
PERFORMED, AND BUILD CONTROL INTO THE PROCESS

In most organizations, those who do the work are distinguished from those who monitor the work and make decisions about it. The tacit assumption is that the people actually doing the work have neither the time nor the inclination to monitor and control it and that they lack the knowledge and scope to make decisions about it. The entire hierarchical management structure is built on this assumption. Accountants, auditors, and supervisors check, record, and monitor work. Managers handle any exceptions.

The new principle suggests that the people who do the work should make the decisions and that the process itself can have built-in controls. Pyramidal management layers can therefore be compressed and the organization flattened.

Information technology can capture and process data, and expert systems can to some extent supply knowledge, enabling people to make their own decisions. As the doers become self-managing and self-controlling, hierarchy—and the slowness and bureaucracy associated with it—disappears.

When Mutual Benefit Life reengineered the insurance application process, it not only compressed the linear sequence but also eliminated the need for layers of managers. These two kinds of compression—vertical and horizontal—often go together; the very fact that a worker sees only one piece of the process calls for a manager with a broader vision. The case managers at MBL provide end-to-end management of the process, reducing the need for traditional managers. The managerial role is changing from one of controller and supervisor to one of supporter and facilitator.

CAPTURE INFORMATION ONCE AND AT THE SOURCE

This last rule is simple. When information was difficult to transmit, it made sense to collect information repeatedly. Each person, department, or unit had its own requirements and forms. Companies simply had to live with the associated delays, entry errors, and costly overhead. But why do we have to live with those problems now? Today when we collect a piece of information, we can store it in an on-line database for all who need it. Bar coding, relational databases, and electronic data interchange (EDI) make it easy to collect, store, and transmit information. One insurance company found that its application review process required that certain items be entered into "stovepipe" computer systems supporting different functions as many as five times. By integrating and connecting these systems, the company was able to eliminate this redundant data entry along with the attendant checking functions and inevitable errors.

Think Big

Reengineering triggers changes of many kinds, not just of the business process itself. Job designs, organizational structures, management systems—anything associated with the process—must be refashioned in an integrated way. In other words, reengineering is a tremendous effort that mandates change in many areas of the organization.

When Ford reengineered its payables, receiving clerks on the dock had to learn to use computer terminals to check shipments, and they had to make decisions about whether to accept the goods. Purchasing agents also had to assume new responsibilities—like making sure the purchase orders they entered into the database had the correct information about where to send the check. Attitudes toward vendors also had to change: vendors could no longer be seen as adversaries; they had to become partners in a shared business process. Vendors too had to adjust. In many cases, invoices formed the basis of their accounting systems. At least one Ford supplier adapted by continuing to print invoices, but instead of sending them to Ford threw them away, reconciling cash received against invoices never sent.

The changes at Mutual Benefit Life were also widespread. The company's job-rating scheme could not accommodate the case manager position, which had a lot of responsibility but no direct reports. MBL had to devise new job-rating schemes and compensation policies. It also had to develop a culture in which people doing work are perceived as more important than those supervising work. Career paths, recruitment and training programs, promotion policies—these and many other management systems are being revised to support the new process design.

The extent of these changes suggests one factor that is necessary for reengineering to succeed: executive leadership with real vision. No one in an organization wants reengineering. It is confusing and disruptive and affects everything people have grown accustomed to. Only if top-level managers back the effort and outlast the company cynics will people take reengineering seriously. As one wag at an electronics equipment manufacturer has commented, "Every few months, our senior managers find a new religion. One time it was quality, another it was customer service, another it was flattening the organization. We just hold our breath until they get over it and things get back to normal." Commitment, consistency—maybe even a touch of fanaticism—are needed to enlist those who would prefer the status quo.

Considering the inertia of old processes and structures, the strain of implementing a reengineering plan can hardly be overestimated. But by the same token, it is hard to overestimate the opportunities, especially for established companies. Big, traditional organizations aren't necessarily dinosaurs doomed to extinction, but they are burdened with layers of unproductive overhead and armies of unproductive workers. Shedding them a layer at a time will not be good enough to stand up against sleek startups or streamlined Japanese companies. U.S. companies need fast change and dramatic improvements.

We have the tools to do what we need to do. Information technology offers many options for reorganizing work. But our imaginations must guide our decisions about technology—not the other way around. We must have the boldness to imagine taking 78 days out of an 80-day turnaround time, cutting 75% of overhead, and eliminating 80% of errors. These are not unrealistic goals. If managers have the vision, reengineering will provide a way.

3

The Reinvention Roller Coaster: Risking the Present for a Powerful Future

Tracy Goss, Richard Pascale, and Anthony Athos

Kodak, IBM, American Express, and General Motors have recently sacked their CEOs. All were capable executives with impressive track records. All had promised turnarounds, and all had spearheaded downsizing, delayering, and reengineering programs in vigorous efforts to deliver those promises. Indeed, most of these efforts lowered costs, increased productivity, and improved profitability—at least for a while. Yet despite this frenzy of activity, the competitive vitality of these companies continued to ebb away until finally their boards felt compelled to act.

What went wrong? The simplistic answer is "leadership." All these boards wound up blaming their CEOs for poor leadership and inadequate strategic vision. But press the members of those boards—or the shaken executives—for a better answer, and you will uncover uncertainty, bafflement, even an occasional muddled insight that the answer lies somewhere deeper than any board or executive is equipped to look.

These experienced businesspeople see the problem as "leadership" because they see the solution as "change." And surely, they tell themselves, any leader deserving of that name can successfully implement change. They are right. With all the practice of the 1980s, every CEO knows how to create cross-functional teams, reduce defects, and redesign business processes in ways that lower costs and improve performance. A CEO who cannot set ambitious new goals and does not know how to try harder to reach them deserves the boot.

But what these CEOs are missing is that such incremental change is not enough for many companies today. Managers groping about for a more fundamental shift in their organizations' capabilities must re-alize that change programs treat symptoms, not underlying conditions. These companies do not need to improve themselves; they need to reinvent themselves.

Reinvention is not changing what is, but creating what isn't. A butterfly is not more caterpillar or a better or improved caterpillar; a butterfly is a different creature. Leaders of three multinational compa-nies with whom we have worked have grappled with this distinction. When British Airways declared itself the world's favorite airline in the 1980s, it faced the challenge of becoming a different company, not just a better company. The same held true when Europcar decided to become the most user friendly and efficient rental-car company in Europe and not just an omnipresent one. And when Häagen-Dazs chose to make a visit to its European ice-cream shops an exciting event, the company didn't need just to change what it did or how work got done.

When a company reinvents itself, it must alter the underlying as-sumptions and invisible premises on which its decisions and actions are based. This *context* is the sum of all the conclusions that members of the organization have reached. It is the product of their experience and their interpretations of the past, and it determines the organiza-tion's social behavior, or culture. Unspoken and even unacknowledged conclusions about the past dictate what is possible for the future.

To reinvent itself, an organization must first uncover its hidden context. Only when an organization is threatened, losing momentum, or eager to break new ground will it confront its past and begin to understand why it must break with its outmoded present. And only then will a company's employees come to believe in a powerful new future, a future that may seem beyond the organization's reach.

Admittedly, the notion that companies should "stretch" themselves to achieve unprecedented goals is not new. But executives have fre-quently under estimated the wrenching shift—the internal conflict and soul-searching—that goes hand in hand with a break from the present way of thinking and operating. And because executives have not understood this as they announced their grandiose "strategic in-tentions," employees have often ignored the call to arms.

Unless managers orchestrate the creation of a new context, all that the organizations are *doing* to improve their competitiveness—whether they are improving service, accelerating product development, or in-creasing the flexibility of manufacturing—will at worst yield unproductive churnings and at best produce meaningful but episodic change.

But if a company authentically reinvents itself, if it alters its context, it not only has the means to alter its culture and achieve unprecedented results in quality, service ratings, cycle time, market share, and, finally, financial performance; it also will have the ability to sustain these improvements regardless of any changes in the business environment.

One company that nearly succeeded in reinventing itself is the Ford Motor Company. From 1980 through 1982, Ford lost $3 billion. By 1986, its earnings surpassed those of much larger General Motors for the first time since the 1920s. By 1988, Ford's profits reached $5.3 billion, and return on stockholders' equity hit 26.3%. Its market share in the United States had increased five points to 22%. Cycle time for the development of an automobile decreased from eight years to five. Quality, according to J.D. Power surveys, jumped from the bottom 25% to the top 10% of all automobiles that were sold in the United States. And surveys and focus groups of both union and salaried employees recorded dramatic shifts in their perceptions of management, morale, and company loyalty.

The key to these remarkable improvements? Employees consistently reported that Ford had somehow become an entirely different company than it had been five years earlier. Ford had left behind its past as a rigidly hierarchical company driven by financial considerations to pursue a future in which a concern for quality and new products became the overriding priority.

Ford's organizational reinvention proved to be successful. But unfortunately, the company's leaders at the time were not similarly reinvented, as their failure to invest sufficiently in the core business revealed. Sustaining the company's momentum in the 1990s, therefore, has become a challenging task.

Creating a New Context

Most executives who have any inkling of what reinvention entails flinch at the prospect of taking on this 500-pound gorilla. "The journey to reinvent yourself and your company is not as scary as they say it is; it's worse," says Mort Meyerson, chairman of Perot Systems, an information-systems company that is assisting in many corporate reinventions. "You step into the abyss out of the conviction that the only way to compete in the long haul is to be a totally different company. It's a sink-or-swim proposition."

It should come as no surprise, then, that many CEOs end up sinking. After creating a context or being the product of one, they either don't have the courage—or see the need—to throw it away. But in defense of these CEOs, it is easy to look for the root cause of declining competitiveness and not see it.

Consider this analogy. You inherit your grandmother's house. Unknown to you is one peculiarity: all the light fixtures have bulbs that give off blue rather than yellow light. You find that you don't like the feel of the rooms and spend a lot of time and money repainting walls, reupholstering furniture, and replacing carpets. You never seem to get it quite right, but nonetheless, you rationalize that at least it is improving with each thing you do. Then one day you notice the blue lightbulbs and change them. Suddenly, all that you fixed is broken.

Context is like the color of the light, not the objects in the room. Context colors everything in the corporation. More accurately, the context alters what we see, usually without our being aware of it.

Much-abused IBM is an example of a company that has been doing things to the objects in the room without changing the color of the light. IBM was among the vanguard in employing most contemporary business techniques, such as pursuing Six Sigma quality (3.4 defects per one million units), empowerment, delayering, and downsizing. But because IBM failed to alter its context—the "IBM way" of controlling and predicting every aspect of the business—these change programs did not serve as steps to a powerful future.

The company leaders sought to instill an entrepreneurial spirit that would lead employees to take bold initiatives with new product ideas and with customers. But the context in which they managed made entrepreneurship at IBM an oxymoron. That context—ever-positive and upbeat—demanded that managers demonstrate how a course of action would play out five steps into the future before they could take step one. This left managers unwilling to risk, let alone abandon, what the company had become for what it might be.

At the other end of the spectrum is Motorola, a familiar example of successful reinvention. Over the course of its 65-year history, Motorola has on several occasions decided that a new future was at hand, first in car radios, then in television, consumer electronics, and semiconductors, and recently in microcomputers, cellular phones, and pagers. Each shift has been marked by fundamentally altering the kind of company that Motorola was in order to compete in entirely different industries. This involved self-imposed upheaval: selling off successful but older businesses and taking big gambles on the new ones.

In facing these challenges, Motorola's leaders realized the importance of context. Motorola was once a collection of fiefdoms dominated by macho engineers who mistakenly thought that they had no serious rivals. But in the late 1970s, CEO Robert Galvin recognized that the inward-looking company was not prepared to face intensifying Japanese competition.

He forced everyone to confront quality problems, divisional limitations, and the Japanese threat. To do so, the company had to become self-questioning, outward looking, and much more humble. A healthy degree of self-criticism replaced the former sense of superiority. In 1989, one year before he stepped down as CEO, Galvin challenged Motorola to become "the world's premier company," a guiding vision that transcended the company's former definition of itself as the best maker of its products.

"The world's premier company" seems too vague to inspire a powerful new future, but as Motorola's employees began to come to terms with the idea, they were spurred by the challenge of being the best in every facet of their business. The vision served as a reminder that the company must constantly challenge its sense of what is possible in order to resist the downward pull of habit and routine.

The Doing Trap

Author Rita Mae Brown defines insanity as doing the same thing again and again but expecting different results. With no awareness of the power of context, we continue to beat our heads against the same wall.

What are we missing? This parallel may help. Scientists at the turn of the century treated time as a constant, a given. But physicists studying light (photons) found increasing experimental evidence that something was amiss. They held fast, however, to the ether-wave theory of light and its central premise that the speed of light was a variable. When Einstein speculated that the speed of light might be a constant, he was drawn to look elsewhere for a variable that could account for the elasticity of the cosmos. Time was the only candidate. Einstein created an intellectual puzzle that forced him to look "outside the box." His consideration of a new possibility launched him on the intellectual odyssey that led to the Special and General Theories of Relativity and revolutionized the world of physics. He created a new context for looking at the universe.

Like time to turn-of-the-century physicists, *doing* is the assumed managerial constant. To manage is to *do* something; managers are selected and promoted based on their ability to get things done. But what if something else is the constant, and doing is the variable?

Like Einstein's thought experiment of riding on a photon of light to see what the world looked like from that perspective, the executive who would master reinvention must journey into a largely unfamiliar and uncomfortable territory, the territory of *being*.[1] Being alters action; context shapes thinking and perception. When you fundamentally alter the context, the foundation on which people construct their understanding of the world, actions are altered accordingly.

Context sets the stage; being pertains to whether the actor lives the part or merely goes through the motions. Organizations and the people in them are being something all the time. On occasion, we describe them as "conservative," or "hard charging," or "resistant to change." Trouble is, aside from such casual generalizations, we concentrate mostly on what we are doing and let being fend for itself.

That may be because we Westerners have few mental hooks or even words for excursions into being. The Japanese chart the journey across life in terms of perfecting one's inner nature, or being. They call it *kokoro*.[2] In contrast, Westerners typically assess their progression through adulthood in terms of personal wealth or levels of accomplishments. To the Japanese, merely *doing* these things is meaningless unless one is able to become deeper and wiser along the way.

Many Western CEOs will undoubtedly say that all this smacks of something philosophical or, far worse, theological and therefore has presumably little relevance for managers. But an organization's being determines its context, its possibilities. Remarkable shifts in context can happen only when there is a shift in being. Since IBM's would-be entrepreneurs continued to act "appropriately" and "conservatively," it is hardly surprising that the context of risk taking that former Chairman and CEO John Akers tried to create never took hold.

Our difficulty in discerning what a business *is* explains why so many efforts at corporate revitalization have failed. Consider all the retail chains throughout the country, including Saks and Macy's, that have tried to counter or capture Nordstrom's magic but with little success. Nordstrom's way of being has enabled it to win in seemingly impossible circumstances. For example, it was able to launch a successful expansion program in the Northeastern United States when that region was gripped by deep recession. That expansion helped Nordstrom become the leading department store chain in the country in terms of sales per square foot. Nordstrom now has 64 stores, annual sales of $2.89 billion, and an annual growth rate of 20%.

While the other chains can copy some of what Nordstrom is doing, they don't seem to realize that Nordstrom is living its motto, "Respond to Unreasonable Customer Requests." This way of being leads employees to relish the challenges that customers toss at them. Usually, meeting these demands entails little more than providing just a bit more service. But occasionally it means hand delivering items purchased by phone to the airport for a customer with a last-minute business trip, changing a customer's flat tire, or paying a customer's parking ticket when in-store gift wrapping has taken longer than expected.

Nordstrom encourages these acts by promoting its best employees, keeping scrapbooks of "heroic" acts, and paying its salespeople entirely on commission, through which they usually earn about twice what they would at a rival's store. For go-getters who really love to sell, Nordstrom is nirvana. But the system weeds out those who can't meet such demanding standards and selects those prepared to be what Nordstrom stands for.

Rivals scrambling to keep up have instituted in-house charm schools and issued vision statements trumpeting the importance of customers and the value of service. They have copied Nordstrom by introducing commissions and incentives. They have loosened their refund policies. Without exception, these actions have failed to close the gap. The problem seems to be an understanding of what it means to respond to unreasonable customer demands. To many salespeople at competing stores, it means that the customer comes first—within reason. Customer demands must be met—unless these demands are ridiculous. But at Nordstrom, each ridiculous customer request is an opportunity for a "heroic" act by an employee, an opportunity to expand on the store's reputation. To compete with Nordstrom, other stores must shift "who they are" in relation to the customer, not just what they do for the customer.

Shifts in being are not merely upbeat intellectual "ah-ha's." "Oh my God" is more likely to be uttered than "Eureka." The acid test of such a shift is whether or not it is intellectually and emotionally jolting. Executives at Europcar, the second largest rental-car company in Europe, understand this phenomenon.

In January 1992, CEO Fredy Dellis surveyed the competitive situation and did not like what he saw. While revenues were rising slowly, profits were plummeting. He estimated that it cost Europcar $13 to process each rental agreement (mostly by hand), compared with $1 at Hertz and Avis. Past attempts at incremental improvement had failed to close this gap. Much of the problem seemed to stem from the company's structure. Europcar had been built through acquisitions and was a loose federation of rental-car companies throughout Europe, each of which was convinced it knew its country best. Worse still, each country fiefdom built and maintained its own operating system, and these incompatible systems could not deal with the increasing number of cross-border travelers. Europcar was a parochial, balkanized organization whose country managers were preoccupied with protecting their national idiosyncrasies and their turf.

Dellis's response was to initiate the Greenway Project, a plan to revamp Europcar's entire operating system—how reservations were made, how rental operations flowed from check-out to check-in, the financially critical activities of fleet purchasing and fleet utilization. But a companywide operating system would drastically change the way the country units did business and would thus threaten their distinct national identities. Bickering between country managers and the design team, whose members themselves were drawn from the separate country operations, threatened the entire project.

But in early 1993, a small miracle happened when the 35 top managers and the design team gathered in Nice, France. The design team had been invited to demonstrate the new system, on which they had made enormous headway with very little input or encouragement from their senior sponsors. But these top managers, finally recognizing the importance of Greenway for lowering Europcar's cost structure to competitors' levels, took on the task of bridging this gulf of distrust and misunderstanding.

As these managers moved through the design team's presentations on the components of the operating system and what it could accomplish in terms of cost reduction and improved service and fleet utilization, the discussion grew animated with much give-and-take. Participants say the disbelief and alienation felt by both designers and senior managers was transformed into growing excitement about the new possibilities for the flow of information throughout the company. Moreover, by uniting all the operations, the whole would become much more formidable than the previous collection of individual parts. The antagonism that had marked relationships between parts of the company began to fade; everyone at the gathering began to behave like part of a team. The shift for Europcar toward becoming a company that could coalesce across geographical borders and through levels of hierarchy to become an innovator in its field was well under way.

Inventing a Powerful Future

Statements of vision from chief executives have bewildered and even amused employees who just don't get why a CEO would describe a future that their experience says can never materialize. The ensuing action plans are built inevitably on company notions about how things *really* work around here and employees' experience of the last change effort. It all adds up to pulling the leaden past toward a future we never seem to reach.[3]

As we have said, reinvention entails creating a new possibility for the future, one that past experiences and current predictions would indicate is impossible. Sir Colin Marshall did this by declaring that British Airways would be the "world's favorite airline" when it ranked among the worst. Before its turnaround in the 1980s, the airline's frequent maintenance-related delays, poor food, and Aeroflot-like standards of service had inspired long-suffering customers to say that its initials actually stood for "bloody awful."

A declaration from a leader generates an essential element of reinvention. It creates the possibility of a new future that evokes widespread interest and commitment. When a declaration is well stated, it is always visually imaginable (putting a man on the moon) or exceptionally simple (becoming the world's favorite airline). The declaration becomes the magnetic North, the focal point. By contrast, a vision provides a more elaborate description of the desired state and the criteria against which success will be measured.

A declaration forces you to stand in the new future, undertaking a series of steps not in order to be the world's favorite airline *someday,* but to be that airline *now.* Sir Colin began leading British Airways down that road by going to those who dealt closely with customers and asking them what needed to happen. The answers included everything from making sure that the concourse lights were always on to seeing that meals on short flights were easy to deliver and unwrap.

Being the best in customers' eyes also meant putting the airline's operations under the marketing department, so that instead of moving people as if they were packages, all operating decisions would start from a concern for the passenger. Today British Airways's service ranks among the best, and it is one of the most profitable airlines in the world.

But what happens when a company reaches its future? Where does it go from there? This was the situation Häagen-Dazs faced after its stunning success in exporting its "Dedicated to Pleasure" brand identity to the European market in 1989. A team of young, hard-charging recruits from the world's leading food-products companies had thought it would take anywhere from three to five years to gain a presence in a market where competitors ranged from giants like Mars and Nestlé to thousands of home recipe boutiques. Against the odds, this team launched the brand in June 1989, with a daring ad campaign featuring scantily clad couples indulging in the pleasures of ice cream. Within 18 months, Häagen-Dazs was the leading dairy ice cream in Western Europe. The team had pulled off one of the most successful new product launches the packaged food industry had ever seen.

Then an interesting thing began to happen. Once victory was achieved, bureaucracy took over. Paris headquarters began to quarrel with country management teams. Marketing began to flex its muscles at the expense of sales and shops operations. Headquarters in the United States was too worried about Ben & Jerry's encroachments to notice. The young hotshots in Europe began to wonder how to protect their position and, more important, what they could do for an encore.

John Riccitiello, general manager of Häagen-Dazs International, concluded that his organization had already used up its future; incremental improvements, he realized, could not restore momentum. He toyed with embracing the ambitious goal of making Häagen-Dazs Europe's leading premium food brand. But this goal seemed compelling only to top managers, not to everyone in the company.

Riccitiello decided to shift the context of "beating the competition, being the best" and a strategy of selling pleasure to a new context of "celebrating the experience of being alive." He believed that there would be more longevity in a future of selling excitement and pizzazz. A visit to a Häagen-Dazs shop, he determined, would be a memorable event for customers.

This new future generated an important shift in the company's recruitment policy. Interviews with job candidates are now treated much like theatrical auditions. "We aren't just looking for people to clear tables and dispense ice cream," Riccitiello says. "So when a group of prospects come in, we give them impromptu situations and see what they do. Do they ad-lib? Do they freeze and look to others for the right answer? We ask them to juggle four ice-cream cones. We want our shops to be an event, a place where customers and staff celebrate the experience of something that tastes great and gives you—even if just for a moment—a sense that it's worth being alive. It became our mission to provide that feeling."

To that end, the company created a senior position. This "Director of Magic," as the woman given the job has been dubbed, works with shop managers and scoopers to help them generate ideas that make them look forward to their work. When coming to a Häagen-Dazs shop becomes an exciting event for staff and customers, the competition has a hard time measuring up.

Executive Reinvention

During our 35 years of research, writing, teaching, and consulting for U.S., European, and Japanese corporations, we have found, particularly in senior executives, an unwillingness to think rigorously and patiently about themselves or their ideas. We often find senior executives perched like a threatened aristocracy, entitled, aloof, and sensing doom. Flurries of restructuring or downsizing are like the desperate attempts of uncomprehending heirs who try to slow the decline of the family estate. Each successive reaction is misconstrued as bold action to "set things right."

When leading an organization into the future, executives come to a fork in the road. As they come face-to-face with their organizations' needs to reinvent themselves, many executives hope for the best and opt for the prudent path of change. Even when they choose reinvention, their feet get cold. Thrown into the unfamiliar territory of reinvention, where the steps along the path and the outcomes themselves are often unpredictable, the responsible thing to do, many executives think, is to get things back on track. It is not surprising that so many senior executives decline invitations to reinvent themselves and their companies. It is like aging: experts tell us that it is difficult, yet most of us hope to go through it without pain.

There is another choice, but it requires executive reinvention, a serious inquiry into oneself as a leader. This is not a psychological process to fix something that's wrong, but an inquiry that reveals the context from which an executive makes decisions. People have contexts just as organizations do. Our individual context is our hidden strategy for dealing with life; it determines all the choices we make. On the surface, our context is our formula for winning, the source of our success. But on closer examination, this context is the box within which a person operates and determines what is possible and impossible for him or her as a leader and, by extension, for the organization.

A good example is a CEO who wanted to increase the annual revenues of his family-run manufacturing business from $80 million to $200 million within five years. He had been working very hard toward this goal for a number of years and was dissatisfied with the slow progress.

But when people proposed expansion plans, like adding a new product line or entering a new market, all he could see were the incredible problems: the outside executives that would have to be brought on board, the new expertise that existing managers, including complacent family members, would have to acquire, and so on. He refused to endorse such plans, or if he did let a plan go forward, he would halt it whenever contention arose.

If you had asked him how he had spent his day, he would say, "I spent it working on the growth of the company." But when he finally stopped to examine what was going wrong, he realized that he was operating from a context of avoiding conflict, which was inconsistent with a commitment to ambitious growth. He understood that this was why all the things he was doing to expand the business were not working.

He could then put a clear choice before the family board: either they pursue becoming a $200 million company with their eyes open to the fact that there would be chaos, conflict, and upheaval, or they settle for incremental growth. The board decided on the latter (sales of $100 million). They left achieving the larger future to the next generation.

Managing the Present from the Future

An organization that has a clear grasp of its own assumptions about the past is often motivated to alter the context in which the company is embedded. This in turn requires a shift in the organization's being and a powerful vision of the future. The activities involved in reinventing an organization require persistence and flexibility. Some extend over the entire effort, and others are steps along the way.

1. ASSEMBLING A CRITICAL MASS OF KEY STAKEHOLDERS

Leading pilgrims on the journey of reinventing an organization should never be left to the top eight or ten executives. It is deceptively easy to generate consensus among this group; they usually are a tight fraternity, and it is difficult to spark deep self-examination among them. If there are revelations, they may never extend beyond this circle.

As proven by the experiences of such companies as Ford, British Petroleum, Chase Bank, AT&T, Europcar, Thomas Cook, and Häagen-Dazs, this group must encompass a critical mass of stakeholders—the employees "who really make things happen around here." Some hold sway over key resources. Others are central to informal opinion networks. The group may often include critical but seldom-seen people like key technologists and leading process engineers. The goal is a flywheel effect, where enough key players get involved and enrolled that it creates a momentum to carry the process forward.

These key stakeholders first must determine if their company has what it takes to remain competitive and, if not, what to do about it. In the process, such a group will typically put unspoken grievances and suspicions on the table. Its members will learn to work together and to respect nonconforming opinions. All this constitutes a shift in the way participants are being, from a relationship of distrust and resignation toward an authentic, powerful partnership. This is not easy, nor is it enough. But it is a beginning.

Once such a shift has taken place, actions and reactions that previously could not have occurred happen quite naturally, and with surprising results.

Such a watershed event occurred during Ford's transformation in the 1980s. The upper-level managers in charge of the Engineering Division and the Power Train Division, which designed engines and transmissions, were called into one room. Lou Ross, then senior vice president in charge of factories, got right to the point. "Here's the problem," he said. "For 25 years, Power Train and Engineering have been fighting with each other, hurting productivity and quality. Enough is enough. We don't care how long it takes, but we want you to answer one question: Will engineering report to manufacturing, or manufacturing to engineering?"

Now picture a meeting room eight months later, after countless hostile debates. Many of the same people from the Engineering and Power Train divisions were on their hands and knees, discussing the merits of the various organizational charts that covered the floor. There was a lot of give-and-take. Someone asked with an edge of frustration, "Which of these organizational charts is best?" Another person answered, "Maybe *this* is!" A hush fell over the room. He was calling attention to the way they were behaving as colleagues. The important thing was how they were working together, not finding the "perfect" organizational structure. It took another month to put an "organization" together that didn't reorganize at all but simply re-aligned the flows of communication across the traditional Engineering and Power Train chimneys. The new relationship and all that flowed from it was one of the pillars of Ford's turnaround. This broad-based shift in being is central to understanding how Ford compressed the time needed to develop a new model from eight years to five and catapulted its product quality from worst to best.

2. DOING AN ORGANIZATIONAL AUDIT

The first task of the key stakeholders is to reveal and confront the company's true competitive situation. This process will also reveal the barriers to significant organizational change—the organization's context. A company cannot get from "here" to "there" without first knowing where "here" is any more than it can choose reinvention without knowing where "there" is.

The best approach is through a diagnosis that generates a complete picture of how the organization really works: What assumptions are we making about our strategic position and customer needs that may no longer be valid? Which functional units are most influential, and will they be as important in the future as they were in the past? What are the key systems that drive the business? What are the core competencies or skills of the enterprise? What are the shared values and idiosyncrasies that comprise the organization's being? If explored in-depth, these types of questions generate responses that, taken together, paint a picture of how things really work.

Europcar created small groups to conduct such an audit. Each took on a crucial issue, such as the company's competitive position, the current system for renting automobiles and tracking information, and the consequences of the country structure. What emerged was a picture of a highly fragmented organization that had no idea what it meant to work together as a whole. As a result of the audit, these crucial stakeholders recognized that without the Greenway Project, Europcar would not be able to compete in the Pan-European market.

3. CREATING URGENCY, DISCUSSING THE UNDISCUSSABLE

There is an unspoken code of silence in most corporations that conceals the full extent of a corporation's competitive weaknesses. But a threat that everyone perceives and no one talks about is far more debilitating to a company than a threat that has been clearly revealed. Companies, like people, tend to be at least as sick as their secrets.

A company must confront its most life-threatening problems in order to summon the courage to break with the past and embrace a new future. *The Book of Five Rings,* a guide for Japanese samurai written four centuries ago, prescribes the practice of visualizing death in battle as vividly as possible before the actual battle. Having experienced "death" beforehand, there is not a lot left to fear, and the warrior fights with complete abandon. Interesting, isn't it, that in confronting the possible, it becomes less probable.

In a sense, managers of companies whose very existence is at stake are lucky; though being honest about the dire situations to which they contributed is painful, it is relatively easy for these managers to convince employees that there is no alternative to a wrenching shift in who and what they are.

4. HARNESSING CONTENTION

There is an obscure law of cybernetics—the law of requisite variety—that postulates that any system must encourage and incorporate variety internally if it is to cope with variety externally. This seems innocuous until you consider how variety shows up in organizations. Usually it takes the form of such behavior as siphoning off scarce resources from mainstream activities for back-channel experiments, disagreeing at meetings, and so forth. Almost all significant norm-breaking opinions or behavior in social systems are synonymous with conflict.

Paradoxically, most organizations suppress contention; many managers, among others, cannot stand to be confronted because they assume they should be "in charge." But control kills invention, learning, and commitment.

Conflict jump-starts the creative process.[4] That is why the group process described earlier included a large number of stakeholders. When you extend participation to those really accountable for critical resources, or who hold entrenched positions, or who have been burned by past change attempts, you guarantee conflicts. But as the group faces and handles difficult issues, there is a shift in how they relate to contention. Participants learn to disagree without being disagreeable.

Emotions often accompany creative tension, and these emotions are not altogether pleasant. At Intel, conflict is blunt, at times brutal. Says one observer: "If you're used to tennis, Intel plays rugby, and you walk away with a lot of bruises. They've created a company that takes direct, hard-hitting disagreement as a sign of fitness. You put it all behind you in the locker room, and it's forgotten by the scrimmage the next day."

On a field trip to Tokyo to assess Intel's competitiveness against Japanese quality and service standards, the top management team of 20 became involved in a fierce argument about the company's approach to the Japanese market. Underlying the finger-pointing were long-smoldering resentments on the part of those representing internal Intel customers who could not get the quality and service they desired from manufacturing. Intel COO Craig Barrett, who then headed manufacturing, was a combative partisan in the melee. As one person who was at the meeting described it: "Four-letter words flew back and forth like ping-pong balls in a Beijing master's tournament."

But two days later, team members sat down, sorted out their differences, and put the actions in motion to help Intel match or surpass its Japanese rivals. Barrett says, "I've got pretty thick skin; it takes a lot to penetrate my strongly held convictions. This kind of hard-hitting session is precisely what we all needed to strip us of our illusions. It made us all realize the games we were playing and how they prevented us from facing Japanese competitive realities."

Contrary to what many Westerners might think about the importance of consensus in Japanese culture, institutionalized conflict is an integral part of Japanese management. At Honda, any employee, however junior, can call for a *waigaya* session. The rules are that people lay their cards on the table and speak directly about problems. Nothing is out of bounds, from supervisory deficiencies on the factory floor to perceived lack of support for a design team. Waigaya legitimizes tension so that learning can take place.

The Japanese have learned to disagree without being disagreeable and to harness conflict in a wide variety of ingenious ways. One of their chief principles of organizational design is redundancy—overlapping charters, business activities, and managerial assignments, duplicative databases, and parallel lines of inquiry.

With our deeply ingrained Western concept of organizations as machines, we are quick to judge such overlaps as inefficient, prime candidates for elimination in the current fervor of business process reengineering. But to the Japanese, redundancy and ambiguity spur tension and encourage frequent dialogue and communication. They also generate internal competition, particularly when parallel paths are pursued in new product development. Honda and Sony often use such techniques, assigning identical tasks to competing teams. Periodic project reviews determine which team gets funded to build the final prototype. Sony's compact disc player was developed in this fashion. The manager in charge handed two teams a block of wood the size of a small paperback book and said, "Build it to fit in this space." He recruited talent from Seiko and Citizen Watch who were familiar with miniaturization and ignorant of the traditional boundaries of audio design. Then he stood back and let them fight it out.

Conflict has its human and organizational costs, but it is also an essential fuel for self-questioning and revitalization. Some Western companies have incorporated conflict into their designs with this trade-off in mind. One is Nordstrom, where there is a built-in tension between providing excellent customer service and taking the idea to such extremes that it threatens economic viability. And since what takes place between staff and customers is the most important piece of Nordstrom's strategy, there are tensions between department heads and buyers, the traditional stars of retailing. Not surprisingly, Nordstrom employees report high tension levels at work. One executive says, "It's wrong to think of Nordstrom as a happy place. But the tensions yield higher performance."

5. ENGINEERING ORGANIZATIONAL BREAKDOWNS

It's clear that reinvention is a rocky path and that there will be many breakdowns along the way: systems that threaten to fall apart, deadlines that can't be met, schisms that seem impossible to mend. But just as contention in an organization can be highly productive, these breakdowns make it possible for organizations and individuals to take a hard look themselves and confront the work of reinvention. When an organization sets out to reinvent itself, breakdowns should happen by design rather than by accident.

We might seem to be proposing the willy-nilly seeding of conflict and chaos. Nothing could be further from the truth. Inventing a seemingly impossible future and then managing from that future entails creating concrete tasks that will inevitably lead to breakdowns. These tasks must be carefully selected for the kind of upsets an organization wishes to generate. The executive team must identify the core competencies they wish to build, the soft spots in existing capabilities, and the projects that, if undertaken, will build new muscles.

Nordstrom's practice of providing extraordinary customer service necessarily places a great deal of stress on the system. But revealing the weak spots in a store's ability to respond to customer requests is the first step in strengthening those areas.

Others in Europcar's industry insisted that the company could not achieve its goal in less than two years; it would more likely take three. But Europcar, along with its partner in the project, Perot Systems, decided on an "impossible" 18-month deadline. Managers knew the resulting stress would reveal that Europcar's network of fiercely independent fiefdoms was preventing the company from competing successfully in the Pan-European market. Many country managers claimed that they did not have enough information on what was being designed and could never implement the new approach in time. Many also insisted on high degrees of tailoring to their individual country markets that ultimately would have compromised the new system's efficiency. These deep-seated territorial behaviors had to be exposed and surmounted if a true reinvention were to take place.

The purpose of generating breakdowns is to provide opportunities to enable both the organization and its executives to operate from the new context. Paradoxically, you can fail at the project (as has often happened on the road to scientific discoveries and in the careers of entrepreneurs) and still achieve a shift in being. Winston Churchill claimed that his repeated failures, from the disastrous Gallipoli invasion to defeat in his campaign for a seat in Parliament in the years between World War I and World War II, caused a sufficient shift in who he was to prepare him for the responsibilities of a wartime prime minister.

Those who climb on the reinvention roller coaster are in for a challenging ride. The organization encounters peaks and troughs in morale, as initial euphoria is dampened by conflict and dogged task-force work. Morale rises again as alignment among stakeholders occurs—then recedes in the long and demanding task of enrolling the cynical ranks below. Reinvention is a demanding up and down journey—an adventure, to be sure. And it is destined to be that way.

Notes

1. We are indebted to numerous philosophers, scholars, and thinkers who have inquired into the nature of being, especially Werner Erhard, "Transformation and Its Implications for Systems-Oriented Research," unpublished lecture, Massachusetts Institute of Technology, Cambridge, Massachusetts, April 1977, and "The Nature of Transformation," unpublished lecture, Oxford University Union Society, Oxford, England, September 1981; Martin Heidegger, *What Is Called Thinking?* (New York: Harper & Row, 1968), *On the Way to Language* (New York: Harper & Row, 1971), *On Time and Being* (New York: Harper & Row, 1972); and Ludwig Wittgenstein, *Culture and Value* (Oxford: Basil Blackwell, 1980).

2. See Thomas P. Rohlen, "The Promise of Adulthood in Japanese Spiritualism," *Daedalus,* Journal of the American Academy of Arts and Sciences, Spring 1976, p. 125.

3. Numerous writers have grappled with the relationship of past, present, and future in the workplace, especially Werner Erhard, "Organizational Vision and Vitality: Forward from the Future," unpublished lecture, Academy of Management, San Francisco, California, August 1990; Edward Lindaman and Ronald Lippitt, *Choosing the Future You Prefer* (Washington, D.C.: Development Publications, 1979); Fritz Roethlisberger, *Training for Human Relations* (Boston: Harvard University, Graduate School of Business Administration, Division of Research, 1954); Marvin R. Weisbord, *Productive Workplaces: Organizing and Managing for Dignity, Meaning, and Community* (San Francisco: Jossey-Bass, 1991), pp. 282–85.

4. See Ikujiro Nonaka, "The Knowledge-Creating Company," *Harvard Business Review* November–December 1991, pp. 96–97.

4
Successful Change Programs
Begin with Results

Robert H. Schaffer and Harvey A. Thomson

The performance improvement efforts of many companies have as much impact on operational and financial results as a ceremonial rain dance has on the weather. While some companies constantly improve measurable performance, in many others, managers continue to dance round and round the campfire—exuding faith and dissipating energy.

This "rain dance" is the ardent pursuit of activities that sound good, look good, and allow managers to feel good—but in fact contribute little or nothing to bottom-line performance. These activities, many of which parade under the banner of "total quality" or "continuous improvement," typically advance a managerial philosophy or style such as interfunctional collaboration, middle management empowerment, or employee involvement. Some focus on measurement of performance such as competitive benchmarking, assessment of customer satisfaction, or statistical process controls. Still other activities aim at training employees in problem solving or other techniques.

Companies introduce these programs under the false assumption that if they carry out enough of the "right" improvement activities, actual performance improvements will inevitably materialize. At the heart of these programs, which we call "activity centered," is a fundamentally flawed logic that confuses ends with means, processes with outcomes. This logic is based on the belief that once managers benchmark their company's performance against competition, assess their customers' expectations, and train their employees in seven-step problem solving, sales will increase, inventory will shrink, and quality will improve. Staff experts and consultants tell management that it need not—in fact should not—focus directly on improving results because eventually results will take care of themselves.

The momentum for activity-centered programs continues to accelerate even though there is virtually no evidence to justify the flood of investment. Just the opposite: there is plenty of evidence that the rewards from these activities are illusory.

In 1988, for example, one of the largest U.S. financial institutions committed itself to a "total quality" program to improve operational performance and win customer loyalty. The company trained hundreds of people and communicated the program's intent to thousands more. At the end of two years of costly effort, the program's consultants summarized progress: "Forty-eight teams up and running. Two completed Quality Improvement Stories. Morale of employees regarding the process is very positive to date." They did not report any bottom-line performance improvements—because there were none.

The executive vice president of a large mineral-extracting corporation described the results of his company's three-year-old total quality program by stating, "We have accomplished about 50% of our training goals and about 50% of our employee participation goals but only about 5% of our results goals." And he considered those results meritorious.

These are not isolated examples. In a 1991 survey of more than 300 electronics companies, sponsored by the American Electronics Association, 73% of the companies reported having a total quality program under way; but of these, 63% had failed to improve quality defects by even as much as 10%. We believe this survey understates the magnitude of the failure of activity-centered programs not only in the quality-conscious electronics industry but across all businesses.

These signs suggest a tragedy in the making: pursuing the present course, companies will not achieve significant progress in their overall competitiveness. They will continue to spend vast resources on a variety of activities, only to watch cynicism grow in the ranks. And eventually, management will discard many potentially useful improvement processes because it expected the impossible of them and came up empty-handed.

If activity-centered programs have yielded such paltry returns on the investment, why are so many companies continuing to pour money and energy into them? For the same reason that previous generations of management invested in zero-based budgeting, Theory Z, and quality circles. Years of frustrating attempts to keep pace with fast-moving competitors make managers prey to almost any plausible approach. And the fact that hundreds of membership associations, professional societies, and consulting firms all promote activity-centered processes lends them an aura of popularity and legitimacy. As a consequence, many senior managers have become convinced that all of these preparatory activities really will pay off some day and that there isn't a viable alternative.

They are wrong on both counts. Any payoffs from the infusion of activities will be meager at best. And there is in fact an alternative: results-driven improvement processes that focus on achieving specific, measurable operational improvements within a few months. This means increased yields, reduced delivery time, increased inventory turns, improved customer satisfaction, reduced product development time. With results-driven improvements, a company introduces only those innovations in management methods and business processes that can help achieve specific goals. (See "Comparing Improvement Efforts.")

Comparing Improvement Efforts

While activity-centered programs and results-driven programs share some common methodologies for initiating change, they differ in very dramatic ways.

Activity-Centered Programs

1. The improvement effort is defined mainly in long-term, global terms. ("We are going to be viewed as number one in quality in our industry.")

2. Management takes action steps because they are "correct" and fit the program's philosophy. ("I want every manager in the division involved in an action.")

3. The program's champion(s) counsels patience and fortitude. ("Don't be looking for results this year or next year. This is a long-term process, not a quick fix.")

4. Staff experts and consultants indoctrinate everyone into the mystique and vocabulary of the program. ("It will be a Tower of Babel if we try to work on these problems before everyone, managers and employees alike, has been through the quality training and has a common vocabulary and a common tool kit.")

5. Staff experts and consultants urge managers and employees to have faith in the approach and to support it. ("True employee involvement will

take a lot of time and a lot of effort, and though it may be a real struggle for managers, they need to understand that it is essential to become a total quality company.")

6. The process requires management to make big investments up front—before results have been demonstrated. ("During the first year, we expect to concentrate on awareness building and skill training. Then, while managers begin to diagnose problems and opportunities in their areas, a consultant will be surveying all of our customers to get their views on the 14 critical dimensions of service. And then . . .")

Results-Driven Programs

1. There are measurable short-term performance improvement goals, even though the effort is a long-term, sustaining one. ("Within 60 days, we will be paying 95% of claims within 10 days.")

2. Management takes action steps because they appear to lead directly toward some improved results. ("Let's put together a small group to work with you to solve this machine downtime problem.")

3. The mood is one of impatience. Management wants to see results now, even though the change process is a long-term commitment. ("If we can't eliminate at least half of the cost disadvantage within the next three months, we should consider closing the plant.")

4. Staff experts and consultants help managers achieve results. ("We could probably work up a way to measure customer attitudes on delivery service within a week or two so that you can start improving it.")

5. Managers and employees are encouraged to make certain for themselves that the approach actually yields results. ("Why don't you send a few of your people to the quality course to test out whether it really helps them achieve their improvement goals in the next month or two.")

6. Relatively little investment is needed to get the process started; conviction builds as results materialize. ("Let's see if this approach can help us increase sales of high-end products in a couple of branches. If it does, we can take the method to the other branches.")

An automotive-parts plant, whose customers were turning away from it because of poor quality and late deliveries, illustrates the difference between the two approaches. To solve the company's problems, management launched weekly employee-involvement team meetings focused on improving quality. By the end of six months, the teams had generated hundreds of suggestions and abundant goodwill in the plant but virtually no improvement in quality or delivery.

In a switch to a results-driven approach, management concentrated on one production line. The plant superintendent asked the manager of that line to work with his employees and with plant engineering to reduce by 30% the frequency of their most prevalent defect within two months. This sharply focused goal was reached on time. The manager and his team next agreed to cut the occurrence of that same defect by an additional 50%. They also broadened the effort to encompass other kinds of defects on the line. Plant management later extended the process to other production lines, and within about four months the plant's scrap rate was within budgeted limits.

Both activity-centered and results-driven strategies aim to strengthen fundamental corporate competitiveness. But as the automotive-parts plant illustrates, the approaches differ dramatically. The activities path is littered with the remains of endless preparatory investments that failed to yield the desired outcomes. The results-driven path stakes out specific targets and matches resources, tools, and action plans to the requirements of reaching those targets. As a consequence, managers know what they are trying to achieve, how and when it should be done, and how it can be evaluated.

The Activity-Centered Fallacy

There are six reasons why the cards are stacked against activity-centered improvement programs:

1. *Not Keyed to Specific Results.* In activity-centered programs, managers reform the way they work with each other and with employees; they train people; they develop new measurement schemes; they increase employee awareness of customer attitudes, quality, and more. The expectation is that these steps will lead to better business performance. But managers rarely make explicit how the activity is supposed to lead to the result.

Seeking to improve quality, senior management at a large telecommunications equipment corporation sent a number of unit managers to quality training workshops. When they returned, the unit heads ordered orientation sessions for middle management. They also selected and trained facilitators who, in turn, trained hundreds of supervisors and operators in statistical process control. But senior management never specified which performance parameters it wanted to improve—costs, reject rates, delivery timeliness. During the following year, some units improved performance along some dimensions, other units improved along others, and still other units saw no improvement at all. There was no way for management to assess whether there was any connection between the investment in training and specific, tangible results.

2. *Too Large Scale and Diffused.* The difficulty of connecting activities to the bottom line is complicated by the fact that most companies choose to launch a vast array of activities simultaneously across the entire organization. This is like researching a cure for a disease by giving a group of patients ten different new drugs at the same time.

In one case, a large international manufacturer identified almost 50 different activities that it wanted built into its total quality effort. The company's list involved so many programs introduced in so many places that just to describe them all required a complex chart. Once top managers had made the investment and the public commitment, however, they "proved" their wisdom by crediting the programs for virtually any competitive gain the company made. But in fact, no one knew for sure which, if any, of the 50 activities were actually working.

3. *Results Is a Four-Letter Word.* When activity-centered programs fail to produce improvement in financial and operational performance, managers seldom complain lest they be accused of preoccupation with the short term at the expense of the long term—the very sin that has supposedly caused companies to defer investment in capital and human resources and thus to lose their competitive edge. It is a brave manager who will insist on seeing a demonstrable link between the proposed investment and tangible payoffs in the short term.

When one company had little to show for the millions of dollars it invested in improvement activities, the chief operations officer rationalized, "You can't expect to overturn 50 years of culture in just a couple of years." And he urged his management team to persevere in its pursuit of the activities.

He is not alone in his faith that, given enough time, activity-centered efforts will pay off. The company cited above, with almost 50 improvement activities going at once, published with pride its program's timetable calling for three years of preparations and reformations, with major results expected only in the fourth year. And at a large electronics company, the manual explaining its management-empowerment process warned that implementation could be "painful" and that management should not expect to see results for a "long time."

4. *Delusional Measurements.* Having conveyed the false message that activities will inevitably produce results, the activities promoters compound the crime by equating measures of activities with actual im-

provements in performance. Companies proclaim their quality programs with the same pride with which they would proclaim real performance improvements—ignoring or perhaps even unaware of the significance of the difference.

In a leading U.S. corporation, we found that a group of quality facilitators could not enumerate the critical business goals of their units. Surprised, we asked how they could possibly assess whether or not they were successful. Their answer: success consisted of getting 100% of each unit's managers and employees to attend the prescribed quality training—a centerpiece of the corporation's total quality program.

The Malcolm Baldrige National Quality Award encourages such practices by devoting only 180 points out of a possible 1,000 points to quality results. The award gives high marks to companies that demonstrate outstanding quality processes without always demanding that the current products and services be equally outstanding.

5. *Staff- and Consultant-Driven.* The focus on activities as ends in themselves is exacerbated by the fact that improvement programs are usually designed by staff specialists, external consultants, or other experts, rather than by operating managers. In many cases, managers seek this outside help because they have exhausted their own ideas about improvement. So when staff experts and improvement gurus show up with their evangelistic enthusiasm and bright promises of total quality and continuous improvement, asking only for faith and funds, managers greet them with open arms.

But the capability of most of these improvement experts is limited to installing discrete, often generic packages of activities that are rarely aimed directly at specific results. They design training courses; they launch self-directed teams; they create new quality-measurement systems; they organize campaigns to win the Baldrige Award. Senior managers plunge wholeheartedly into these activities, relieving themselves, momentarily at least, of the burden of actually having to improve performance.

The automotive-parts plant described earlier illustrates the pattern. Senior managers had become very frustrated after a number of technical solutions failed to cure the plant's ills. When a staff group then asserted that employee involvement could produce results, management quickly accepted the staff group's suggestion to initiate employee-involvement team meetings—meetings that failed to deliver results.

The futility of expecting staff-driven programs to yield performance improvement was highlighted in a study conducted by a Harvard Business School team headed by Michael Beer. It analyzed a number of large-scale corporate change programs, some of which had succeeded, others of which had failed. The study found that company-wide change programs installed by staff groups did not lead to successful transformation. As the authors colorfully put it, "Wave after wave of programs rolled across the landscape with little positive impact."[1]

6. *Bias to Orthodoxy, Not Empiricism.* Because of the absence of clear-cut beginnings and ends and an inability to link cause and effect, there is virtually no opportunity in activity-centered improvement programs to learn useful lessons and apply them to future programs. Instead, as in any approach based on faith rather than evidence, the advocates—convinced they already know all the answers—merely urge more dedication to the "right" steps.

One manufacturing company, for example, launched almost 100 quality improvement teams as a way to "get people involved." These teams produced scores of recommendations for process changes. The result was stacks of work orders piling up in maintenance, production engineering, and systems departments—more than any of these groups were capable of responding to. Senior managers, however, believed the outpouring of suggestions reinforced their original conviction that participation would succeed. Ignoring mounting evidence that the process was actually counterproductive, they determined to get even more teams established.

Results-Driven Transformation

In stark contrast to activity-centered programs, results-driven improvements bypass lengthy preparation rituals and aim at accomplishing measurable gains rapidly. Consider the case of the Morgan Bank. When told that his units would have to compete on an equal footing with outside vendors, the senior vice president of the bank's administrative services (responsible for 20 service functions including printing, food services, and purchasing) realized that the keys to survival were better service and lower costs. To launch a response, he asked the head of each of the service functions to select one or two service-improvement goals that were important to internal "customers" and could be achieved quickly. Unit heads participated in several workshops and worked with consultants but always maintained a clear focus on launching the improvement processes that would enable them to achieve their goals.

In the bank's microfilm department, for example, the first goal was to meet consistently a 24-hour turn around deadline for the work of a stock-transfer department. The microfilm department had frequently missed this deadline, sometimes by several days. The three shift supervisors and their manager laid out a five-week plan to accomplish the goal. They introduced a number of work-process innovations, each selected on the basis of its capacity to help achieve the 24-hour turnaround goal, and tracked performance improvements daily.

This project, together with similar results-driven projects simultaneously carried out in the other 19 units, yielded significant service improvements and several million dollars of cost savings within the first year of the initiative—just about the time it usually takes to design the training programs and get all employees trained in a typical activity-centered effort. The experience of the Morgan Bank illustrates four key benefits of a results-driven approach that activity-centered programs generally miss:

1. *Companies introduce managerial and process innovations only as they are needed*. Results-driven projects require managers to prioritize carefully the innovations they want to employ to achieve targeted goals. Managers introduce modifications in management style, work methods, goal setting, information systems, and customer relationships in a just-in-time mode when the change appears capable of speeding progress toward measurable goals. Contrast this with activity-centered programs, where all employees may be ritualistically sent off for training because it is the "right" thing to do.

In the Morgan Bank's microfilm department project, the three shift supervisors worked together as a unified team—not to enhance teamwork but to figure out how to reduce customer delivery time. For the first time ever, they jointly created a detailed improvement work plan and week-by-week subgoals. They posted this work plan next to a chart showing daily performance. Employees on all three shifts actively participated in the project, offering suggestions for process changes, receiving essential training that was immediately applied, and taking responsibility for implementation.

Thus instead of making massive investments to infuse the organization with a hodgepodge of improvement activities, the microfilm department and each of the other administrative services introduced innovations incrementally, in support of specific performance goals.

2. *Empirical testing reveals what works*. Because management intro-

duces each managerial and process innovation sequentially and links them to short-term goals, it can discover fairly quickly the extent to which each approach yields results. In the Morgan Bank's microfilm department, for example, the creation of a detailed improvement work plan and week-by-week subgoals—which were introduced during the first two weeks of the program—enabled management to assess accurately and quickly the impact of its actions in meeting the 24-hour turnaround goal.

New procedures for communicating between shifts allowed management to anticipate workload peaks and to reassign personnel from one shift to another. That innovation contributed to meeting deadlines. A new numbering system to identify the containers of work from different departments did not contribute, and management quickly abandoned the innovation. By constantly assessing how each improvement step contributed to meeting deadlines, management made performance improvement less an act of faith and more an act of rational decision making based on evidence.

3. *Frequent reinforcement energizes the improvement process.* There is no motivator more powerful than frequent successes. By replacing large-scale, amorphous improvement objectives with short-term, incremental projects that quickly yield tangible results, managers and employees can enjoy the psychological fruits of success. Demonstrating to themselves their capacity to succeed not only provides necessary reinforcement but also builds management's confidence and skill for continued incremental improvements.

The manager of the bank's microfilm department, for example, had never had the experience of leading a significant upgrading of performance. It was not easy for her to launch the process in the face of employee skepticism. Within a few weeks, however, when the chart on the wall showed the number of missed deadlines going down, everyone took pleasure in seeing it, and work went forward with renewed vigor. The manager's confidence grew and so did employee support for the subsequent changes she implemented.

In another example, a division of Motorola wanted to accelerate new product development. To get started, a management team selected two much-delayed mobile two-way radios and focused on bringing these products to the market within 90 days. For each product, the team created a unified, multifunction work plan; appointed a single manager to oversee the entire development process as the product moved from department to department; and designated an interfunctional team to monitor progress. With these and other innovations, both radios were launched on time. This success encouraged management to extend the innovations to other new product projects and eventually to the entire product development process.

4. *Management creates a continuous learning process by building on the lessons of previous phases in designing the next phase of the program.* Both activity-centered and results-driven programs are ultimately aimed at producing fundamental shifts in the performance of the organization. But unlike activity-centered programs that focus on sweeping cultural changes, large-scale training programs, and massive process innovation, results-driven programs begin by identifying the most urgently needed performance improvements and carving off incremental goals to achieve quickly.

By using each incremental project as a testing ground for new ways of managing, measuring, and organizing for results, management gradually creates a foundation of experience on which to build an organization-wide performance improvement. Once the manager of Morgan's microfilm department succeeded in meeting the 24-hour turnaround goal for one internal customer department, she extended the process to other customer departments.

In each of the other 19 service units, the same expansion was taking place. Unit managers shared their experiences in formal review conferences so that everyone could benefit from the best practices. Within six months, every manager and supervisor in administrative services was actively leading one or more improvement projects. From a base of real results, managers were able to encourage a continuous improvement process to spread, and they introduced dozens of managerial innovations in the course of achieving sizable performance gains.

Putting the Ideas into Practice

Taking advantage of the power of results-driven improvements calls for a subtle but profound shift in mind-set: management begins by identifying the performance improvements that are most urgently needed and then, instead of studying and preparing and gearing up and delaying, sets about at once to achieve some measurable progress in a short time.

The Eddystone Generating Station of Philadelphia Electric, once the world's most efficient fossil-fuel plant, illustrates the successful shift from activity-centered to results-driven improvement. As Eddystone approached its thirtieth anniversary, its thermal efficiency—the amount of electricity produced from each ton of coal burned—had declined significantly. The problem was serious enough that top management was beginning to question the plant's continued operation.

The station's engineers had initiated many corrective actions, including installing a state-of-the-art computerized system to monitor furnace efficiency, upgrading plant equipment and materials, and developing written procedures for helping operating staff run the plant more efficiently. But because the innovations were not built into the day-to-day operating routine of the plant, thermal efficiency tended to deteriorate when the engineers turned their attention elsewhere.

In September 1990, the superintendent of operations decided to take a results-driven approach to improve thermal efficiency. He and his management team committed to achieve a specific incremental improvement of thermal efficiency worth about $500,000 annually— without any additional plant investment. To get started, they identified a few improvements that they could accomplish within three months and established teams to tackle each one.

A five-person team of operators and maintenance employees and one supervisor took responsibility for reducing steam loss from hundreds of steam valves throughout the plant. The team members started by eliminating all the leaks in one area of the plant. Then they moved on to other areas. In the process, they invented improvements in valve-packing practices and devised new methods for reporting leaks.

Another employee team was assigned the task of reducing heat that escaped through openings in the huge furnaces. For its first subproject, the group ensured that all 96 inspection doors on the furnace walls were operable and were closed when not in use. Still another team, this one committed to reducing the amount of unburned carbon that passed through the furnace, began by improving the operating effectiveness of the station's coal-pulverizer mills in order to improve the carbon burn rate.

Management charged each of these cross-functional teams not merely with studying and recommending but also with producing measurable results in a methodical, step-by-step fashion. A steering committee of station managers met every two weeks to review progress and help overcome obstacles. A variety of communication mechanisms built awareness of the project and its progress. For example, to launch the process, the steering committee piled two tons of coal in the station manager's parking space to dramatize the hourly cost of poor thermal efficiency. In a series of "town meetings" with all employees, managers explained the reason for the effort and how it would work. Newsletters reviewed progress on the projects—including the savings realized—and credited employees who had contributed to the effort.

As each team reached its goal, the steering committee, in consultation with supervisors and employees, identified the next series of performance improvement goals, such as the reduction of the plant's own energy consumption, and commissioned a number of teams and individuals to implement a new round of projects. By the end of the first year, efficiency improvements were saving the company over $1 million a year, double the original goal.

Beyond the monetary gains—gains achieved with negligible investment—Eddystone's organizational structure began to change in profound ways. What had been a hierarchical, tradition-bound organization became more flexible and open to change. Setting and achieving ambitious short-term goals became part of the plant's regular routine as managers pushed decisions further and further down into the organization. Eventually, the station manager disbanded the steering committee, and now everyone who manages improvement projects reports directly to the senior management team.

Eddystone managers and workers at all levels continue to experiment and have invented a number of highly creative efficiency-improving processes. A change so profound could never have happened by sending all employees to team training classes and then telling them, "Now you are empowered; go to it."

In the course of accomplishing its results, Eddystone management introduced many of the techniques that promoters of activity-centered programs insist must be drilled into the organization for months or years before gains can be expected: employees received training in various analytical techniques; team-building exercises helped teams achieve their goals more quickly; teams introduced new performance measurements as they were needed; and managers analyzed and redesigned work processes. But unlike activity-centered programs, the results-driven work teams introduced innovations only if they could contribute to the realization of short-term goals. They did not inject innovations wholesale in the hope that they would somehow generate better results. There was never any doubt that responsibility for results was in the hands of accountable managers.

Philadelphia Electric—and many other companies as well—launched its results-driven improvement process with a few modest pilot projects. Companies that want to launch large-scale change, however, can employ a results-driven approach across a broad front.

In 1988, chairman John F. Welch, Jr. launched General Electric's "Work-Out" process across the entire corporation. The purpose was to overcome bureaucracy and eliminate business procedures that interfered with customer responsiveness. The response of GE's $3 billion Lighting Business illustrates how such a large-scale improvement process can follow a results-driven pathway.

Working sessions attended by a large cross-section of Lighting employees, a key feature of Work-Out, identified a number of "quick wins" in target areas. These were initiatives that employees could take right away to generate measurable improvement in a short time. To speed new product development, for example, Work-Out participants recommended that five separate functional review sessions be combined into one, a suggestion that was eagerly adopted. To get products to customers more quickly, a team tested the idea of working with customers and a trucking company to schedule, in advance, regular delivery days for certain customers. The results of the initial pilot were so successful that GE Lighting has extended the scheduling system to hundreds of customers.

Another team worked to reduce the breakage of fragile products during shipment—costly both in direct dollars and in customer dissatisfaction. Subteams, created to investigate package design and shipping-pallet construction, followed sample shipments from beginning to end and asked customers for their ideas. Within weeks, the team members had enough information to shift to remedial action. They tried many innovations in the packaging design; they modified work processes in high-risk areas; they reduced the number of times each product is handled; they collaborated with their shippers, suppliers, and customers. The payoff was a significant reduction in breakage within a few months.

The Lighting Business has launched dozens of such results-oriented projects quickly—and as each project achieves results, management has launched additional projects and has even extended the process to its European operations.

Opportunities for Change

There is no reason for senior-level managers to acquiesce when their people plead that they are already accomplishing just about all that can be accomplished or that factors beyond their control—company policy, missing technology, or lack of resources—are blocking accelerated performance improvement. Such self-limiting ideas are universal. Instead, management needs to recognize that there is an abundance of both underexploited capability and dissipated resources in the organization.

This orientation frees managers to set about translating potential into results and to avoid the cul-de-sac of fixing up and reforming the organization in preparation for future progress. Here is how management can get started in results-driven programs:

1. *Ask each unit to set and achieve a few ambitious short-term performance goals.* There is no organization where management could not start to improve performance quickly with the resources at hand—even in the face of attitudinal and skill deficiencies, personnel and other resource limitations, unstable market conditions, and every other conceivable obstacle. To begin with, managers can ask unit heads to commit to achieve in a short time some improvement targets, such as faster turn-around time in responding to customers, lower costs, increased sales, or improved cash flow. They should also be asked to test some managerial, process, or technical innovations that can help them reach their goals.

2. *Periodically review progress, capture the essential learning, and reformulate strategy.* Results-driven improvement is an empirical process in which managers use the experience of each phase as data for shaping the next phase. In scheduled work sessions, senior management should review and evaluate progress on the current array of results-focused projects and learn what is and what isn't working.

Fresh insights flood in from these early experiments: how rapidly project teams can make gains; what kind of support they need; what changes in work methods they can implement quickly; what kinds of obstacles need to be addressed at higher levels in the organization. Managers and employees develop confidence in their capacity to get things done and to challenge and overturn obsolete practices.

Armed with this learning, senior management can refine strategies and timetables and, in consultation with their people, can carve out the next round of business goals. The cycle repeats and expands as confidence and momentum grow.

3. *Institutionalize the changes that work—and discard the rest.* As management gains experience, it can take steps to institutionalize the practices and technologies that contribute most to performance improvement and build those into the infrastructure of the company. In Motorola's Mobile Division, for example, in its new product development project, a single manager was assigned responsibility for moving

each new product from engineering to production and to delivery, as opposed to having this responsibility handed off from function to function. This worked so well it became standard practice.

Such change can also take place at the policy level. A petroleum company, for example, experimented with incentive compensation in two sales districts. When the trials produced higher sales growth, senior management decided to install throughout the marketing function a performance-based compensation plan that reflected what it had learned in the experiments. In this way, a company can gradually build successful innovations into its operations and discard unsuccessful ones before they do much harm.

4. *Create the context and identify the crucial business challenges.* Senior management must establish the broader framework to guide continuing performance improvement in the form of strategic directions for the business and a "vision" of how it will operate in the future. A creative vision can be a source of inspiration and motivation for managers and employees who are being asked to help bring about change. But no matter how imaginative the vision might be, for it to contribute to accelerated progress, managers must translate it into sharp and compelling expectations for short-term performance achievements. At Philadelphia Electric, for example, the Eddystone improvement work responded to top management's insistent call for performance improvement and cost reduction.

A results-driven improvement process does not relieve senior management of the responsibility to make the difficult strategic decisions necessary for the company's survival and prosperity. General Electric's Work-Out process augmented but could never substitute for Jack Welch's dramatic restructuring and downsizing moves. By marrying long-term strategic objectives with short-term improvement projects, however, management can translate strategic direction into reality and resist the temptation to inculcate the rain dance of activity-centered programs.

Note

1. See Michael Beer, Russell A. Eisenstat, and Bert Spector, "Why Change Programs Don't Produce Change," *Harvard Business Review* November–December 1990, p. 158.

5

Leveraging Processes for Strategic Advantage: A Roundtable with Xerox's Allaire, USAA's Herres, SmithKline Beecham's Leschly, and Pepsi's Weatherup

David A. Garvin

Reengineering efforts are sweeping the country as companies shift from purely functional organizations to those that better accommodate horizontal work flows. Broad, crosscutting processes such as product development and order fulfillment have become the new organizational building blocks, replacing narrowly focused departments and functions. Managers, in turn, have begun to develop new ways of working. But much remains to be learned about how these new organizations are crafted and led. The critical questions involve strategy and management practice. Which strategic purposes are best served by processes? How do the roles and responsibilities of senior managers change in these new organizations? What skills are required to manage through processes?

To address those questions, I invited four senior executives who have pioneered the shift to process-based organizations to a roundtable discussion of their experiences. The group consisted of Paul Allaire, chairman and CEO of Xerox; Robert Herres, chairman and CEO of United Services Automobile Association (USAA); Jan Leschly, chief executive of SmithKline Beecham; and Craig Weatherup, president and CEO of Pepsi-Cola North America. They represent diverse industries—document processing, insurance, pharmaceuticals, and soft drinks—and a wide range of competitive challenges. But their observations about processes and process management are strikingly similar. The discussion was held at the Harvard Business School in Boston, Massachusetts.

David A. Garvin: In recent years, there has been an enormous surge of interest in processes. What caused you and your organizations to make the shift?

Jan Leschly: The customer completely changed on us. In the past, we were always a physician-driven business; now we're payer driven. In the United States today, employers and insurance companies pay our bills; in Europe, the government pays. So we figured we'd better find out how to satisfy these new customers, and that led us to a powerful realization: The way we do business had to change completely.

For a long time, we had four separate businesses—pharmaceuticals, consumer health care, animal health, and clinical laboratories—each working in silos, independent of the others, developing strategies of their own. But when we looked at the health care system as a whole and tried to understand how it was changing, we had trouble fitting these businesses into the new world. We simply had no idea which parts of the system to participate in and which to avoid. After a fair amount of work, we decided to focus on three key areas: care delivery, care management, and care coverage. Each is a collection of broad processes driving the health care system rather than a narrowly defined business. We then defined strategies for each area and looked into the capabilities that were necessary for success. We ended up with a list of six critical capabilities: pioneer discovery, product development, low-cost production, customer intimacy, alliance building, and continuous improvement.

Eventually, that list led us to processes. Why? Because we realized that a capability comes only by combining a competence with a reliable process. To be a leader in biotechnology, you first need the best cellular and molecular biologists in the world. But that isn't enough. You must also have a reliable, repeatable discovery and development process; otherwise, products won't emerge regularly from the pipeline. These larger processes are themselves divided into many smaller ones—in the case of product development, more than 3,000 in all. Today each of these processes is charted and on the way to being repeatable and controllable. But I believe that we have at least five years to go before we become a fully process-oriented organization.

Paul Allaire: The incentive for us to shift to processes was similar: a fundamental change in customers' requirements and competitive forces. You can't survive if you don't respond to those new conditions. But first you have to understand them, so we began in 1989 with a broad review of trends in our environment. We called the review Xerox 2000 and used it to generate and examine assumptions about technology, markets, customers, and competitors over the coming decade. After studying position papers and meeting with experts in each of those areas, our senior team created a list of some 60 possible assumptions about the future. Then we voted on the ones that we deemed most likely to prove valid. Some of the assumptions were particularly thorny, such as whether paper would continue to be widely used in offices or whether digital technology would replace analog products altogether. The validated assumptions led us to a new set of imperatives—things we must do to succeed in the future—as well as to a new strategic direction, which we call the Document Company. Our goal shifted from being a manufacturer of copier, printer, and facsimile products to becoming a provider of document tools and services that enhance our customers' productivity. We soon realized that the organization had to be redesigned to reflect our strategy, and that's when we began focusing on processes.

So your motivation for shifting to processes was fundamentally strategic?

Allaire: Absolutely. You can't redesign processes unless you know what you're trying to do. What you're after is congruence among strategic direction, organizational design, staff capabilities, and the processes you use to ensure that people are working together to meet the company's goals. So you start by looking at the competition and reviewing your strategic direction; then you figure out how to organize to achieve the new goals. Today the toughest competition comes from smaller companies. Unless large companies like ours are able to change the way we operate, smaller companies will win because they are able to react to the marketplace so quickly.

We decided to respond to competitive forces by breaking our business into smaller pieces. But, at the same time, we didn't want to lose the effectiveness of a large organization. We wanted to be more customer focused but no less efficient. That, we found, is the magic of processes—you can have it both ways. A process orientation allows you to take huge amounts of cost out of the system while still improving customer satisfaction. It keeps your eye on both objectives simultaneously. Today we have nine separate divisions, each drawing on common research laboratories, a shared sales force, and a set of aligned processes. We realized pretty quickly that the only way to manage this kind of structure was to focus on core processes.

Craig Weatherup: Our motivation was a bit more internal, although

I suppose it could also be traced to a changing environment. We've competed against Coke forever. But, in the late 1980s, we made a $4 billion bet, buying up many of our independent bottlers to gain more control over distribution. Almost overnight, we went from a company with 600 customers—the franchised bottlers—to a company with 600,000 customers. And we moved aggressively into a wide range of alternative beverages, such as juices and teas, and added lots of new packaging. All of a sudden, we had an explosion of complexity in various shapes, forms, and sizes. To give one example, between 1990 and 1992 we introduced 8 new stock-keeping units; in the next two years we introduced 110.

At the same time, we were still a company with a "big event" marketing mentality. Our entire mindset was geared to superstar entertainers such as Michael Jackson and Ray Charles. However, we now had several hundred thousand customers, and we weren't spending enough time thinking about them. The complexity was a huge challenge and drove us to this compelling commitment: to devote as much time, energy, and passion to operations and service as we had historically devoted to marketing. That quickly pointed us toward processes. As we got into it, we began to recognize the tremendous leverage that we would gain by improving our operating skills. We had processes, of course, since we were producing and selling every day. But they weren't working well enough. We have focused over the last four years on installing the context, tools, training, and incentives to make all our processes more effective.

Couldn't the changes you three have described been made years ago?

Allaire: Yes and no. The concept of processes really isn't that new. Effective managers have long known that you manage by processes—they're an essential tool for getting things done. What's different now is the enabling technology. Today's information systems allow you to do things that weren't possible in the past, such as accessing information simultaneously from multiple locations and diverse functional groups. With that ability, you can enjoy the efficiency of a process orientation without losing the responsiveness of a divisional orientation. The less developed information systems that supported command-and-control structures couldn't do that. In fact, those structures—which can probably be traced to the church and to the military as far back as Caesar—persisted precisely because for many years they were the *only* way to manage large, complex organizations.

Robert Herres: When I was taking management courses, we used to describe management as a process. I'm not sure that everybody got it. But the old rule that you plan, organize, direct, and control always seemed to me to be a pretty good description of what management is all about.

At USAA, we have always had processes linking together our basic activities. There's an underwriting process, a rate-setting process, a loss-management process, a catastrophe-management process, as well as the usual collection of functional processes. They've been there for years, although we haven't always been conscious of them. In fact, in some cases I think those processes were working in spite of our organizational structure.

Like Xerox, we were helped enormously by new developments in information technology. How? They forced us to think about the most effective ways of managing by process. We found that if you really want to exploit new technology—and for us, that includes both communications and information systems—you have to analyze how the work in your organization actually gets done and decide which steps can be tailored to a machine and which are best left to people. To do that, you have to develop detailed process maps and get the whole organization thinking in process terms.

Could you say a bit more about the links between information technology and processes?

Herres: Let me begin with a bit of history. USAA was started in 1922 as a direct writer of insurance. We never had agents; everything was done by mail and telephone. In fact, at one time we were the largest mail-order house in the country, maybe even in the world. Everything came to one centralized location in San Antonio, Texas, where the paperwork was processed. When we began to think about new technology, we discovered that lots of traditions had built up in this administrative organization, and many unnecessary steps. Paper was forever getting lost. My predecessor tells a wonderful story of trying to break into one of our processes. He was prowling the corridors one night when he looked into an office and noticed stacks of piled-up folders. None of them had been touched since his last visit a few evenings earlier, so he took a folder to see if anybody would notice. It was his way of testing whether our processes were under control. Unfortunately, many of them weren't, which meant that we had much cleaning up to do before we could meld those processes with modern information systems.

Technology also forced us to think about how and where our processes intersect. Alignment across businesses is critical for us because our goal is to exploit the efficiencies of centralized information management while we decentralize service delivery. Someone has to be master-at-arms to ensure that we don't have one of our companies— say, life insurance—creating systems and processes that don't interface well with the corporate system. Otherwise, we'd have a terrible time leveraging technology across the company.

Let me give you an example. About four years ago, I decided that the company needed to do something about address changes. Our customers are a mobile group; they move once every three years. And they didn't enjoy having to call each and every one of our lines of business to register the same change of address. They kept asking, "Don't you guys ever talk to one another?" Unfortunately, at the time the answer was no. It took us a year and a half to get the necessary systems and processes lined up so that a person could call any of our lines of business, report an address change, and have it posted immediately in our other businesses as well. It sounds like a simple process—changing addresses. But we found that the process cut across all parts of the organization.

Leschly: I think Bob raises an important point. Process improvement isn't limited to large-scale reengineering or fixing macro processes. (See Beyond Total Quality Management and Reengineering: Managing through Processes.) Real power comes from working with small processes—that's where the inefficiencies are. For example, we examined the problem of changing business cards when our sales representatives move from one of our sales forces to another. It typically took a couple of weeks; today it takes 24 hours. That may seem insignificant until you realize that we have 2,000 sales reps. Then the savings in time, money, energy, and communication with customers become quite substantial.

Beyond Total Quality Management and Reengineering: Managing through Processes

Virtually all efforts to redesign business processes today have their roots in two movements: total quality management (TQM) and reengineering. Both have provided managers with a powerful means of reshaping individual processes so that they serve existing categories of customers more efficiently. Reengineering, in particular, has helped managers harness the formidable power of information technology to improve process performance. But a growing number of managers are discovering that TQM and reengineering have three severe limitations.

First, these techniques assume that process redesign can be divorced from rethinking business strategy. Most TQM and reengineering programs take a strong operational view of improvement. They target processes that have grown with little rationale or planning; measure progress by reductions in cycle times, defect rates, and costs; and define success as better or faster execution. Those are laudable goals. But, in an era of volatile and rapidly changing markets and technologies, TQM and reengineering can generate a much improved process for competing in an environment that no longer exists.

Second, while TQM and reengineering are powerful tools for redesigning individual business processes, they often treat processes as unconnected islands. But the success of most businesses depends on how a bundle of their critical processes interact—something that TQM and reengineering programs often don't address.

Third, TQM and reengineering efforts typically focus on redesigning business processes and ignore management processes—the ways senior managers make, communicate, implement, monitor, and adjust decisions, and measure and compensate performance. But senior managers' role in a process-oriented organization is radically different than in a functional, command-and-control hierarchy. Unless management processes are redesigned, too, chances are the company will not come close to reaping the full benefits of its TQM or reengineering plan.

When I say that TQM and reengineering have limitations, I do not mean that they are inherently flawed. I am merely arguing that they are tools for achieving operational improvements, not total solutions. But the level of disappointment among companies that have embraced TQM or reengineering—reengineering experts report failure rates as high as 70%—suggests that many managers see them as panaceas rather than as tools for fixing particular problems.

Thus, before setting out to redesign a critical process, a manager first should ask whether the chief problem is the quality, cost, or speed of the process or, rather, the fundamental inability of the process to support the strategy. In other words, should the process be improved or should it be radically transformed to accommodate strategic requirements?

Consider a semiconductor manufacturer that has historically competed in slow-moving niche markets with limited competition. The company's managers describe its traditional resource-allocation process as "covering the roulette table"—avoiding difficult choices by spreading R&D dollars among a large number of small-scale, low-payoff projects. Product development has always been a leisurely and extended affair: Work on a product's next generation would begin only after work on its predecessor had been completely finished.

Today, however, changes in underlying technologies and customer preferences mean that instead of selling components, the company now must bundle components into complex systems. The required level of research per product is therefore rising rapidly, at the same time that product life cycles are shrinking from 10 to 15 years to 3 to 5 years. The company's mainstay customers have also changed. Formerly a virtually exclusive supplier to many companies in niche markets, the manufacturer now serves a handful of automakers and disk-drive producers and faces aggressive competition.

In short, the new strategy requires that the company excel at two tasks: making a few large R&D investments that can generate significant payoffs and developing new generations of products concurrently. Does the company need to adapt its resource-allocation and product-development processes to accommodate this strategy? If so, in what ways? Neither TQM nor reengineering experts deal with those questions, beyond suggesting that the two processes be made swifter, more productive, and less prone to error. Neither would necessarily lead the company to create a new resource-allocation process—one that is capable of identifying and funding a few high-impact investments. Such a process would require a more elaborate system for gathering customer information as well as revised procedures for choosing among investment proposals.

Nor would TQM and reengineering naturally bring about the radical changes in the product-development process that are critical for carrying out the new strategy. Because the company's product life cycles are much shorter, it needs a development process that enables it to work simultaneously on current and future generations of products. Such a process means engineers must develop new forms of collaboration and better ways to communicate across projects.

Managers should also try to answer a second question before redesigning a critical process: How much of the problem stems from the individual process and how much from the complex interaction among processes? Few processes unfold in isolation; most depend heavily on one another for information and resources. A greatly improved product-development process won't generate the desired results if the market-research process is not aligned to provide timely information about customers. Similarly, strategic planning is a mere exercise if the resource-allocation process uses different criteria to rank investment proposals. (In the case of the semiconductor company, the two processes remain distinct. The two top-level executives, both industry veterans, are continuing to rely mostly on their instincts, rather than on the company's formal strategic analysis, to place bets.) Before redesigning a process, therefore, managers need to make sure they understand the upstream and downstream linkages among processes; they must learn to think about processes as a collective organism rather than as isolated streams of activity.

Finally, managers should consider whether existing management processes will be compatible with the redesigned business processes. Most management processes are woven into the organizational fabric of a company. For this reason, they profoundly influence the likely success of reengineering initiatives. It makes little sense to reengineer a logistics process around information technology that allows rapid, autonomous decision making in the field if the company's norms and incentives continue to require sign-offs from corporate staff. Nor is a redesigned service process likely to deliver superior advice to customers if the evaluation system continues to judge telephone representatives on their efficiency and productivity.

Will senior management groups need to relinquish authority to ensure that processes function as planned? Will they have to change the rules and the systems for accessing information to ensure that everyone needing to share it can do so? How do senior managers plan to interact with processes once inefficiencies have been eliminated? Will the reward system support the team behavior required of new processes? As Christopher Meyer noted in "How the Right Measures Help Teams Excel" (*Harvard Business Review* May–June 1994), traditional measurement and reward systems for governing hierarchical, functional organizations often disempower teams charged with executing cross-functional processes.

TQM and reengineering experts—other than saying the goal should be to eliminate waste and minimize deviations from standard—are virtually silent on the subject of how to manage business processes once they have been improved. There is a wide range of possible approaches, depending on the nature of the process, the company's culture and management style, the organization's size, and competitive demands. Consider the strategic-planning process of Emerson Electric, an $8.6 billion company that competes in a wide range of stable, cost-competitive businesses. Charles F. Knight, the company's chairman and CEO, is the architect of the company's strategy and its strategic-planning process, including its accompanying performance-measurement system. By committing 50% of his time to planning and review meetings that focus on financial performance, he shapes the way that the process unfolds. In these meetings he rigorously questions the division presidents' goals and assumptions, but the division heads are ultimately responsible for devising and executing their own plans.

Standing in sharp contrast is the way the strategic-planning process needs to be managed at small, narrowly focused high-technology companies contending with rapid change. Their senior managers need to track real-time operating data, such as shipments. They also need to develop multiple strategic alternatives simultaneously; they cannot wait for review meetings to redirect misguided strategies and must play a much more hands-on role in crafting their businesses' strategies.

When a company has "fixed" its processes through TQM or reengineering, it hopes to end up with superior processes. But those processes still have to be managed. *How* they are managed will determine whether the company realizes their full potential.

As you make these shifts, you are implicitly changing the company's culture and behavior patterns. Organizations, after all, are more than collections of processes; they are made up of people who have become accustomed to long-standing norms and ways of working together. How have the members of your organizations responded to the increased attention to processes?

Weatherup: We struggled at first. Pepsi has always been an action-oriented organization with a "take-the-hill, get-it-done, can-do" mentality. Results were what mattered, whether you got them in an ad hoc or an orderly fashion. At the start, people were afraid that processes would slow them down. They feared they would lead to standardization, bureaucracy, and less freedom to act. It took time to overcome those concerns.

Allaire: I think there's a danger of falling into a trap here, of thinking of processes as a constraint. At Xerox, we're very keen on empowering people and unleashing their creative juices–and we see processes as liberating. After all, if you have processes that are in control, you know how the organization is working. There's no guesswork because variances are small and operating limits are well defined. Couple that with objectives that are consistent with your strategy and communicated all the way down the line—to individuals on the production floor as well as to those who deal directly with customers—and you get quality output without a lot of checking. You don't need the old command-and-control approach, which was designed to keep people in line; instead, you can tell people to do their own thing provided they respect the process. You wind up with an environment that frees people to be creative. This connection to empowerment turned out to be critical for us: If people don't understand it, they tend to resist a process approach because they think it will restrict their creativity. But it does exactly the opposite.

Weatherup: I agree with you one thousand percent. A process approach *is* liberating. It helps us build reliability and winning consistency, and our people love to win. So over time, they've bought in completely. But our starting point was totally different. People felt that processes meant standardization and less freedom. I'm curious to know how you dealt with that at USAA.

Herres: We decided to keep our experiments with processes focused in the early stages and designated the Great Lakes area as our test region for business-process improvement. That allowed us to work the bugs out of new ideas before we exposed them to the total membership; in addition, it helped us ensure consistency and seamless service. It was also a great opportunity to provide career-broadening experiences for promising managers, and it gave us a new way for us to think about change. Once the process approach was proven in the test region—and the goal there was revolutionary rather than evolutionary change—it could be rolled out to the rest of the organization with much less resistance.

Leschly: Sometimes you can get the same results by changing the players. I came to SmithKline Beecham in June 1990, just a year after the merger took place. I was a newcomer who had no association with the previous cultures and was put in charge of the worldwide pharmaceutical business. There were about 12 people on my management team. Today, I have to admit, only 2 of them are left. It was a gradual process. Some people retired; some didn't think the job was fun any longer; a few enjoyed it and stayed. We found that we needed people who were capable of adapting to a completely new way of running the business and who weren't wedded to either of the premerger cultures.

Weatherup: Bless you! It's good to know I have company. I also had 12 people reporting to me at the start of our change process. That was four years ago, and today only 2 of them remain.

Leschly: Unfortunately, people don't recognize these shifts at the top, because nobody in our position is going to stand up and say, "I'm proud to report that management has changed." But even with new people at the top, we found that we had to work hard on education and training. People have a tough time understanding what it means for processes to be reliable, repeatable, and in control. Every one of our employees was asked to embrace a set of problem-solving and process-improvement tools, which we've labeled a "Simply Better Way" of working. We now have 57 coach-trainers, who teach our trainers, plus 170 country/site trainers, who ensure a local presence in every country and major site. They, in turn, have trained 1,200 frontline facilitators, who support our process-improvement teams. And we still think it's going to take us years before we can honestly say that all 50,000 people at SmithKline Beecham understand what it means to standardize and improve a process. It's important to note that the trainers are not full-time; they all wear two hats. We have avoided having an organization within the organization to manage process improvements.

Weatherup: We actually developed a formal enrollment process to win acceptance of our changes. It took us 15 months—from December 1990 to March 1992—with separate meetings for each level of the organization. Every 3 months we worked with a different group, starting with the 70 people who are on the rung below my direct reports, moving to larger groups of 400 and 1,200, then to a huge meeting of 5,500 in Dallas, and finally to a one-day video presentation to all 20,000 of our frontline employees.

Every enrollment had the same format. The process was kicked off with a 3-day meeting, followed immediately by a 90-day work period. I always opened up the meeting with a "burning platform" speech that I borrowed from a consultant of ours to get people tuned in to the need for change. Apparently, a few years ago there was a fire on a North Sea oil rig. Because the rigs were 150 feet high, the workers had been instructed not to jump but to wait for help, no matter how bad things got. Despite the injunction, one worker jumped—and survived. Asked later to explain his actions, he said that he had looked behind, seen an approaching wall of fire, then looked down and seen the icy sea below. His rationale? "I chose probable death over certain death." Only 11 others survived the fire, out of several hundred workers.

That image set the stage. I then made the case for change with detailed data on the financial, market, and organizational pains we were facing. Members of the previous enrollment group followed, describing our new vision and reporting their findings from interviews with customers and employees. After discussion, training was presented; most of the time was devoted to basic process analysis. Participants then divided into teams to plan their "real" work. All groups were given 90 days to complete assigned activities, which included interviewing customers, charting work processes, and designing and leading the enrollment meeting for the next group of employees.

That last step was the secret for us. We ended up calling it "head, heart, hands" because we believed that for change to occur, people had to do three things: develop a conceptual understanding of the rationale and proposed direction of change, internalize and commit emotionally to the new vision, and acquire new skills to ensure that the vision would be realized. Each group had 90 days to get comfortable, to think about what was said and digest it, to conduct their own little process-improvement projects, and to work through the vision statement and company values. Not that you could get fully comfortable in 90 days. But our basic message was, Don't go underground. Either sign up or we'll be happy to give you a nice severance package—and you can go to work for somebody else.

It sounds as if a new type of manager with a different set of skills is required to work effectively in a process environment.

Leschly: Twenty years ago, it was simple to select people. You just looked at results. Anybody who could bring home the bacon was, by definition, a terrific person. Today we go through an elaborate selection process that goes well beyond bottom-line numbers. It focuses more on soft skills, on communication and the ability to work as a team player. All those skills are necessary if you are going to oversee or participate in cross-functional processes. And there are the intangibles that don't show up on a résumé–things like intelligence, judgment, a sense of humor, and energy level. Those are the qualities I use to pick my own team. Take a sense of humor. If there is no smile, no laugh, you can bet the candidate isn't any good with people and won't be able to create the right atmosphere. We also don't want any clones. We want some mavericks who are different—but still aligned. Because then you can create a team of wide-ranging differences that is more than the sum of its parts.

Herres: We've recognized the growing importance of technical skills. One of our biggest problems in the past was the gulf that separated our information technology people, who are centralized, from our lines of business. The business people had a simple approach to technology: They defined their business requirements, threw them over the transom to information services, and told them to call back when they were finished. That was okay when systems requirements were easy to define, but not today when complex processes are involved.

I've seen it time and time again with the programs that have gotten into trouble. They all lacked a continuing, interactive dialogue between systems developers and the business people who wound up using the technology.

So we decided to foster an understanding of systems in the minds of our business people, especially those in key positions. I just announced a replacement for the head of our property and casualty group, and I picked someone who understands information technology. He hasn't been a technologist all his life, but he has a good grasp of systems design and systems analysis. For those employees who don't yet have the background, we've launched an ambitious program to subsidize their purchase of personal computers. Because it's open to any USAA employee, it's going to cost us a few million dollars. But it's worth it. Computer literacy is essential for succeeding in business today.

Weatherup: When I was considering someone for promotion a few years ago, I looked at only two criteria. One was idea leadership. The person had to have the ability to find, create, borrow, steal, or reshape ideas, especially big ideas, because that was the essence of our culture. The other thing I looked for was people leadership. Pepsi's managers had to be able to mobilize the troops and energize the organization, to get it moving fast and aggressively. Today we've added a third category, capability leadership, by which I mean a manager's ability to build and institutionalize the capabilities of people, the organization, and systems. To do that well requires a focus on core processes.

Have you assigned individuals or created special roles for overseeing processes?

Allaire: Right now, we're trying to reengineer four key processes: market to collection, or the order-fulfillment cycle; time to market, which is really the product-delivery process; integrated supply chain; and customer service. Each of these efforts has both a process champion and a process owner. The process owner is responsible for orchestrating the daily details of redesign and improvement; it's a full-time job for a vice president. Process champions, in contrast, are members of my senior team, with broad oversight responsibilities.

We have assigned process champions to each of the four major processes being reengineered. The symbolism is important; their mere existence makes senior management more process oriented. But champions are more than figureheads. Sometimes process owners, who sit one organizational level below our business-division presidents, run into interference. Their efforts stall, perhaps because of local loyalties or because a division manager is reluctant to provide funding for the additional investments required to upgrade a process. Traditionally, in situations like these, process owners had no recourse since they were outranked by the division presidents. But now there is a senior champion to turn to, a representative from the corporate office who understands the issues and has the clout to work across the entire business. With these people in place, our reengineering efforts no longer get sidetracked.

Leschly: We have a similar approach but use slightly different terms. We call them owners and sponsors. Ownership means that you jump into the soup: You roll up your sleeves and get intimately involved in improving the process. Sponsorship means that you manage the process: You have responsibility, but you don't necessarily get your hands dirty. That sounds like Paul's description, although sometimes—especially for a core process such as drug development—a member of the corporate management team serves as sponsor and owner simultaneously.

It sounds as though processes are becoming an accepted management responsibility even at senior levels. That poses a problem of evaluation. Companies have years of experience evaluating the performance of department and function heads but are still novices in evaluating process responsibility. How do you accurately judge the work of someone who is overseeing a cross-functional process? What measures do you use, and how do you conduct an assessment?

Allaire: For process owners, we use outcome-oriented measures such as quality and productivity. The only difference is that they apply to total processes rather than to individual functions or units. For example, the integrated supply chain has all the usual customer satisfaction, inventory, and efficiency metrics that a business division does. In this case, however, the process owner has companywide responsibility, and his numbers are the sum total of those reported by all divisions and departments. This part of the evaluation is pretty straightforward, although it took us a while to develop the right measurements. For individuals who are overseeing reengineering projects, we add other objectives that are geared to project management, like meeting budgets and progressing according to preset milestones.

Weatherup: My focus right now is on evaluating the members of my executive team, who have responsibility for broad, systemic processes. Take my senior vice president of marketing. To get a good evaluation, he first needs to "own" the Super Bowl, to have the most talked about, memorable ads, the best copy, and great reviews in the popular press. That's still important, and if he doesn't deliver he gets a bad grade. But now he is also responsible for a process we call single-voice communication. It governs how we go to market with promotional campaigns and new products. A tremendous amount of material has to be sent to the field each trimester in a coordinated fashion, so that all market units are able to act in concert. Otherwise, we don't get the necessary alignment, and the phones start ringing with complaints.

In the past, this process didn't exist. Our advertising was terrific, but we broke down in execution. Now the senior vice president of marketing owns the process. It's one of his top four priorities and figures heavily in the calculation of his annual bonus. That makes a huge difference. We discuss the process regularly, and I evaluate him on the timeliness and completeness of his communications to the field. The subject also comes up at our weekly senior-staff meetings. Remember, this is a core process. If the materials don't show up in the field, it's not merely of passing interest; it's a disaster. Feedback from angry customers tends to pour in pretty quickly.

Does the shift to processes alter your concept of how senior managers should work together?

Allaire: I think the challenge now is that, for the first time, you must have a team at the top. We always *talked* teams, but today they really are necessary to make companywide processes work effectively. It's not just the people reporting to me but those several layers down, as well. I have six direct reports who form the top management team. But we also have nine division heads, who run their own businesses yet depend on the same laboratories and sales force. They therefore share processes and have to make joint decisions for the betterment of the company. In their minds, we're giving them contradictory advice: Be independent, but cooperate and work together.

At a minimum, they need to buy into what we're trying to do as a company. That's why the strategic intent has to be crystal clear. But, at the same time, they need to understand that even though they're running their own divisions, their success very much depends on the success of the larger organization and its core processes.

Leschly: I would love to get some input here, because we've hit a roadblock in moving toward a team-based organization. No matter how much we emphasize teams, individual managers still want to make their bonuses and tend to stay focused on their personal and departmental goals. How do you develop an incentive system that makes it worthwhile for people to work in teams?

Allaire: When we shifted to our new organization, we also put a new compensation plan in place. In a traditional plan, you get rated against your objectives in three areas—how the corporation does, how your division does, and how you as an individual perform—with the ratings then added together to determine your bonus. But ultimately what happened with this approach was that bonuses varied little year to year and became virtual entitlements at Xerox.

Not anymore. Now the ratings are multiplied together rather than added. We use a simple graph with two axes. The vertical axis represents performance against corporate objectives, which have been set for the whole company. They're not just financials—although they're a big part of it—but also include market share, customer satisfaction, and employee satisfaction. The horizontal axis reflects how your division has done and how you have performed against personal objectives. That's usually where we pick up the process dimension. For instance, process owners will be evaluated according to their progress against milestones that are part of their personal objectives. To compute the overall bonus factor, we multiply the horizontal and vertical ratings together.

With this system, if you perform well but the company doesn't, you're not going to do very well financially. Because if you achieve 100% of your goals and the company as a whole only performs at 80%, you're only going to get a score of 80. One result of this system is that the variability of bonuses has gone way up—they've been as low as 35% of target and as high as 250%—so that people have begun to pay more attention to the drivers of performance. Risk taking and entrepreneurship are more likely because the payoffs for success have increased so dramatically. The multiplicative factor also encourages managers to broaden their focus beyond their own needs to consider the needs of other departments and divisions. That has been especially important for our division presidents, who compete for resources yet must work together to oversee common processes like selecting R&D projects.

Let's turn now to your own jobs. How has a process orientation affected the work you do and the way you spend your time?

Weatherup: It has changed *everything* about my job, as well as the jobs of my senior team. Our focus is completely different. Let me give you an example. We spend every Monday morning in a senior-staff meeting, and much of the time is now devoted to discussions of our core, capability-building processes. Whether it's new product development, single-voice communication, or coaching and support for sales, we're constantly asking, How do we leverage these processes for maximum advantage? It's not as though we'd asked these questions before; they never came up. We were much too tactical and reactive.

At a personal level, there's even a difference in the questions I ask. As soon as I stepped off the plane on field visits, my first question used to be, "Are you going to deliver your volume and NOPAT [net operating profits after taxes] for the month?" You can imagine the message that sent. Now the questions are completely different: "Are we giving great customer service? How is our relationship with Wal-Mart? Where are you on coaching and support for sales? Were there any problems with the rollout of this trimester's promotion?" The focus is much more on the doing, much more attuned to our major processes. I never would have asked those questions before. Why? Because I grew up under the old Pepsi philosophy that said, Here's the big idea. Run with it and carry the flag up the hill. That's fine for getting things started. But if you don't create structured, repeatable processes, you don't develop a long-term capability, and the work doesn't get done.

Perhaps most important, processes have brought us discipline. They force you to be very precise about what you're looking for and how you make decisions. In the past, I could usually get away with vague advice or meddling because I was the boss. Take new product development. Before we had a well-defined process, people would come to me with partially developed plans for review. I would usually propose changes, but they weren't always helpful. I might say, "I like the new flavor, but try to make it sweeter. Why don't you experiment with a few additional variables and get back to me as soon as you can?" In hindsight, those instructions weren't very clear. They often required guesswork by employees and resulted in repeated visits and requests for clarification.

Today we have a structured seven-step process that governs all product and package development. There are exit criteria for each stage, which lay out the hurdles that a new idea has to clear before it can move from one stage to the next. These hurdles are crystal clear, and all fuzziness and guesswork are gone. For instance, new products are not allowed to move beyond test marketing unless they are able to produce a 60/40 win in blind taste tests against the competition. Criteria like these force me to be more disciplined in my responses and more attentive to implementation. Either I override the exit criteria consciously—and live with the consequences—or allow the remainder of the process to unfold as planned.

Leschly: Like Craig, I'm also restructuring my work habits. I now spend about 90% of my time on strategic issues and 10% on operational issues. I am almost totally disengaged from day-to-day, tactical implementation. But that doesn't mean I'm removed from processes. I remain heavily involved in the development and measurement of the capabilities of our key management and business processes, and devote special attention to two of them—innovation, for which I am the process sponsor, and alliance formation. Both are tightly linked to our major strategic initiatives.

It seems that there has been a subtle shift at the top, from managing by results to managing through direction setting and processes. Direction setting is establishing the "where"; it's making sure that everyone is working toward achieving the same goals. Processes are the "how"; they ensure that the work gets done efficiently and effectively.

Leschly: That's right, but you still have to keep score. Maybe it goes back to my competitive tennis-playing days, but I have always felt that if you don't keep score, you're just practicing. And that requires very clear objectives. We have one-year, three-year, and ten-year plans, and we know exactly what has to be achieved for each one.

Herres: We also put great effort into setting objectives. But we've learned that you can't set them and then just walk off and assume they're good forever; there's a constant process of adjustment and change. That's especially true of new products because customers' needs are always evolving. Managers need to be careful not to get completely captured by the customer-driven perspective. I spend a lot of time on customers' expectations and evaluations; I even try to sign the response to every complaint letter addressed to me. Two or three times a week, a small team and I meet to review the most recent letters, and at almost every session I hear something that inspires me to start a project that will fix a problem or hone a process. So we listen to our customers. But at the same time, when it comes to new and better products for the future, the customer doesn't know enough to tell us what to do. The minivan is a good example. The American public didn't know it wanted minivans until they were out on the market, and then it seemed that nearly every family had to have one. Our job is to anticipate what customers will want three or four years from now, before they can articulate it.

Let me play devil's advocate for a moment. Suppose we had been sitting around this table 25 years ago. I bet we would have heard the very same things from chief executives then. That they try to spend their time on strategic issues, not operational issues. That they focus on direction setting and keeping score. That they attend to innovation, product development, and customers' needs because of their links to strategic goals. What really is different today? Has process thinking had an impact? Or is the job the same as always?

Allaire: There's definitely a difference. But to understand it, you need to define processes more precisely. We've actually been talking about three very different kinds of processes. At the highest level, there are management processes—how the CEO runs the company, how management interacts with employees, how decisions get made, and how communication takes place. Those processes set the organizational context and style of working, like "the IBM way." Then there are business processes, which are the focus of reengineering efforts. Business processes are large, crosscutting collections of activities, like product design, order fulfillment, and customer service. Finally, there are work processes, which are the basic building blocks of business processes. Work processes are focused and operational; they are how the work actually gets done. Examples include such activities as prototype development, finished-goods warehousing, and purchasing.

With these definitions, we can distinguish the old from the new. Chief executives have always focused on management processes. They're the way you get things done. What's different now is that senior managers are also involved in business and work processes. Today those processes are explicit rather than implicit, and senior managers are examining them from a perspective that encompasses the entire company. For the first time, they are reshaping business and work processes to align them with strategy while making them more customer oriented and efficient.

There are good reasons for this shift. In the past, most processes were divided up on a functional basis. They were unintegrated, and the pieces were allowed to operate independently, without tight links. Because functional expertise was regarded as the key to success, there was little place for senior-management involvement. Now, however, we are trying to focus our processes on the customer. That requires much tighter integration and the involvement of a higher level of management. Unless each function has a different customer—and in our business, they don't—you have to link together activities that were always run separately. They're not going to integrate themselves; they haven't for a hundred years.

Herres: I think Paul's three-level map has real merit. It not only fits our own approach but also suggests another reason why senior managers are more involved with processes today. As technology improves and the pace of change accelerates, all three types of processes become faster moving and more interactive. Decision-making cycles tighten, feedback loops are shorter, and there's less room for error. The risks go up because you can get left behind a lot more quickly. For that reason alone, managers now have to pay more attention to processes. In the past, the pace was less intense–you could plan, organize, direct, and control processes in a more leisurely fashion.

As you reflect on the changes you have described, what advice would you offer other chief executives about to embark on the same path?

Leschly: First and foremost, if you're not willing to go through the pain, do something else. I mean that seriously. Getting people to change is extremely difficult—exciting, yes, but terribly painful. Second, recognize that in the final analysis success rests on selecting the right people to work with. If you have the right people, the rest will follow.

Weatherup: I second Jan's comments. If you aren't willing to be relentless and persevere, don't even think about launching a change process. It takes years of hard work, and you have to be the one driving it forward. At the same time, make sure that you understand your company's culture. Leverage the strengths of the culture—it's your only advantage—while working around or eliminating the weaknesses. Finally, make sure that your message reaches the grass roots. We shut down all locations for a day to enroll our 20,000 frontline employees in our new vision. These are the people who do the work day in and day out. If they're not on board, you aren't going to make much progress.

Herres: I'd also suggest paying attention to the human side of the equation. Try to establish the notion that change is a way of life and that success in the new environment requires the sharing of obligations. At USAA, we now expect that in a 20- to 25-year career, a typical employee will hold six different jobs. We want to keep our employees when we shift to new processes. They come with assets like loyalty, commitment to customers, and understanding of our culture and our mission. We've therefore struck a bargain: We'll provide them with the training they need if they're willing to do their part and invest in self-development and education. CEOs need to accept the challenge of retraining their employees just as they retool their machinery and equipment.

Allaire: Changes in culture are what make the shift to processes so difficult. They can't be mandated; instead, they have to be formed over time through continual reinforcement. Communication becomes enormously important yet incredibly difficult. In fact, every time we make one of these changes, we find that we undercommunicate it. After four or five times repeating the same message, we assume that it has been heard. In reality, many people have not absorbed the information. It takes a lot of time to win understanding and acceptance of major changes.

PART

III

The New Role of Management

1
The New Managerial Work

Rosabeth Moss Kanter

Managerial work is undergoing such enormous and rapid change that many managers are reinventing their profession as they go. With little precedent to guide them, they are watching hierarchy fade away and the clear distinctions of title, task, department, even corporation, blur. Faced with extraordinary levels of complexity and interdependency, they watch traditional sources of power erode and the old motivational tools lose their magic.

The cause is obvious. Competitive pressures are forcing corporations to adopt new flexible strategies and structures. Many of these are familiar: acquisitions and divestitures aimed at more focused combinations of business activities, reductions in management staff and levels of hierarchy, increased use of performance-based rewards. Other strategies are less common but have an even more profound effect. In a growing number of companies, for example, horizontal ties between peers are replacing vertical ties as channels of activity and communication. Companies are asking corporate staffs and functional departments to play a more strategic role with greater cross-departmental collaboration. Some organizations are turning themselves nearly inside out—buying formerly internal services from outside suppliers, forming strategic alliances and supplier-customer partnerships that bring external relationships inside where they can influence company policy and practice. I call these emerging practices "postentrepreneurial" because they involve the application of entrepreneurial creativity and flexibility to established businesses.

Such changes come highly recommended by the experts who urge organizations to become leaner, less bureaucratic, more entrepreneurial. But so far, theorists have given scant attention to the dramatically altered realities of managerial work in these transformed corporations. We don't even have good words to describe the new relationships. "Superiors" and "subordinates" hardly seem accurate, and even "bosses" and "their people" imply more control and ownership than managers today actually possess. On top of it all, career paths are no longer straightforward and predictable but have become idiosyncratic and confusing.

Some managers experience the new managerial work as a loss of power because much of their authority used to come from hierarchical position. Now that everything seems negotiable by everyone, they are confused about how to mobilize and motivate staff. For other managers, the shift in roles and tasks offers greater personal power. The following case histories illustrate the responses of three managers in three different industries to the opportunities and dilemmas of structural change.

Hank is vice president and chief engineer for a leading heavy equipment manufacturer that is moving aggressively against foreign competition. One of the company's top priorities has been to increase the speed, quality, and cost-effectiveness of product development. So Hank worked with consultants to improve collaboration between manufacturing and other functions and to create closer alliances between the company and its outside suppliers. Gradually, a highly segmented operation became an integrated process involving project teams drawn from component divisions, functional departments, and external suppliers. But along the way, there were several unusual side effects. Different areas of responsibility overlapped. Some technical and manufacturing people were co-located. Liaisons from functional areas joined the larger development teams. Most unusual of all, project teams had a lot of direct contact with higher levels of the company.

Many of the managers reporting to Hank felt these changes as a loss of power. They didn't always know what their people were doing, but they still believed they ought to know. They no longer had sole input into performance appraisals; other people from other functions had a voice as well, and some of them knew more about employees' project performance. New career paths made it less important to please direct superiors in order to move up the functional line.

Moreover, employees often bypassed Hank's managers and interacted directly with decision makers inside and outside the company.

Some of these so-called subordinates had contact with division executives and senior corporate staff, and sometimes they sat in on high-level strategy meetings to which their managers were not invited.

At first Hank thought his managers' resistance to the new process was just the normal noise associated with any change. Then he began to realize that something more profound was going on. The reorganization was challenging traditional notions about the role and power of managers and shaking traditional hierarchy to its roots. And no one could see what was taking its place.

When George became head of a major corporate department in a large bank holding company, he thought he had arrived. His title and rank were unmistakable, and his department was responsible for determining product-line policy for hundreds of bank branches and the virtual clerks—in George's eyes—who managed them. George staffed his department with MBAs and promised them rapid promotion.

Then the sand seemed to shift beneath him. Losing market position for the first time in recent memory, the bank decided to emphasize direct customer service at the branches. The people George considered clerks began to depart from George's standard policies and to tailor their services to local market conditions. In many cases, they actually demanded services and responses from George's staff, and the results of their requests began to figure in performance reviews of George's department. George's people were spending more and more time in the field with branch managers, and the corporate personnel department was even trying to assign some of George's MBAs to branch and regional posts.

To complicate matters, the bank's strategy included a growing role for technology. George felt that because he had no direct control over the information systems department, he should not be held fully accountable for every facet of product design and implementation. But fully accountable he was. He had to deploy people to learn the new technology and figure out how to work with it. Furthermore, the bank was asking product departments like George's to find ways to link existing products or develop new ones that crossed traditional categories. So George's people were often away on cross-departmental teams just when he wanted them for some internal assignment.

Instead of presiding over a tidy empire the way his predecessor had, George presided over what looked to him like chaos. The bank said senior executives should be "leaders, not managers," but George didn't know what that meant, especially since he seemed to have lost control over his subordinates' assignments, activities, rewards, and careers. He resented his perceived loss of status.

The CEO tried to show him that good results achieved the new way would bring great monetary rewards, thanks to a performance-based bonus program that was gradually replacing more modest yearly raises. But the pressures on George were also greater, unlike anything he'd ever experienced.

For Sally, purchasing manager at an innovative computer company, a new organizational strategy was a gain rather than a loss, although it changed her relationship with the people reporting to her. Less than ten years out of college, she was hired as an analyst—a semiprofessional, semiclerical job—then promoted to a purchasing manager's job in a sleepy staff department. She didn't expect to go much further in what was then a well-established hierarchy. But after a shocking downturn, top management encouraged employees to re-think traditional ways of doing things. Sally's boss, the head of purchasing, suggested that "partnerships" with key suppliers might improve quality, speed innovation, and reduce costs.

Soon Sally's backwater was at the center of policy-making, and Sally began to help shape strategy. She organized meetings between her company's senior executives and supplier CEOs. She sent her staff to contribute supplier intelligence at company seminars on technical innovation, and she spent more of her own time with product designers and manufacturing planners. She led senior executives on a tour of supplier facilities, traveling with them in the corporate jet.

Because some suppliers were also important customers, Sally's staff began meeting frequently with marketing managers to share information and address joint problems. Sally and her group were now also acting as internal advocates for major suppliers. Furthermore, many of these external companies now contributed performance appraisals of Sally and her team, and their opinions weighed almost as heavily as those of her superiors.

As a result of the company's new direction, Sally felt more personal power and influence, and her ties to peers in other areas and to top management were stronger. But she no longer felt like a manager directing subordinates. Her staff had become a pool of resources deployed by many others besides Sally. She was exhilarated by her personal opportunities but not quite sure the people she managed should have the same freedom to choose their own assignments. After all, wasn't that a manager's prerogative?

Hank's, George's, and Sally's very different stories say much about the changing nature of managerial work. However hard it is for managers at the very top to remake strategy and structure, they themselves will probably retain their identity, status, and control. For the managers below them, structural change is often much harder. As work units become more participative and team oriented, and as professionals and knowledge workers become more prominent, the distinction between manager and nonmanager begins to erode.

To understand what managers must do to achieve results in the post entrepreneurial corporation, we need to look at the changing picture of how such companies operate. The picture has five elements:

1. There are a greater number and variety of channels for taking action and exerting influence.
2. Relationships of influence are shifting from the vertical to the horizontal, from chain of command to peer networks.
3. The distinction between managers and those managed is diminishing, especially in terms of information, control over assignments, and access to external relationships.
4. External relationships are increasingly important as sources of internal power and influence, even of career development.
5. As a result of the first four changes, career development has become less intelligible but also less circumscribed. There are fewer assured routes to success, which produces anxiety. At the same time, career paths are more open to innovation, which produces opportunity.

To help companies implement their competitive organizational strategies, managers must learn new ways to manage, confronting changes in their own bases of power and recognizing the need for new ways to motivate people.

The Bases of Power

The changes I've talked about can be scary for people like George and the managers reporting to Hank, who were trained to know their place, to follow orders, to let the company take care of their careers, to do things by the book. The book is gone. In the new corporation, managers have only themselves to count on for success. They must learn to operate without the crutch of hierarchy. Position, title, and authority are no longer adequate tools, not in a world where subordinates are encouraged to think for themselves and where managers have to work synergistically with other departments and even other companies. Success depends increasingly on tapping into sources of good ideas, on figuring out whose collaboration is needed to act on those ideas, on working with both to produce results. In short, the new managerial work implies very different ways of obtaining and using power.

The postentrepreneurial corporation is not only leaner and flatter, it also has many more channels for action. Cross-functional projects, business-unit joint ventures, labor-management forums, innovation funds that spawn activities outside mainstream budgets and reporting lines, strategic partnerships with suppliers or customers—these are all overlays on the traditional organization chart, strategic pathways that ignore the chain of command. (For examples and the questions that arise from the changing powerbase, see "The New Managerial Quandries.")

The New Managerial Quandaries

At American Express, the CEO instituted a program called "One Enterprise" to encourage collaboration between different lines of business. One Enterprise has led to a range of projects where peers from different divisions work together on such synergistic ventures as cross-marketing, joint purchasing, and cooperative product and market innovation. Employees' rewards are tied to their One Enterprise efforts. Executives set goals and can earn bonuses for their contributions to results in other divisions.

But how do department managers control their people when they're working on cross-departmental teams? And who determines the size of the rewards when the interests of more than one area are involved?

At Security Pacific National Bank, internal departments have become forces in the external marketplace. For example, the bank is involved in a joint venture with local auto dealers to sell fast financing for car purchases. And the MIS department is now a profit center selling its services inside and outside the bank.

But what is the role of bank managers accountable for the success of such entrepreneurial ventures? And how do they shift their orientation from the role of boss in a chain of command to the role of customer?

At Digital Equipment Corporation, emphasis on supplier partnerships to improve quality and innovation has multiplied the need for cross-functional as well as cross-company collaboration. Key suppliers are included on product planning teams with engineering, manufacturing, and purchasing staff. Digital uses its human resources staff to train and do performance appraisals of its suppliers, as if they were part of the company. In cases where suppliers are also customers, purchasing and marketing departments also need to work collaboratively.

But how do managers learn enough about other functions to be credible, let alone influential, members of such teams? How do they maintain adequate communication externally while staying on top of what their own departments are doing? And how do they handle the extra work of responding to projects initiated by other areas?

At Banc One, a growing reliance on project teams spanning more than 70 affiliated banks has led the CEO to propose eliminating officer titles because of the lack of correlation between status as measured by title and status within the collaborative team.

But then what do "rank" and "hierarchy" mean anymore, especially for people whose careers consist of a sequence of projects rather than a sequence of promotions? What does "career" mean? Does it have a shape? Is there a ladder?

At Alcan, which is trying to find new uses and applications for its core product, aluminum, managers and professionals from line divisions form screening teams to consider and refine new-venture proposals. A venture manager, chosen from the screening team, takes charge of concepts that pass muster, drawing on Alcan's worldwide resources to build the new business. In one case of global synergy, Alcan created a new product for the Japanese market using Swedish and American technology and Canadian manufacturing capacity.

But why should senior managers release staff to serve on screening and project teams for new businesses when their own businesses are making do with fewer and fewer people? How do functionally oriented managers learn enough about worldwide developments to know when they might have something of value to offer someplace else? And how do the managers of these new ventures ever go back to the conventional line organization as middle managers once their venture has been folded into an established division?

At IBM, an emphasis on customer partnerships to rebuild market share is leading to practices quite new to the company. In some cases, IBM has formed joint development teams with customers, where engineers from both companies share proprietary data. In others, the company has gone beyond selling equipment to actually managing a customer's management information system. Eastman Kodak has handed its U.S. data center operations to IBM to consolidate and manage, which means lower fixed costs for Kodak and a greater ability to focus on its core businesses rather than on ancillary services. Some 300 former Kodak people still fill Kodak's needs as IBM employees, while two committees of IBM and Kodak managers oversee the partnership.

But who exactly do the data center people work for? Who is in charge? And how do traditional notions of managerial authority square with such a complicated set of relationships?

Their existence has several important implications. For one thing, they create more potential centers of power. As the ways to combine resources increase, the ability to command diminishes. Alternative paths of communication, resource access, and execution erode the authority of those in the nominal chain of command. In other words, the opportunity for greater speed and flexibility undermines hierarchy. As more and more strategic action takes place in these channels, the jobs that focus inward on particular departments decline in power.

As a result, the ability of managers to get things done depends more on the number of networks in which they're centrally involved than on their height in a hierarchy. Of course, power in any organization always has a network component, but rank and formal structure used to be more limiting. For example, access to information and the ability to get informal backing were often confined to the few officially sanctioned contact points between departments or between the company and its vendors or customers. Today these official barriers are disappearing, while so-called informal networks grow in importance.

In the emerging organization, managers add value by deal making, by brokering at interfaces, rather than by presiding over their individual empires. It was traditionally the job of top executives or specialists to scan the business environment for new ideas, opportunities, and resources. This kind of environmental scanning is now an important part of a manager's job at every level and in every function. And the environment to be scanned includes various company divisions, many potential outside partners, and large parts of the world. At the same time, people are encouraged to think about what they know that might have value elsewhere. An engineer designing windshield wipers, for example, might discover properties of rubber adhesion to glass that could be useful in other manufacturing areas.

Every manager must think cross-functionally because every department has to play a strategic role, understanding and contributing to other facets of the business. In Hank's company, the technical managers and staff working on design engineering used to concentrate only on their own areas of expertise. Under the new system, they have to keep in mind what manufacturing does and how it does it. They need to visit plants and build relationships so they can ask informed questions.

One multinational corporation, eager to extend the uses of its core product, put its R&D staff and laboratory personnel in direct contact with marketing experts to discuss lines of research. Similarly, the superior economic track record of Raytheon's New Products Center—dozens of new products and patents yielding profits many times their development costs—derives from the connections it builds between its inventors and the engineering and marketing staffs of the business units it serves.

This strategic and collaborative role is particularly important for the managers and professionals on corporate staffs. They need to serve as integrators and facilitators, not as watchdogs and interventionists. They need to sell their services, justify themselves to the business units they serve, literally compete with outside suppliers. General Foods recently put overhead charges for corporate staff services on a pay-as-you-use basis. Formerly, these charges were either assigned uniformly to users and nonusers alike, or the services were mandatory. Product managers sometimes had to work through as many as eight layers of management and corporate staff to get business plans approved. Now these staffs must prove to the satisfaction of their internal customers that their services add value.

By contrast, some banks still have corporate training departments that do very little except get in the way. They do no actual training, for example, yet they still exercise veto power over urgent divisional training decisions and consultant contracts.

As managers and professionals spend more time working across boundaries with peers and partners over whom they have no direct control, their negotiating skills become essential assets. Alliances and partnerships transform impersonal, arm's-length contracts into relationships involving joint planning and joint decision making. Internal competitors and adversaries become allies on whom managers depend for their own success. At the same time, more managers at more levels are active in the kind of external diplomacy that only the CEO or selected staffs used to conduct.

In the collaborative forums that result, managers are more personally exposed. It is trust that makes partnerships work. Since collaborative ventures often bring together groups with different methods, cultures, symbols, even languages, good deal making depends on empathy—the ability to step into other people's shoes and appreciate their goals. This applies not only to intricate global joint ventures but also to the efforts of engineering and manufacturing to work together more effectively. Effective communication in a cooperative effort rests on more than a simple exchange of information; people must be adept at anticipating the responses of other groups. "Before I get too excited about our department's design ideas," an engineering manager told me, "I'm learning to ask myself, 'What's the marketing position on this? What will manufacturing say?' That sometimes forces me to make changes before I even talk to them."

An increase in the number of channels for strategic contact within the postentrepreneurial organization means more opportunities for people with ideas or information to trigger action: salespeople encouraging account managers to build strategic partnerships with customers, for example, or technicians searching for ways to tap new-venture funds to develop software. Moreover, top executives who have to spend more time on cross-boundary relationships are forced to delegate more responsibility to lower level managers. Delegation is one more blow to hierarchy, of course, since subordinates with greater responsibility are bolder about speaking up, challenging authority, and charting their own course.

For example, it is common for new-venture teams to complain publicly about corporate support departments and to reject their use in favor of external service providers, often to the consternation of more orthodox superiors. A more startling example occurred in a health care company where members of a task force charged with finding synergies among three lines of business shocked corporate executives by criticizing upper management behavior in their report. Service on the task force had created collective awareness of a shared problem and had given people the courage to confront it.

The search for internal synergies, the development of strategic alliances, and the push for new ventures all emphasize the political side of a leader's work. Executives must be able to juggle a set of constituencies rather than control a set of subordinates. They have to bargain, negotiate, and sell instead of making unilateral decisions and issuing commands. The leader's task, as Chester Barnard recognized long ago, is to develop a network of cooperative relationships among all the people, groups, and organizations that have something to contribute to an economic enterprise. Postentrepreneurial strategies magnify the complexity of this task. After leading Teknowledge, a producer of expert systems software, through development alliances with six corporations including General Motors and Procter & Gamble, company chairman Lee Hecht said he felt like the mayor of a small city. "I have a constituency that won't quit. It takes a hell of a lot of balancing." The kind of power achieved through a network of stakeholders is very different from the kind of power managers wield in a traditional bureaucracy. The new way gets more done, but it also takes more time. And it creates an illusion about freedom and security.

The absence of day-to-day constraints, the admonition to assume responsibility, the pretense of equality, the elimination of visible status markers, the prevalence of candid dialogues across hierarchical levels—these can give employees a false sense that all hierarchy is a thing of the past. Yet at the same time, employees still count on hierarchy to shield them when things go wrong. This combination would create the perfect marriage of freedom and support—freedom when people want to take risks, support when the risks don't work out.

In reality, less benevolent combinations are also possible, combinations not of freedom and support but of insecurity and loss of control. There is often a pretense in postentrepreneurial companies that status differences have nothing to do with power, that the deference paid to top executives derives from their superior qualifications rather than from the power they have over the fates of others. But the people at the top of the organization chart still wield power—and sometimes in ways that managers below them experience as arbitrary. Unprecedented individual freedom also applies to top managers, who are now free to make previously unimaginable deals, order unimaginable cuts, or launch unimaginable takeovers. The reorganizations that companies undertake in their search for new synergies can uncover the potential unpredictability and capriciousness of corporate careers. A man whose company was undergoing drastic restructuring told me, "For all of my ownership share and strategic centrality and voice in decisions, I can still be faced with a shift in direction not of my own making. I can still be reorganized into a corner. I can still be relocated into oblivion. I can still be reviewed out of my special project budget."

These realities of power, change, and job security are important because they affect the way people view their leaders. When the illusion of simultaneous freedom and protection fades, the result can be a loss of motivation.

Sources of Motivation

One of the essential, unchanging tasks of leaders is to motivate and guide performance. But motivational tools are changing fast. More and more businesses are doing away with the old bureaucratic incentives and using entrepreneurial opportunity to attract the best talent. Managers must exercise more leadership even as they watch their bureaucratic power slip away. Leadership, in short, is more difficult yet more critical than ever.

Because of the unpredictability of even the most benign restructuring, managers are less able to guarantee a particular job—or any job at all—no matter what a subordinate's performance level. The reduction in hierarchical levels curtails a manager's ability to promise promotion. New compensation systems that make bonuses and raises dependent on objective performance measures and on team appraisals deprive managers of their role as the sole arbiter of higher pay. Cross-functional and cross-company teams can rob managers of their right to direct or even understand the work their so-called subordinates do. In any case, the shift from routine work, which was amenable to oversight, to "knowledge" work, which often is not, erodes a manager's claim to superior expertise. And partnerships and ventures that put lower level people in direct contact with each other across departmental and company boundaries cut heavily into the managerial monopoly on information. At a consumer packaged-goods manufacturer that replaced several levels of hierarchy with teams, plant team members in direct contact with the sales force often had data on product ordering trends before the higher level brand managers who set product policy.

As if the loss of carrots and sticks was not enough, many managers can no longer even give their people clear job standards and easily mastered procedural rules. Postentrepreneurial corporations seek problem-solving, initiative-taking employees who will go the unexpected extra mile for the customer. To complicate the situation further still, the complexities of work in the new organization—projects and relationships clamoring for attention in every direction—exacerbate the feeling of overload.

With the old motivational tool kit depleted, leaders need new and more effective incentives to encourage high performance and build commitment. There are five new tools:

Mission. Helping people believe in the importance of their work is essential, especially when other forms of certainty and security have disappeared. Good leaders can inspire others with the power and excitement of their vision and give people a sense of purpose and pride in their work. Pride is often a better source of motivation than the traditional corporate career ladder and the promotion-based reward system. Technical professionals, for example, are often motivated most effectively by the desire to see their work contribute to an excellent final product.

Agenda Control. As career paths lose their certainty and companies' futures grow less predictable, people can at least be in charge of their own professional lives. More and more professionals are passing up jobs with glamour and prestige in favor of jobs that give them greater control over their own activities and direction. Leaders give their subordinates this opportunity when they give them release time to work on pet projects, when they emphasize results instead of procedures, and when they delegate work and the decisions about how to do it. Choice of their next project is a potent reward for people who perform well.

Share of Value Creation. Entrepreneurial incentives that give teams a piece of the action are highly appropriate in collaborative companies. Because extra rewards are based only on measurable results, this approach also conserves resources. Innovative companies are experimenting with incentives like phantom stock for development of new ventures and other strategic achievements, equity participation in project returns, and bonuses pegged to key performance targets. Given the cross-functional nature of many projects today, rewards of this kind must sometimes be systemwide, but individual managers can also ask for a bonus pool for their own areas, contingent, of course, on meeting performance goals. And everyone can share the kinds of rewards that are abundant and free—awards and recognition.

Learning. The chance to learn new skills or apply them in new arenas is an important motivator in a turbulent environment because it's oriented toward securing the future. "The learning organization" promises to become a 1990s business buzzword as companies seek to learn more systematically from their experience and to encourage continuous learning for their people. In the world of high technology, where people understand uncertainty, the attractiveness of any company often lies in its capacity to provide learning and experience. By this calculus, access to training, mentors, and challenging projects is more important than pay or benefits. Some prominent companies— General Electric, for example—have always been able to attract top talent, even when they could not promise upward mobility, because people see them as a training ground, a good place to learn, and a valuable addition to a résumé.

Reputation. Reputation is a key resource in professional careers, and the chance to enhance it can be an outstanding motivator. The professional's reliance on reputation stands in marked contrast to the bureaucrat's anonymity. Professionals have to make a name for themselves, while traditional corporate managers and employees stayed behind the scenes. Indeed, the accumulation of reputational "capital" provides not only an immediate ego boost but also the kind of publicity that can bring other rewards, even other job offers. Managers can enhance reputation—and improve motivation—by creating stars, by providing abundant public recognition and visible awards, by crediting the authors of innovation, by publicizing people outside their own departments, and by plugging people into organizational and professional networks.

The new, collaborative organization is predicated on a logic of flexible work assignments, not of fixed job responsibilities. To promote innovation and responsiveness, two of today's competitive imperatives, managers need to see this new organization as a cluster of activity sets, not as a rigid structure. The work of leadership in this new corporation will be to organize both sequential and synchronous projects of varying length and breadth, through which varying combinations of people will move, depending on the tasks, challenges, and opportunities facing the area and its partners at any given moment.

Leaders need to carve out projects with tangible accomplishments, milestones, and completion dates and then delegate responsibility for these projects to the people who flesh them out. Clearly delimited projects can counter overload by focusing effort and can provide short-term motivation when the fate of the long-term mission is uncertain. Project responsibility leads to ownership of the results and sometimes substitutes for other forms of reward. In companies where product development teams define and run their own projects, members commonly say that the greatest compensation they get is seeing the advertisements for their products. "Hey, that's mine! I did that!" one engineer told me he trumpeted to his family the first time he saw a commercial for his group's innovation.

This sense of ownership, along with a definite time frame, can spur higher levels of effort. Whenever people are engaged in creative or problem-solving projects that will have tangible results by deadline dates, they tend to come in at all hours, to think about the project in their spare time, to invest in it vast sums of physical and emotional energy. Knowing that the project will end and that completion will be an occasion for reward and recognition makes it possible to work much harder.

Leaders in the new organization do not lack motivational tools, but the tools are different from those of traditional corporate bureaucrats. The new rewards are based not on status but on contribution, and they consist not of regular promotion and automatic pay raises but of excitement about mission and a share of the glory and the gains of success. The new security is not employment security (a guaranteed job no matter what) but *employability* security—increased value in the internal and external labor markets. Commitment to the organization still matters, but today managers build commitment by offering project opportunities. The new loyalty is not to the boss or to the company but to projects that actualize a mission and offer challenge, growth, and credit for results.

The old bases of managerial authority are eroding, and new tools of leadership are taking their place. Managers whose power derived from hierarchy and who were accustomed to a limited area of personal control are learning to shift their perspectives and widen their horizons. The new managerial work consists of looking outside a defined area of responsibility to sense opportunities and of forming project teams drawn from any relevant sphere to address them. It involves communication and collaboration across functions, across divisions, and across companies whose activities and resources overlap. Thus rank, title, or official charter will be less important factors in success at the new managerial work than having the knowledge, skills, and sensitivity to mobilize people and motivate them to do their best.

2
Changing the Role of Top Management: Beyond Systems to People

Christopher A. Bartlett and Sumantra Ghoshal

The postwar decades were boom years for management systems. A generation of top-level managers embraced the development of a rich portfolio of planning and control tools designed to help them deal with the rapid pace of corporate growth and diversification. No company participated in the managerial revolution more enthusiastically than the Norton Company, an industrial abrasives manufacturer and a competitor of 3M.

In its search for profitable growth through diversification, Norton in the early 1970s pioneered the use of profit impact of market strategies, known as PIMS, the computer model that analyzed the impact of 37 factors on a business's profit potential. It became one of the first companies to adopt the Boston Consulting Group's growth/share matrix, which allocated strategic roles to a company's businesses based on their cash-flow characteristics. Always eager to adopt the latest management system, Norton was also an early convert to the nine-block grid, which allowed companies to match strategies to each of their businesses according to their competitive strengths and the attractiveness of their particular industry environments. Backed by planning and control reports and supported by staff analysis, Norton's

This article is the third in a series called "Changing the Role of Top Management"; the first article, subtitled "Beyond Strategy to Purpose," appeared in the *Harvard Business Review* November–December 1994 issue, and the second article, subtitled "Beyond Structure to Process," appeared in the *Harvard Business Review* January–February 1995 issue.

corporate executives used these and similar tools to screen acquisitions while pushing existing businesses to improve profits constantly.

Yet, in spite of all Norton's state-of-the-art management systems, its diversification efforts never met management's or shareholders' expectations, and the performance of its core abrasives business remained disappointing. Persistently poor results left the company vulnerable, and, in 1990, it was absorbed into the French giant, Compagnie de Saint-Gobain.

Meanwhile, 3M achieved the diversification aims that eluded Norton by taking a very different tack. Leaders there placed little emphasis on top-down planning and control. Instead, they nurtured the innovative ideas of frontline engineers and sales representatives, thereby building an entrepreneurial engine that generated a stream of profitable new products and promising new technologies. Going into the postwar boom, 3M and Norton were roughly the same size. By the mid-1980s, 3M was reporting sales eight times those of its old competitor. Ironically, just as Norton was swallowed up by Saint-Gobain, 3M was named for the fifth time in six years to *Fortune*'s list of the Ten Most Admired Corporations.

One factor chiefly explains such different results for two companies with similar origins and goals: their management philosophies and styles. If Norton was an archetype of a systems-driven company, 3M epitomized a people-centered entrepreneurial model. That model is essential to competing in today's postindustrial, global markets.

Over the years, 3M's top management developed a very different relationship with its organization's members than the one that evolved at Norton. Although information, planning, and control systems were clearly part of the management process, they did not define 3M's primary communication channels. Individual entrepreneurs there have always been able to present their ideas directly to management and to discuss them in face-to-face meetings. As a result, 3M's top management has seen its role much less as directing and controlling employees' activities and more as developing their initiatives and supporting their ideas. Chairman and CEO Livio D. DeSimone believes that 3M's philosophy has been at the core of its ability to renew itself continuously: "Senior management's primary role is to create an internal environment in which people understand and value our way of operating. . . . Our job is one of creation and destruction—supporting individual initiative while breaking down bureaucracy and cynicism. It all depends on developing a personal trust relationship between those at the top and those at lower levels."

From Organization Man to Individualized Corporation

Norton's systems-based approach to management was part of what we described in the first article in this series as the strategy-structure-systems doctrine. The doctrine took hold before World War II, when increasing size and complexity led the CEOs of several prominent companies to delegate most of their operating decisions to newly installed division-level managers. Senior managers recast their own jobs as defining strategy, developing structure, and managing the systems required to link and control the company's parts. The role of systems in that troika of tasks was crucial. As the divisional structure first made diversification possible and then competitively necessary, systems became the essential tools that top-level managers needed to understand and control their sprawling enterprises.

The strategy-structure-systems management model enabled companies to grow for more than 50 years. But, while those at the top saw increasingly sophisticated systems as the lifelines that linked them to their distant and diverse operations, those deeper in the organization felt them as chains that pulled them to heel. The problems that many companies are experiencing today are inherent in the philosophy underlying that model, which originated with the teachings of Frederick Winslow Taylor.

Early in this century, Taylor wrote that management's role was to ensure that workers' tasks were well defined, measured, and controlled. With the objective of making people as consistent, reliable, and efficient as the machines they supported, managers came to regard their subordinates as little more than another factor of production. In that context, managers designed systems, procedures, and policies that would ensure that all employees conformed to the company way. The goal was to make the middle managers' and workers' activities more predictable and thus more controllable. In doing so, they helped create what William H. Whyte, Jr., in 1956 labeled "the organization man."

A problem with that management approach was that its assumptions about the unpredictability and pathology of human behavior became self-fulfilling prophecies. The systems that ensured control and conformity also inhibited creativity and initiative. Stripped of individuality, people often engaged in the very behaviors that the system had been designed to control. At best, the resulting organizational culture grew passive; with amused resignation, employees implemented corporate-led initiatives that they knew would fail. At worst, the tightly controlled environment triggered antagonism and even subversion; people deep in the organization found ways to undermine the system that constrained them.

For instance, by the end of the 1980s, Paul Lego, then president of Westinghouse Electric Corporation, was boasting to *Fortune* that the company had "the most sophisticated strategic-planning system in the United States . . . allowing us to portfolio-plan on a micro basis." The managers running that portfolio of businesses, however, soon began to spend much of their time simply justifying their units' survival. They stretched projections, inflated estimates, and disguised data—sometimes with ruinous results. Eventually, bad loans and poor investment decisions surfaced, and the resulting write-offs cost Westinghouse $5 billion.

Westinghouse executives had allowed their management systems to impede rather than support relationships with those below them in the organization. The generation and transmission of consolidated and formatted reports replaced direct communication from people representing their own ideas, analyses, and proposals. And the opportunity to discuss the proposals was lost in the ritualized presentations and reviews of the data. One manager likened systems-based communication to a narrow and unstable rope bridge looping across the widening information and knowledge gap that separated senior executives from frontline managers.

In our study of 20 large companies that have either avoided or successfully navigated such difficulties, we found top-level managers who have been able to reconnect with the people in their organizations. Their objective was to reinforce the rope bridge of systems-based communication with the steel girders of frequent personal contact. They sought not only to improve communication but also to stimulate those who felt alienated under the systems-dominated management approach.

Percy Barnevik, CEO and president of ABB Asea Brown Boveri, frequently challenges his management team to tap more of the talents of their people. "Our organizations are constructed so that most of our employees are asked to use only 5% to 10% of their capacity at work," he says. "It is only when those same individuals go home that they can engage the other 90% to 95%—to run their households, lead a Boy Scout troop, or build a summer home. We have to be able to recognize and employ that untapped ability that each individual brings to work every day."

Leaders such as Barnevik are beginning to articulate management's challenge in terms of engaging the unique knowledge, skills, and capabilities of each member in the organization. They are questioning the assumptions of Taylorism that encouraged the use of systems and policies to force individuals into a corporate mold and are instead developing a management philosophy based on a more personalized approach that encourages a diversity of views and empowers employees to develop their own ideas. By building organizations that reflect the abilities of their members, managers are attempting to exchange the organization man for what we call "the individualized corporation."

That shift is part of a broader redefinition of top management's role that results from the need to replace the obsolete strategy-structure-systems doctrine with a leadership philosophy built on purpose, process, and people. The shift from systems-driven to people-oriented management is pivotal because only then can top-level managers broaden their roles as we have argued that they must: from defining strategy to building corporate purpose and from framing structure to developing organizational processes.

Creating an individualized corporation does not mean stripping the organization of all its formal systems, policies, and procedures. It does require redefining them so that they support rather than subvert top management's ability to focus on the organization's people. Top management can:

- reduce its reliance on strategic-planning systems by influencing the organization's direction through the development and deployment of key people;
- lighten the burden of control systems by developing personal values and interpersonal relationships that encourage self-monitoring; and
- replace much of its dependence on information systems by developing personal communications with those who have access to vital intelligence and expertise.

Setting Direction by Deploying Key People

The ways in which top management at 3M and Norton shaped strategic direction contrast strikingly. The planning and forecasting system that Norton had developed in its early years allowed owner-managers to control the company's strategic direction through corporate-level investment decisions. As late as 1956, all capital appropriations of more than $1,000 still required board approval. And, when professional executives began to replace family management in the late 1960s, they pushed the tradition of systems-based, top-down direction and control to even higher levels.

By contrast, 3M's formal planning and capital budgeting systems developed much later and played a secondary role in top management's decision making. The company did not even have a corporate strategic-planning system until the early 1980s. Under the enduring influence of longtime CEO William L. McKnight, successive generations of top-level managers believed that their primary job was to develop and support the entrepreneurs who operated on the company's front lines.

More large companies have followed Norton's approach than 3M's. But, as the industrial era is overtaken by the information age, those at the top of large companies have found that their strategic-planning and capital-budgeting systems are increasingly inappropriate in an environment that demands knowledge-based flexibility and responsiveness. The cost in dollars and time of collecting, analyzing, and transporting operational information up through the hierarchy has begun to exceed the benefit that top management's input provides. As a result, many corporate leaders have begun to embrace a new philosophy of strategic management. In the organizations that we studied, leaders are downplaying their strategic decision-making role and delegating much of that responsibility to frontline managers, who are closer to the business. Top-level managers still influence long-term direction, but they recognize that they have their greatest impact by working internally to develop the organization's resources, knowledge, and capabilities as strategic assets.

That is not to say that managers are no longer involved in formal planning. ABB, for instance, operates a highly sophisticated strategic-planning system. But executives view it as only one component of an organizational infrastructure that they can use to build relationships with the managers reporting to them.

Goran Lindahl, ABB's executive vice president responsible for power transmission and distribution, sees his most important role as coach and developer of his management team. He estimates that he spends 50% to 60% of his time communicating directly with his people in a process he calls "human engineering." Lindahl begins with "unlearning experiences," designed to help managers recognize their limiting assumptions and break old habits. Those experiences might involve little more than a series of informal discussions focused on honest self-appraisal, or they could entail a visit, a temporary assignment, or even a transfer so that managers are exposed to different ideas and practices that have succeeded elsewhere in the organization. Once developing managers are open and receptive, Lindahl spends time discussing overall objectives and standards with them, always leaving room for them to embrace the goals as their own. Over months and years of working together, he watches as individuals internalize the objectives and develop the competence to implement them. Gradually, he gives his managers more and more autonomy.

Thus, to Lindahl, the empowerment of a manager is not an overnight transfer or an abdication of responsibility from a boss to a subordinate. It is a gradual delegation process that requires substantial top-management involvement. He summarizes his role this way: "People want to learn and are greatly motivated and satisfied when they do. Top management's challenge is not only to help people develop themselves but also to ensure that they do so in ways that support and reinforce the company's objectives. My first task is to provide the frameworks to help engineers and other specialists develop as managers; the next challenge is to loosen the frameworks and let them become leaders—those who are ready to take responsibility for setting their own objectives and standards. When I have created the environment that allows all the managers to transform themselves into leaders, we will have a self-driven, self-renewing organization."

As they become more directly involved in developing their management teams, senior managers find that the process is also an effective means of shaping the company's goals. For example, soon after being named vice chairman of PepsiCo in late 1993, Roger Enrico decided he could add value best by devoting himself to coaching up-and-coming executives. Instead of just increasing the executive-development budget, Enrico committed half of his own time to being an on-call coach to PepsiCo's division presidents. He organized a series of retreats for the managers most likely to be the next generation of PepsiCo leaders. He asked all the participants to bring a "big idea"—a proposal that they believed could have a major impact on their business. Eschewing the usual outside management gurus and facilitators, Enrico conducted all the sessions himself. After five days, the managers returned to their units to implement their projects. Ninety days later, they reconvened to report on their progress and discuss follow-up action.

Through such retreats, Enrico has created an effective way to develop the skills and confidence of a group of high-potential managers while building his own relationship with them and learning about their thinking. Equally important is that he can learn more about the key issues facing the company's businesses and can directly influence his managers' response to them. For Enrico, the retreats are a far more dynamic means of shaping the company's direction and priorities than any formal strategic-planning system.

As important as such development efforts are, however, there are clearly limits to the number of people whom any executive can work with on a personal basis. To leverage their commitment to developing people, top-level managers in most of the companies that we studied have begun to spend at least as much time with the top human resources executive as with the chief financial officer.

In the first article in this series, we described the efforts of Komatsu's president, Tetsuya Katada, to replace his company's strategic intent "to catch up with and beat Caterpillar" with the broader objective of "Growth, Global, Groupwide," which was designed to liberate rather than constrain the organization. As part of the change, Katada radically revised Komatsu's top-down planning model and softened the systems-driven management style. He also began to overhaul Komatsu's human resources policies to ensure that they reinforced the new corporate goals.

For instance, "Groupwide" in the new corporate slogan was shorthand for a strategic goal of turning Komatsu's capabilities in electronics, robotics, and plastics into new, self-sustaining businesses that would eventually account for 50% of the company's sales. Rather than forcing the necessary linkages through the company's traditional top-down "management-by-policy" approach, Katada realized that he could move the organization toward that goal by adjusting the company's personnel recruitment, development, and assignment policy.

Komatsu had typically recruited its best people into corporate staffs, the central research laboratory, or the construction equipment division, and it transferred those not destined for top corporate jobs into subsidiaries and affiliates. Katada broke that habit by declaring that, for at least five years, Komatsu would commit 70% of its new university recruits to its nonconstruction businesses; at the time, those operations accounted for little more than a quarter of the company's sales. Next, to develop a web of relationships across the company, he proposed a new career-path concept. It includes two innovative features: a "return ticket" policy to encourage the transfer of young employees to subsidiaries and affiliate companies that had previously been viewed as banishment; and the Strategic Employee Exchange

Program, which allows employees to work on projects in other parts of the company on a short-term basis. Furthermore, Katada gradually gave about half the company's top 27 executives oversight responsibility for the new nonconstruction businesses that he was trying to develop. His intention was both to broaden the perspectives of those at the top and to create new career paths and role models for the company's rising managers. By focusing as much on assignment patterns as on strategic planning, Katada signaled the company's commitment to nonconstruction businesses and began to build the management capabilities that those businesses would demand. The year before his appointment as president, nonconstruction sales were 27% of total sales; just four years later, they climbed to 37%.

In companies such as ABB, PepsiCo, and Komatsu, strategic planning is alive and well. Yet the senior managers in those companies recognize that their traditional roles—final review and approval of abstract plans and proposals—gave them limited ability to shape their companies' directions. Today, they're having a more lasting impact by becoming more involved in shaping the skills and relationships of key people in the middle levels and on the front lines of their organizations.

Achieving Control Through Internalized Behaviors

More difficult than modifying top-level managers' role in strategic planning has been breaking their dependence on formal control systems. As rapid growth and diversification have required companies to become more decentralized, corporate-level executives created systems that would permit them to retain control even as they delegated authority.

At Norton, for instance, a corporate controller named Henry Duckworth became the company's most powerful nonfamily manager in the early 1920s. Duckworth designed, installed, and, for nearly 50 years, managed an elaborate financial-reporting system through which owner-managers exercised their commitment to thrift and control. At the outset of the Great Depression, the systems-driven, control-based model allowed Norton's top management to respond quickly to a 75% drop in sales by slashing costs, halting investment, and shrinking the organization. As late as the 1960s, Norton's owner-managers were still using Duckworth's systems to make all major pricing changes, to approve all expenses of more than $100, and to conduct performance reviews of all salaried managers.

Over several generations of corporate leadership, the role of top management as operational controller was firmly established at Norton and at most other large, modern companies. Even as the growing diversity and increasing dispersion of frontline operations stretched senior managers' ability to understand many of the decisions they were reviewing, no one questioned their responsibility to exercise that control—or the system that gave them the power to do so.

In the past couple of decades, however, the problems inherent in such systems have begun to appear. When product and process technologies begin to change swiftly, standard costs become obsolete. In increasingly dynamic markets, last year's sales have diminishing value as a performance benchmark. Even budgeted objectives have little relevance when external conditions are unpredictable, and the internal budgeting process is flawed by managers' temptation to game the system.

Most control systems were designed to take the pulse of an organization on a monthly or quarterly basis; they simply cannot detect—never mind, respond to—operational changes that occur weekly or even daily. The lag is amplified by the time it takes to record, consolidate, transmit, and analyze data, move it up the hierarchy for review, then back down for implementation.

The most basic problem for companies that depend heavily on formal controls is the assumption that those at the top are the most competent to act on the data and analyses that the system generates. Many corporate executives have recognized their dwindling ability to make good judgments on the basis of abstract and outdated information about operations of which they have limited understanding. As a result, they are supplementing or replacing their control systems by finding more subtle means of influencing the people in their organizations who are closer to the action. Instead of intervening with corrective action, they are finding ways to affect individual motivation by coaching managers in self-monitoring, self-correcting behavior.

At IKEA, the Swedish homefurnishings stores in 20 countries that together represent more than $5 billion in sales, top management decided to abolish the company's budgeting system al together in 1992. Today, it relies instead on a set of simple financial ratios that act more as benchmarks for carefully managed internal competition than as standards for top-management control. Even giant General Electric has changed its budget system, deemphasizing the control aspect that led to game playing and to setting minimal acceptable targets. Today, managers focus on a set of self-generated stretch targets that are aimed more at igniting ambition than at imposing control.

In the companies we studied, the most basic characteristic that top managements were developing to supplement formal control systems and reduce their dependence on those systems was organizational transparency. Corporate leaders found that when people in the organization clearly understand corporate objectives, they measure their own performance against those objectives. Given the same information as their supervisors, those in middle and frontline positions usually reach the same conclusions as their bosses. More important, the arrangement allows frontline managers to fix problems at their own level instead of sending variance reports up the hierarchy and then waiting for top-down judgments.

An example is ISS-International Service System, the cost-conscious Danish company that has grown from a local office-cleaning contractor into a $2 billion multinational business employing more than 10,000 people. The company's entire control process is built around founder and president Poul Andreassen's belief that people at all levels of the organization will make the right decisions if they are properly informed. He encourages the thousands of cleaning-team supervisors to run their operations as if they were independent businesses. To help them, he provides them with financial reports by individual cleaning contract. The detailed reports show direct labor, material, and equipment costs, as well as overhead charges allocated by the branch, district, and regional offices. Once frontline supervisors are thoroughly trained, they are able to interpret the data and understand the business's economics. Andreassen finds that they use that information to control costs—even exerting pressure on middle and senior managers to provide value for the overhead they generate. He could never achieve that kind of control through a controller's office.

Besides teaching those at lower levels how to monitor and correct themselves, as the ISS program clearly does, companies also have had to instill the self-discipline that motivates people to do so. Andersen Consulting inculcates in each of its recruits the standards of performance that have become institutionalized as "the Andersen way." New associates from around the world attend the Andersen Consulting Client Engagement Training Course, a six-week program known as ACCENT, half of which is held at the firm's campus in St. Charles, Illinois. There, participants not only receive training in the most current tools and concepts in their profession but also are indoctrinated in the firm's core values. For example, the requirement to attend class in business attire emphasizes the firm's professional discipline, the 80-hour workweeks underline its strong work ethic, and the mutual support required by the demanding workload demonstrates the importance of strong interpersonal relationships. The Andersen acculturation process continues on the job. New employees receive an additional 1,000 hours of instruction in their first five years. The uniform values, professionalism, and dedication displayed by Andersen employees prompt competitors to call them Andersen androids. But the derision may contain a hint of envy because the internalized norms allow Andersen to give its personnel a great deal of freedom without endangering the firm's standards.

Some companies that we studied create a self-regulating process by harnessing competition among peers. As we discussed in the second article in this series, Intel's norm of "constructive confrontation" encourages—indeed, requires—those with the most relevant information and expertise to enter the debate on key decisions. Thus the company has built an effective control mechanism right into the organization's ongoing activities.

Banc One Corporation, a bank based in Columbus, Ohio, which ranked eighth in the United States in assets and second in market value in 1992, uses what it calls "share-and-compare" management. In an industry known for its tight systems and restrictive policies for frontline managers, Banc One develops entrepreneurs in its subsidiary banks. Although its Management Information and Control System (MICS) is among the most sophisticated in commercial banking, corporate managers pride themselves on how little they intervene in the operation of their affiliates. Banc One's legendary chairman and CEO John B. McCoy believes that MICS is his most powerful tool precisely because it reduces the need for corporate intervention. Each bank's managers have access to the performance of every other bank in the system. Because managers do not want to see their bank at the bottom of the monthly peer-comparison report, they actively seek out best practice to improve performance.

In each of the companies that we have described, strong management control is vital: IKEA has to control the costs and flow of 10,000 products from 1,800 suppliers to 100 stores in 20 countries; ISS operates in a highly competitive contract-cleaning business with razor-thin margins; and Banc One must ensure that its 100 affiliate banks are able to deal with the risks and vicissitudes of financial markets. Yet in each of those companies and in most of the others in our study, top-level managers use control systems in a supporting rather than a dominating role. Particularly in the past decade, the systems-driven approach of hierarchical review and corrective action has taken a backseat to a people-centered management model. In that model, top management's key role is to create an environment in which managers and employees monitor and correct themselves.

Managing Information Flows Through Personal Relationships

Historically, formal systems have also given top management control over the information flows that are the lifeblood of any organization. As Norton's businesses grew larger and more complex, the company created a business analysis department to handle the flood of data. By the mid-1920s, statistical analysts were generating 80 different reports to feed top management's growing appetite for information. The more authority top-level managers had to delegate, the more information they needed to maintain their control.

When the computer arrived, the corporate executives at Norton, as at most other large companies, saw the new data-processing capacity simply as a supercharger for existing manual information systems. They commissioned studies to determine future information needs, and they invested in the prescribed hardware and software. Yet the returns on those huge investments have ranged from disappointing to disastrous.

The problem in many companies lies in the way they defined the opportunities of the information revolution. They thought the challenge lay in harnessing the power of data processing when it really lay in understanding information technology's potential for developing and diffusing knowledge as a source of competitive advantage. Most corporate leaders manage information the way they manage capital— that is, as a scarce resource that they can collect, store, and allocate as they see fit. But far from being lifeless and timeless, information is vital and volatile. To have value, information must be linked to other information. Only then does it become a source of knowledge and the basis of organizational learning. Thus top management's principal challenge is not to design systems that will process data more efficiently but to create an environment in which people can exploit information more effectively.

Discussions with top-level managers in our study revealed that data processing systems are neither the most important nor the most effective means of collecting, evaluating, and transporting information; personal communication best serves that role. The challenge for managers is to prevent the organization from devoting huge amounts of time to serving the needs of information systems. Instead, managers must realign the systems so that they serve the needs of the members of the organization—particularly their need to communicate with one another.

As self-evident as that statement may seem, there are many companies in which systems are not only the primary source of information used to make decisions but also the dominant topic of internal communication, with managers debating the accuracy and relevance of the data they generate. Top management takes a major step when it realizes that the organization's information systems must support rather than dominate the discussions about core business issues.

At ABB, CEO Percy Barnevik took such a step when he ordered the development of the ABB Accounting and Communicating System, called Abacus. It provides people at all levels of the organization with simultaneous access to precise reports generated from a single database. Barnevik's intent was to create an undisputed basis for productive discussions, in which frontline managers could decide on action rather than debate the validity of the data. In that respect, Abacus has been a success, but as Ulf Gundemark, an ABB worldwide business manager, explains, the system alone is insufficient: "Abacus is fine, but it can provide only historical financial information. To anticipate problems and understand alternative courses of action, you need a strong personal network. We all work intensively at that."

Top-level managers in other companies are coming to the same conclusion: Personal relationships are much more effective in communicating complex information, sensing subtle signals, and transferring embedded knowledge. Anita Roddick, the founder and managing director of the Body Shop International, abhors formal systems. She believes that communication is much more effective than reports at capturing employees' attention and triggering action. Her organization is designed "to maintain a constant sense of change, even anarchy," she says. As a way to convey her excitement about the products and her interest in customers to the employees and franchisees in 700 Body Shops in more than 40 countries, Roddick has installed a bulletin board, a fax machine, and a videocassette recorder in every shop. She continually bombards her employees with images and messages designed to get them talking. She visits stores to tell stories and listen to employees' concerns, and she holds regular meetings with cross sections of employees, often at her home. In all her personal communications, Roddick taps into the organization's informal networks, even by planting ideas with the office gossips. She encourages upward communication through a suggestion scheme run by the irreverently named Department of Damned Good Ideas. Another process allows any employee to bypass the formal systems and communicate directly with a director-level executive on any issue.

Ingvar Kamprad, founder of IKEA, also prefers to communicate through personal networks rather than formal systems. Throughout his 30-year leadership of the company, Kamprad has transferred priorities on what he describes as "a mouth-to-ear basis." He seeds the organization with "culture bearers," individuals who exhibit management potential and share the company's values. Throughout the 1980s, Kamprad led weeklong training sessions on IKEA's history, culture, and values. Then, the company assigned the ambassadors who attended the sessions to key positions worldwide. By the early 1990s, more than 300 cultural agents were serving as nodes in a personal communication network that could collect and transmit information without the distortion that more formal information systems often introduce.

Most managers also realize, however, that the challenge goes beyond creating their own communication links. They must build a network through which all members of the organization can exchange information, develop ideas, and support one another. To do so, they must nurture the horizontal information flows that vertically driven, financially biased formal systems long ago short-circuited.

At Becton Dickinson and Company (BD), a healthcare-products company, domestic and international managers had long been insulated from each other, despite the existence of an information system that was designed to prevent that problem. Although formal reports could identify common problems and opportunities and assess their importance, they could not so easily communicate their causes and potential solutions. Such subjective information required personal interaction.

For example, when BD's blood-collection product, Vacutainer, performed below expectations in Europe in the mid-1980s, the U.S.-based product development managers refused to modify it. Their formal reporting system confirmed the lower-than-forecast European conversion rate, but it did not help them understand the cause of the problem. The European managers knew that their customers were worried about the safety of the new product, but U.S. managers had dismissed that explanation as an excuse for poor marketing implementation. And although the system was able to calibrate precisely the shortfall in market penetration, it was never able to bridge that gap in communication. Not until AIDS made blood-handling safety a larger concern in the United States did BD's domestic managers understand what the European managers had tried to tell them.

Such incidents convinced the company's top management that its heavy reliance on formal, systems-driven communication was restricting its ability to learn from its overseas managers. Ray Gilmartin, who was BD's CEO at the time, helped create global teams in each of its businesses in the hope that improved communications would lead to more effective cooperation between domestic and international managers. The supposition has proved to be accurate. The worldwide blood-collection team and others like it have helped develop cross-border strategies and launch global products. Team membership has become a mark of status, and a global network has become an important career asset. Indeed, Gilmartin cites such cross-border relationships as one of the keys to BD's success in expanding its international sales from less than 30% to almost 50% of the company's total sales in just six years.

At BD, ABB, and most of the companies that we studied, executives have been rethinking their role in managing organizational information. Instead of building systems to collect data solely to help them make top-level decisions, they now realize that they must ensure that all employees have access to information as a vital organizational resource. In the information age, a company's survival depends on its ability to capture intelligence, transform it into usable knowledge, embed it as organizational learning, and diffuse it rapidly throughout the company. In short, information can no longer be abstracted and stored at the corporate level; it must be distributed and exploited as a source of competitive advantage.

A Changing Employment Contract

The strategy-structure-systems management doctrine rests on a relationship between the company and its employees that is fast becoming irrelevant. The assumption has been that capital was the company's most critical and scarcest resource and that labor's role was simply to leverage the company's investment in equipment and machinery. An implicit employment contract held that top management's job was to ensure the company's short-term profitability and long-term competitiveness by making sound investment decisions, and employees were to support those investments by doing as they were told. In exchange for their loyalty and sacrifice of autonomy, employees got wages and job security. Those assumptions provided the foundation for the modern corporation's authority-based structure and the logic for the systems and processes that were required to pull plans, proposals, and performance data up the hierarchy for top management's input and control.

In a postindustrial environment, most companies are no longer well served by the old management doctrine or its implicit employment contract. In the emerging information age, the critical scarce resource is knowledge—composed of information, intelligence, and expertise. Unlike capital, knowledge is most valuable when it is controlled and used by those on the front lines of the organization. In a fast-changing, competitive, global environment, the ability to exploit knowledge is what gives companies their competitive advantage.

The implications for top-level managers are profound. If frontline employees are vital strategic resources instead of mere factors of production, corporate executives can no longer afford to be isolated from the people in their organizations. Furthermore, roles and responsibilities must be reallocated, with those deeper in the organization taking on many of the tasks formerly reserved for those at the top. In short, corporate executives must adopt the people-oriented model of management that General Electric's Jack Welch described in an interview with Noel Tichy and Ram Charan (*Harvard Business Review* September–October 1989): "Above all else . . . good leaders are open. They go up, down, and around their organization to reach people. . . . It is all about human beings coming to see and accept things through a constant interactive process aimed at consensus."

Thus, behind the delayering and downsizing in most companies, a quieter revolution has been taking place. It has redefined employees' roles and, in doing so, has rewritten the implicit contract they had with their employers. GE's old assumption of lifetime employment had produced what Welch calls "a paternal, feudal, fuzzy kind of loyalty." Now Welch advocates a change: "My concept of loyalty is not 'giving time' to some corporate entity and, in turn, being shielded and protected from the outside world. Loyalty is an affinity among people who want to grapple with the outside world and win. . . . The new psychological contract, if there is such a thing, is that jobs at GE are the best in the world for people who are willing to compete. We have the best training and development resources and an environment committed to providing opportunities for personal and professional growth."

What Welch and other corporate leaders now advocate is a complete reversal of the traditional company-employee contract. When employees "grapple with the outside world and win," as Welch puts it, they are essentially taking over what was previously assumed to be a corporate responsibility. Meanwhile, many companies are seeing their responsibility not in terms of ensuring long-term job security but as what Welch describes as "providing opportunities for personal and professional growth," changing the implicit contract from a guarantee of employment to a commitment to employability.

Such a change demolishes the core tenets of the strategy-structure-systems doctrine, which instructs managers to minimize risk by controlling the idiosyncratic individual. Today's top-level managers recognize that the diversity of human skills and the unpredictability of the human spirit make possible initiative, creativity, and entrepreneurship. The most basic task of corporate leaders is to recapture those valuable human attributes by individualizing the corporation. To do so, they need to adopt a management philosophy that is based on purpose, process, and people.

3
Whatever Happened to the Take-Charge Manager?

Nitin Nohria and James D. Berkley

Many managers felt that the emergence of new managerial ideas during the 1980s signaled the rejuvenation of U.S. business. By readily adopting innovations such as total quality programs and self-managed teams, managers believed that they were demonstrating the kind of decisive leadership that kept companies competitive. But such thinking doesn't jibe with the facts. American managers did not take charge in the 1980s. Instead, they abdicated their responsibility to a burgeoning industry of management professionals.

The 1980s witnessed the spectacular rise of management schools, consultants, media, and gurus who fed on the insecurities of American managers fearful of foreign competition and economic decline. (See Exhibit I.) Mistrustful of their own judgment, many managers latched on to these self-appointed pundits, readily adopting their latest panaceas. Off-the-shelf programs addressing quality, customer satisfaction, time-to-market, strategic focus, core competencies, alliances, global competitiveness, organizational culture, and empowerment swept through U.S. corporations with alarming speed.

Adopting "new" ideas became a way for companies to signal to the world that they were progressive, that they had come to grips with their misguided pasts, and that they were committed to change. After all, the worst thing one could do was stick with the status quo.

For some businesses, the new ideas worked. They enabled companies to stem decline and challenge their foreign competitors. But in the majority of cases, research shows, the management fads of the last 15 years rarely produced the promised results.

Between 1980 and 1990, market share in most key U.S. industries

Exhibit I.　　The Rise of the Management Industry

	1982	1992	Growth
Management Schools and MBAs			
Number of management schools	545	670	23%
Number of MBAs granted	60,000	80,000	33
Consulting Industry			
Number of consulting firms	780	1,533	97
Number of consultants	30,000	81,000	170
Total consulting revenues	$3.5 billion	$15.2 billion	334
Corporate Training			
Number of people trained	33.5 million	40.9 million	22
Total training hours	1.1 billion	1.3 billion	18
Total corporate expenditures	$10 billion	$45 billion	350
Business Media			
Number of business stories	125,000	680,000	444
Number of new business books	1,327	1,831	38
Sales of business books	$225 million	$490 million	118

Source: Authors' estimates, drawn from multiple sources. The authors gratefully acknowledge the assistance of Michael Stevenson *and George Jenkins, both business information analysts at the Harvard Business School, in compiling these data.*

declined as much as or more than it had between 1970 and 1980. (See Exhibit II.) Recent surveys at the Harvard Business School, McKinsey & Company, and Ernst & Young and the American Quality Foundation suggest that managers themselves are dissatisfied with the new management programs. In a study we conducted in 1993 at the Harvard Business School, we polled managers at nearly 100 companies on more than 21 different programs and found 75% of them to be unhappy with the results in their organizations.

What accounts for such disastrous results? We believe it is the failure of U.S. management to address its most serious problem: a lack of pragmatic judgment. The widespread adoption of trendy management techniques during the 1980s allowed managers to rely on readymade answers instead of searching for creative solutions. Although some companies are starting to question this reliance on quick fixes, the adoption of off-the-shelf "innovations" continues at a disturbing rate.

If managers want to reverse this trend, they must start by reclaiming managerial responsibility. Instead of subscribing impulsively to fads, they must pick and choose carefully the managerial ideas that promise

Exhibit II. The Competitive Decline of U.S. Businesses

U.S. Share as Percentage of Worldwide Sales of the 12 Largest Companies in Each Industry

Industry	1960	1970	1980	1990
Autos	83%	66%	42%	38%
Banking	61	67	26	0
Chemicals	68	40	31	23
Computers	95	90	86	70
Electricals	71	59	44	11
Iron and Steel	74	31	26	0
Textiles	58	44	41	21

Source: Lawrence G. Franko, "Global Corporate Competition II: Is the Large American Firm an Endangered Species?" *Business Horizons,* November–December 1991, adaptation of Table 1, p. 15. Copyright 1991 by the Foundation for the School of Business at Indiana University. Used with permission.

to be useful. And they must adapt those ideas rigorously to the context of their companies. Managers will often profit most by resisting new ideas entirely and making do with the materials at hand. However unfashionable this may seem, it is precisely as it should be. The manager's job is not to seek out novelty; it is to make sure the company gets results. Pragmatism is the place to start.

"Flavor of the Month" Managing

Given that managerial innovations disappoint with such regularity, we are surprised that companies continue to adopt them with such abandon. The lure of new management fads remains irresistible to managers looking for easy answers. And some companies seem particularly vulnerable to the gurus' hype.

We have identified three basic syndromes that perpetuate the adoption of ineffective, off-the-shelf solutions. The first might be called the "we didn't get it right the first time, let's do it better this time" syndrome. In this case, managers attribute the failure of an imported practice or concept to some missing element in how the idea was formulated and implemented. Old management consultants and champions are thrown out, and new ones are brought in. Eager to succeed where others have failed, the new pundits introduce variations on the original idea that promise to set things right.

Unfortunately, in most cases, this syndrome has led only to a proliferation of ideas, each one claiming—with little justification—to be the correct one. Consider, for example, today's increasingly fuzzy notion of total quality management (TQM). The Ernst & Young and American Quality Foundation study surveyed 584 companies and found they used a total of 945 standardized programs, each promoted by different "experts."[1] In such an environment, managers find themselves adrift in a sea of competing ideas, increasingly insecure about whether the right approach will ever be found.

Frustration with this all-too-common scenario leads to a second pattern, which we term the "flavor of the month" syndrome. In this scenario, managers cast aside old ideas as misguided and introduce new ones that will finally—this time—deliver the business to the promised land. Thus, for instance, TQM programs are derided for their incremental nature, while reengineering is championed as the key to achieving "breakthrough" performance. The half-life of such ideas is becoming so short that we find managers shifting abruptly from one idea to the next. Employees wise up to this syndrome very quickly. Experience teaches them not to get terribly enthused about any new idea. They learn to shrug it off, reasoning, "If we wait until Monday, this too shall pass."

Other companies fall into a third syndrome: they "go for it all." We know of one large U.S. bank where the vice president of HR proudly declared that his organization had implemented every new management program it could find. It had more than 1,000 self-managed teams, over 500 quality initiatives, more than 300 reengineering initiatives, and a host of other programs. Of course, if you probed a bit, you discovered that the majority of these initiatives addressed such crucial management issues as what color to paint the walls. Employees found all their time taken up participating in initiatives of varying importance. And this was happening in an organization where the core business was eroding at an alarming rate.

What happens when managers or their gurus are confronted with the situations we have been depicting? In our experience, they tend to respond with a few unchallengeable replies: "It's only natural to expect some failures—look at the great successes that other companies have had;" "It's not easy to change decades of existing practice;" or, "In time, we'll see results." By deflecting all possibility of judgment into the future like this, it is possible to sustain faith in a managerial promised land almost indefinitely.

But what about the success stories of the new management? Certainly, there have been some, but they have happened because managers used their ingenuity to adapt new ideas, such as TQM, to the particular contexts of their companies. When tailored to fit specific situations, and often changed beyond recognition, these new ideas can prove invaluable. This is pragmatic management at its best.

The Four Faces of Pragmatism

We are calling for a return to pragmatism as espoused by the nineteenth-century American pragmatists: to judge any idea by its practical consequences, by seeing what it allows you to do, rather than by chasing after an elusive notion of truth. Or as the pragmatist philosopher William James put it, "Theories are instruments, not answers to enigmas in which we can rest." Every managerial situation, we believe, demands a pragmatic attitude. For purposes of discussion, we can divide this approach into four general components: sensitivity to context, willingness to make do, focus on outcomes, and openness to uncertainty.

SENSITIVITY TO CONTEXT

We cannot stress enough that the central concept of pragmatic management is the need to adapt ideas to a given context. Being able to judge the parameters of a particular situation and decide what ideas and actions will work in that context is what distinguishes the truly effective manager.

Context includes both the macro and micro—from the cultural milieu of a host country, for example, to the personalities of employees on a management team. Managers who are sensitive to context have a keen sense of the company's history, including the successes and failures of past management programs. They know the company's resources intimately, from physical assets to human capital. And they understand the organization's and the employees' strengths and weaknesses, so they can discern what actions are possible and how much the organization can be stretched.

Pragmatic managers understand that a change initiative that worked in one context could just as easily fail in another and that programs must be continually reevaluated as circumstances evolve. Otherwise, change programs can get stuck at lofty levels of abstraction and ambiguity and have little relevance to the day-to-day workings of the corporation. Even when an overall program like TQM has been adopted, managers should make frequent pragmatic judgments about how best to implement it. Management gurus may peddle a glossary of rules that describe how to do this, but universal answers rarely meet particular needs.

Many of the most successful managerial innovations in recent years have come from companies that have adapted, rather than adopted, popular ideas. Consider an example that has been much in the news in recent years, GE's Work-Out program.[2] Before developing Work-Out in the late 1980s, GE tried to implement the popular Japanese quality circles, teams of employees dedicated to significant quality improvement, throughout the company.

In Japanese quality circles, people are isolated in small groups that often receive substantial direction from above. This approach, GE soon discovered, had limited value in an American context, however. CEO Jack Welch believed the top-down model would never foster the trust necessary to convince line employees to buy into major change. Nor would it sway many middle and upper level managers, whom he saw as "actively resistant to new ideas."

In 1989, Welch began replacing quality circles with the broader, homespun Work-Out program. Instead of gathering in small groups, workers and managers met in large forums dedicated to airing new ideas, the more radical the better. Frequency and duration of work-outs were flexible, according to need, and the town-meeting-like settings fostered a sense of community while ensuring the visibility of individual contributions. The public setting also forced reticent managers to face up to pressures for change. Welch insisted that managers give on-the-spot responses to employee proposals. Nothing was considered sacred in the Work-Out program. Even major changes like overhauling an existing business process (now hyped as reengineering) could be brought up and dealt with in less than a day. In sum, by following the pragmatic strategy of tailoring a program to fit the company, GE was able to avoid the pitfalls of generic quality management.

Homespun solutions are not always the answer, however. Sometimes it makes the most sense for companies to abandon ideas entirely, even those touted as "the next big thing." Some companies have discovered, for example, that just-in-time manufacturing, while beautiful theoretically, doesn't make sense in their manufacturing contexts. Even some Japanese companies that use JIT at home have found that American marketing methods and distribution systems make JIT less attractive in the United States.

In stressing the importance of sensitivity to context, however, we are not advocating a rejection of any idea that originates outside the company. We would hate to see managers conclude too quickly, "It won't work because our context is so different." That will stop the flow of ideas. We are urging only that innovative ideas, such as TQM, and basic management practices, such as strategic planning, be adopted with an acute sensitivity to the situation at hand. Careful forethought and monitoring should determine how practices are used and to what extent they are followed. Managers should also bear in mind that a solution that works today may fail tomorrow. After all, even the best management ideas, such as portfolio planning, have had a half-life of no more than 10 to 15 years.

WILLINGNESS TO MAKE DO

Pragmatic managers, we have found, are particularly adept at "making do." They know what resources are available and how to round up more on short notice; they seek pragmatic answers based on the materials at hand.

We call this aspect of pragmatism *bricolage,* a word French anthropologist Claude Lévi-Strauss used to describe the thought processes of primitive societies. Against prevailing stereotypes of these societies as intellectually inferior, Lévi-Strauss argued that they have ingenious, nonrational ways of thinking. They reason inductively, deriving principles from their daily experience to guide them. For example, these societies have developed elaborate systems of medicine by continually experimenting with local herbs and flowers until they discover the right mixtures to cure their ailments.

Effective managers are *bricoleurs* in this same sense. They play with possibilities and use available resources to find workable solutions. They tinker with systems and variables, constantly on the lookout for improved configurations.

One of our favorite examples of bricolage comes from a director we met a few years ago at a large telecommunications company. While most other people were focusing on the massive IT overhaul the company needed, she directed her attention to how it could use the existing computer resources more creatively.

The engineers who maintained the huge telecommunications network stored data on a trio of aging, overstuffed, and incompatible mainframes. Most people believed it was time to scrap them and install a new, cutting-edge information architecture that would integrate all the company's computer resources. The director concurred that the mainframes would eventually have to go, but she believed it didn't have to happen right away, and, given the time necessary for planning such a change, it couldn't. Why not get the most we can from the mainframes in the interim, she asked. Why not use computer workstations to simulate the multimillion-dollar information architecture that the company would have in the future? With little direction from above, she and her team developed a series of software applications that delayed the need for mainframe replacement while, at the same time, cutting the system-project time from months to weeks.

When a bricoleur is making do, solutions are never fixed or final. This innovative director's project evolved constantly from the day it was conceived until it was sent on-line. Indeed, being a bricoleur entails a willingness to take actions without a clear sense of how things are going to unfold in the future. This doesn't mean that bricoleurs don't care about results, but that they are willing to experiment to get there.

Motorola CEO Bob Galvin's skillful management of a change effort during the 1980s is another good example of bricolage. In 1983, Motorola had just come off a very good year, but Galvin was aware of rumblings throughout the company that the organizational structure wasn't working because it was too bureaucratic. A recent trip to Japan had also convinced him that Motorola was slow to respond to changes in the marketplace.

Rather than waiting for a crisis to erupt, postponing action until he could come up with the perfect strategy, or hiring outside consultants to implement a prepackaged program, Galvin plunged his managers into the change process. At a May meeting of more than 100 senior officers, he announced that the corporation would begin a large-scale change initiative. What he neglected to say was how.

Understandably, the officers were confused. No one was clear about the CEO's agenda or what anyone was expected to do. And this is precisely what Galvin was after. He wanted the officers to be creative and to experiment with different ways of addressing the problems they were confronting in their particular situations. While some managers became preoccupied with "not really knowing what Galvin wanted," others used his challenge as a jumping-off point for experimentation. They came up with numerous structural changes and product innovations, from more market-driven business units to a new line of cellular products, which enabled Motorola to weather an economic downturn and emerge as the most powerful player in the cellular industry. An intuitive pragmatist, Galvin had created a situation that allowed those closest to the problems to come up with solutions.

FOCUS ON OUTCOMES

Pragmatists are concerned with getting results. But they don't get overly hung up on how to get them. The telecommunications director didn't mind a Rube Goldberg approach to system design if it could make a positive contribution to the business. The managers who rejected just-in-time manufacturing realized that the most elegant theory would mean nothing if it couldn't improve delivery time.

Failure to focus on outcomes can spell disaster. Consider the case of the large bank we referred to earlier that had "gone for it all," adopting every change program in the book. Progress was defined in terms of the number of people who had received quality training and the number of quality and reengineering teams that had been established. This had created the illusion of progress. But the bank's performance continued to decline.

Allen-Bradley, a Rockwell-owned manufacturer of industrial controls, learned the hard way about the value of focusing on outcomes. The company's early experience with team-based management at its Industrial Computer and Communications Group had been successful because the teams had a clear mission: to deliver an innovative computer-integrated manufacturing product as quickly as possible. Their focus on outcomes made them flexible and pragmatic; when it was more reasonable for a few people to tackle a problem instead of a team, they went off on their own and did it.

When ICCG switched the whole organization to teams, however, the mission became more diffuse. Teams became a virtue unto themselves, and suddenly all problems had to be solved through teams, whether or not this was the most pragmatic solution. People became caught up in the novelty of teams, and the company took on a summer-camp atmosphere. "Whoever dies with the most teams wins," an employee joked.

Eventually, senior managers noticed that the proliferation of teams had led to a lack of discipline, while failing to get rid of the negative bureaucratic elements of the old system. Chastened by this experience, ICCG began using teams much more cautiously. Today senior managers decide when, where, and how teams are used. First, they ask three critical questions: Is a team necessary? What will we gain? How will we measure our gains? The emphasis is less on fostering camaraderie than on seeing concrete results.

An incident at a major computer company shows what happens when a manager focuses on the *wrong* outcome. After years of indifferent performance, the company's PC division was finally beginning to show some signs of life. The hardware group had developed a full line of PCs that could compete on price. A third-party software group had made promising alliances with major software vendors. And an internal software development group had produced a networking product that had great market potential.

To promote these new products, the managers of each group asked the division's marketing director to assign additional people to their marketing efforts. Had this director been thinking pragmatically, she might have assigned a couple of key staff members to each group. But she refused because she did not want to take the focus off her first priority, improving the performance of her overall marketing department.

With this goal in mind, she hired internal and external consultants to initiate a formal strategic planning exercise. To empower her people and maintain a spirit of participation, she solicited input at a series of off-site meetings and undertook team-building exercises. Of course, while all this was going on, the three managers felt like Nero was fiddling while Rome burned. Eventually, they appealed to the division's vice president, who intervened and broke up the marketing department. He assigned the director's star employees to the three groups and left her with only a skeletal staff. The marketing director had become so caught up in developing a trendy new strategy for her department that she had lost sight of the outcomes critical to her company's success. And she lost her employees in the process.

OPENNESS TO UNCERTAINTY

The last important component of a pragmatic attitude is a willingness to embrace uncertainty and surprise. We believe that most of today's off-the-shelf managerial innovations foster a regimentation that discourages managers from dealing effectively with the unexpected. The fashionable emphasis on being "proactive" can give a false sense that all circumstances can be anticipated. But more often than not, managers are thrown into situations in which they must act quickly and without certainty. To quote economist Kenneth Arrow, in many situations, "we must simply act, fully knowing our ignorance of possible consequences."

For those who associate pragmatism with conservatism or prudence, stressing an openness to uncertainty may seem counterintuitive. But the two concepts are linked. Pragmatists understand that it is unrealistic to try to avoid uncertainty. Attempts to deny or ignore it can blind managers to the real contexts in which they are working and prevent them from responding effectively. Instead of fearing sudden changes, pragmatic managers welcome them as unanticipated opportunities. They learn to capitalize on the unexpected, whether implementing a companywide change initiative or making a critical business decision.

Reebok CEO Paul Fireman is a manager who knows how to profit from uncertainty. At a shoe manufacturers' show in Europe in 1989, Fireman was unimpressed by the merchandise displayed on the floor. He noticed that members of the trade press, looking for a good story, seemed bored with the show as well. Fireman realized that this situation presented an opportunity for Reebok; if he could come up with something new and exciting, he could generate a lot of publicity. A Reebok product that was still in development, THE PUMP, boasted an innovative, inflatable technology that could give the wearer a close personal fit. He knew it would make a great story. But the marketing plan for the shoe had not been completed, and many details had not been worked out, including the price. But Fireman decided to "just do it." He introduced THE PUMP at the show.

The early launch turned out to be a hit. These rave reviews, according to Fireman, not only created market anticipation for the shoe but also helped "light a fire inside the company to get the product developed and released quickly." It was produced in record time and turned out to be a huge success in the marketplace.

Fireman's boldness could have gotten the company in trouble had

Reebok not been able to deliver on time. Many companies have been skewered in the press for making new product promises they couldn't keep. But Fireman's move was not quite as brash as it seemed. He based it on a quick but careful assessment of the state of the industry, his company's capabilities, and just how much Reebok could be stretched in a pinch. Because he understood the context in which he was operating, Fireman was able to seize the moment. No time-to-market program could have produced such positive results. No companywide initiative can ever be a substitute for the pragmatic judgment of an individual manager.

Pragmatism in an Age of Ready-Made Answers

Management ideas should be:

> Adopted only after careful consideration
> Purged of unnecessary buzzwords and clichés
> Judged by their practical consequences
> Tied to the here and now
> Rooted in genuine problems
> Adapted to suit particular people and circumstances
> Adaptable to changing and unforeseen conditions
> Tested and refined through active experimentation
> Discarded when they are no longer useful

American management is at a crossroads. It must decide whether to continue on its present path, on the fruitless quest for managerial Holy Grails, or whether to face up to the challenge of pragmatism. It is worth noting that in many academic disciplines, this sort of pragmatism has witnessed something of a revival. American management may stand to gain the most from looking back to this indigenous style of thought, particularly to its pragmatic successes of the past.

A case in point is the long list of uncommon accomplishments of the United States during World War II. Planes were designed, built, and flown safely in combat in less than two years. Today it takes more than ten years to accomplish the same. During the war, ships were built in weeks; today it takes years. And one could go on and on with stories of achievements that now seem beyond the realm of possibility. A crisis like World War II focuses people on pragmatic action in an uncommon way. It unites national and personal interests. Of course, it may be nearly impossible to replicate such conditions, but creating this kind of urgency is exactly what effective managers have always known how to do. And they have always been able to create urgency with or without the invocation of a brand-new management paradigm.

We are by no means arguing that the new ideas hyped to managers are without worth or that managers should go back to focusing on the much-maligned bureaucratic practices of the past. Instead, we are saying that the time has come to reconsider the relative balance between management innovations and management fundamentals. If the eighties were the time for the flowering of new perspectives on managerial practice, the remainder of the nineties may be the time for a sober reevaluation of managerial responsibility.

Notes

1. "The International Quality Study—Best Practices Report" (Cleveland, Ohio: American Quality Foundation and Ernst & Young, 1992).
2. Work-Out is discussed in detail in Noel M. Tichy and Stratford Sherman, *Control Your Destiny or Someone Else Will: How Jack Welch Is Making G.E. the World's Most Competitive Corporation* (New York: Doubleday, 1993).

4
Managers and Leaders: Are They Different?

Abraham Zaleznik

What is the ideal way to develop leadership? Every society provides its own answer to this question, and each, in groping for answers, defines its deepest concerns about the purposes, distributions, and uses of power. Business has contributed its answer to the leadership question by evolving a new breed called the manager. Simultaneously, business has established a new power ethic that favors collective over individual leadership, the cult of the group over that of personality. While ensuring the competence, control, and the balance of power among groups with the potential for rivalry, managerial leadership unfortunately does not necessarily ensure imagination, creativity, or ethical behavior in guiding the destinies of corporate enterprises.

Leadership inevitably requires using power to influence the thoughts and actions of other people. Power in the hands of an individual entails human risks: first, the risk of equating power with the ability to get immediate results; second, the risk of ignoring the many different ways people can legitimately accumulate power; and third, the risk of losing self-control in the desire for power. The need to hedge these risks accounts in part for the development of collective leadership and the managerial ethic. Consequently, an inherent conservatism dominates the culture of large organizations. In *The Second American Revolution*, John D. Rockefeller III describes the conservatism of organizations:

"An organization is a system, with a logic of its own, and all the weight of tradition and inertia. The deck is stacked in favor of the tried and proven way of doing things and against the taking of risks and striking out in new directions."[1]

Out of this conservatism and inertia, organizations provide succession to power through the development of managers rather than individual leaders. Ironically, this ethic fosters a bureaucratic culture in business, supposedly the last bastion protecting us from the encroachments and controls of bureaucracy in government and education.

Manager vs. Leader Personality

A managerial culture emphasizes rationality and control. Whether his or her energies are directed toward goals, resources, organization structures, or people, a manager is a problem solver. The manager asks: "What problems have to be solved, and what are the best ways to achieve results so that people will continue to contribute to this organization?" From this perspective, leadership is simply a practical effort to direct affairs; and to fulfill his or her task, a manager requires that many people operate efficiently at different levels of status and responsibility. It takes neither genius nor heroism to be a manager, but rather persistence, tough-mindedness, hard work, intelligence, analytical ability, and perhaps most important, tolerance and goodwill.

Another conception of leadership, however, attaches almost mystical beliefs to what a leader is and assumes that only great people are worthy of the drama of power and politics. Here leadership is a psychodrama in which a brilliant, lonely person must gain control of himself or herself as a precondition for controlling others. Such an expectation of leadership contrasts sharply with the mundane, practical, and yet important conception that leadership is really managing work that other people do.

Two questions come to mind. Is this leadership mystique merely a holdover from our childhood—from a sense of dependency and a longing for good and heroic parents? Or is it true that no matter how competent managers are, their leadership stagnates because of their limitations in visualizing purposes and generating value in work? Driven by narrow purposes, without an imaginative capacity and the ability to communicate, do managers then perpetuate group conflicts instead of reforming them into broader desires and goals?

If indeed problems demand greatness, then judging by past performance, the selection and development of leaders leave a great deal to chance. There are no known ways to train "great" leaders. Further, beyond what we leave to chance, there is a deeper issue in the relationship between the need for competent managers and the longing for great leaders.

What it takes to ensure a supply of people who will assume practical responsibility may inhibit the development of great leaders. On the other hand, the presence of great leaders may undermine the development of managers who typically become very anxious in the relative disorder that leaders seem to generate.

It is easy enough to dismiss the dilemma of training managers, though we may need new leaders or leaders at the expense of managers, by saying that the need is for people who can be both. But just as a managerial culture differs from the entrepreneurial culture that develops when leaders appear in organizations, managers and leaders are very different kinds of people. They differ in motivation, personal history, and in how they think and act.

Attitudes Toward Goals

Managers tend to adopt impersonal, if not passive, attitudes toward goals. Managerial goals arise out of necessities rather than desires and, therefore, are deeply embedded in their organization's history and culture.

Frederic G. Donner, chairman and chief executive officer of General Motors from 1958 to 1967, expressed this kind of attitude toward goals in defining GM's position on product development:

"To meet the challenge of the marketplace, we must recognize changes in customer needs and desires far enough ahead to have the right products in the right places at the right time and in the right quantity.

"We must balance trends in preference against the many compromises that are necessary to make a final product that is both reliable and good looking, that performs well and that sells at a competitive price in the necessary volume. We must design not just the cars we would like to build but, more important, the cars that our customers want to buy."[2]

Nowhere in this statement is there a notion that consumer tastes and preferences arise in part as a result of what manufacturers do. In reality, through product design, advertising, and promotion, consumers learn to like what they then say they need. Few would argue that people who enjoy taking snapshots need a camera that also develops pictures. But in response to a need for novelty, convenience, and a shorter interval between acting (snapping the picture) and gaining pleasure (seeing the shot), the Polaroid camera succeeded in the marketplace. It is inconceivable that Edwin Land responded to impressions of consumer need. Instead, he translated a technology (polarization of light) into a product, which proliferated and stimulated consumers' desires.

The example of Polaroid and Land suggests how leaders think about goals. They are active instead of reactive, shaping ideas instead of responding to them. Leaders adopt a personal and active attitude toward goals. The influence a leader exerts in altering moods, evoking images and expectations, and in establishing specific desires and objectives determines the direction a business takes. The net result of this influence changes the way people think about what is desirable, possible, and necessary.

Conceptions of Work

Managers tend to view work as an enabling process involving some combination of people and ideas interacting to establish strategies and make decisions. They help the process along by calculating the interests in opposition, planning when controversial issues should surface, and reducing tensions. In this enabling process, managers' tactics appear flexible: on one hand, they negotiate and bargain; on the other, they use rewards, punishments, and other forms of coercion.

Alfred P. Sloan's actions at General Motors illustrate how this process works in situations of conflict. The time was the early 1920s when Ford Motor Company still dominated the automobile industry using, as did General Motors, the conventional water-cooled engine. With the full backing of Pierre du Pont, Charles Kettering dedicated himself to the design of an air-cooled copper engine, which, if successful, would be a great technical and marketing coup for GM. Kettering believed in his product, but the manufacturing division heads opposed the new design on two grounds: first, it was technically unreliable, and second, the corporation was putting all its eggs in one basket by investing in a new product instead of attending to the current marketing situation.

In the summer of 1923, after a series of false starts and after its decision to recall the copper engine Chevrolets from dealers and customers, GM management scrapped the project. When it dawned on Kettering that the company had rejected the engine, he was deeply discouraged and wrote to Sloan that, without the "organized resistance" against the project, it would have succeeded and that, unless the project were saved, he would leave the company.

Alfred Sloan was all too aware that Kettering was unhappy and indeed intended to leave General Motors. Sloan was also aware that, while the manufacturing divisions strongly opposed the new engine, Pierre du Pont supported Kettering. Further, Sloan had himself gone on record in a letter to Kettering less than two years earlier expressing full confidence in him. The problem Sloan had was how to make his decision stick, keep Kettering in the organization (he was much too valuable to lose), avoid alienating du Pont, and encourage the division heads to continue developing product lines using conventional water-cooled engines.

Sloan's actions in the face of this conflict reveal much about how managers work. First, he tried to reassure Kettering by presenting the problem in a very ambiguous fashion, suggesting that he and the executive committee sided with Kettering, but that it would not be practical to force the divisions to do what they were opposed to. He presented the problem as being a question of the people, not the product. Second, he proposed to reorganize around the problem by consolidating all functions in a new division that would be responsible for the design, production, and marketing of the new engine. This solution appeared as ambiguous as his efforts to placate Kettering. Sloan wrote: "My plan was to create an independent pilot operation under the sole jurisdiction of Mr. Kettering, a kind of copper-cooled car division. Mr. Kettering would designate his own chief engineer and his production staff to solve the technical problems of manufacture."[3]

Sloan did not discuss the practical value of this solution, which included saddling an inventor with management responsibility, but in effect, he used this plan to limit his conflict with Pierre du Pont.

Essentially, the managerial solution that Sloan arranged limited the options available to others. The structural solution narrowed choices, even limiting emotional reactions to the point where the key people could do nothing but go along. It allowed Sloan to say in his memorandum to du Pont, "We have discussed the matter with Mr. Kettering at some length this morning, and he agrees with us absolutely on every point we made. He appears to receive the suggestion enthusiastically and has every confidence that it can be put across along these lines."[4]

Sloan placated people who opposed his views by developing a structural solution that appeared to give something but in reality only limited options. He could then authorize the car division's general manager, with whom he basically agreed, to move quickly in designing water-cooled cars for the immediate market demand.

Years later, Sloan wrote, evidently with tongue in cheek, "The copper-cooled car never came up again in a big way. It just died out; I don't know why."[5]

To get people to accept solutions to problems, managers continually need to coordinate and balance opposing views. Interestingly enough, this type of work has much in common with what diplomats and mediators do, with Henry Kissinger apparently an outstanding practitioner. Managers aim to shift balances of power toward solutions acceptable as compromises among conflicting values.

Leaders work in the opposite direction. Where managers act to limit choices, leaders develop fresh approaches to long-standing problems and open issues to new options. To be effective, leaders must project their ideas onto images that excite people and only then develop choices that give those images substance.

John F. Kennedy's brief presidency shows both the strengths and weaknesses connected with the excitement leaders generate in their work. In his inaugural address he said, "Let every nation know, whether it wishes us well or ill, that we shall pay any price, bear any burden, meet any hardship, support any friend, oppose any foe, in order to assure the survival and the success of liberty."

This much-quoted statement forced people to react beyond immediate concerns and to identify with Kennedy and with important shared ideals. On closer scrutiny, however, the statement is absurd because it promises a position, which, if adopted, as in the Vietnam War, could produce disastrous results. Yet unless expectations are aroused and mobilized, with all the dangers of frustration inherent in heightened desire, new thinking and new choice can never come to light.

Leaders work from high-risk positions; indeed, they are often temperamentally disposed to seek out risk and danger, especially where the chance of opportunity and reward appears promising. From my observations, the reason one individual seeks risks while another approaches problems conservatively depends more on his or her personality and less on conscious choice. For those who become managers, a survival instinct dominates the need for risk, and with that instinct comes an ability to tolerate mundane, practical work. Leaders sometimes react to mundane work as to an affliction.

Relations with Others

Managers prefer to work with people; they avoid solitary activity because it makes them anxious. Several years ago, I directed studies on the psychological aspects of careers. The need to seek out others with whom to work and collaborate seemed to stand out as an important characteristic of managers. When asked, for example, to write imaginative stories in response to a picture showing a single figure (a boy contemplating a violin or a man silhouetted in a state of reflection), managers populated their stories with people. The following is an example of a manager's imaginative story about the young boy contemplating a violin:

"Mom and Dad insisted that their son take music lessons so that someday he can become a concert musician. His instrument was ordered and had just arrived. The boy is weighing the alternatives of playing football with the other kids or playing with the squeak box. He can't understand how his parents could think a violin is better than a touchdown.

"After four months of practicing the violin, the boy has had more than enough, Dad is going out of his mind, and Mom is willing to give in reluctantly to their wishes. Football season is now over, but a good third baseman will take the field next spring."

This story illustrates two themes that clarify managerial attitudes toward human relations. The first, as I have suggested, is to seek out activity with other people (that is, the football team), and the second is to maintain a low level of emotional involvement in those relationships. Low emotional involvement appears in the writer's use of conventional metaphors, even clichés, and in the depiction of the ready transformation of potential conflict into harmonious decisions. In this case, the boy, Mom, and Dad agree to give up the violin for sports.

These two themes may seem paradoxical, but their coexistence supports what a manager does, including reconciling differences, seeking compromises, and establishing a balance of power. The story further demonstrates that managers may lack empathy, or the capacity to sense intuitively the thoughts and feelings of others. Consider another story written to the same stimulus picture by someone thought of as a leader by his peers:

"This little boy has the appearance of being a sincere artist, one who is deeply affected by the violin, and has an intense desire to master the instrument.

"He seems to have just completed his normal practice session and appears to be somewhat crestfallen at his inability to produce the sounds that he is sure lie within the violin.

"He appears to be in the process of making a vow to himself to expend the necessary time and effort to play this instrument until he satisfies himself that he is able to bring forth the qualities of music that he feels within himself.

"With this type of determination and carrythrough, this boy became one of the great violinists of his day."

Empathy is not simply a matter of paying attention to other people. It is also the capacity to take in emotional signals and make them meaningful in a relationship. People who describe another person as "deeply affected," with "intense desire," "crestfallen," and as one who can "vow to himself" would seem to have an inner perceptiveness that they can use in their relationships with others.

Managers relate to people according to the role they play in a sequence of events or in a decision-making process, while leaders, who are concerned with ideas, relate in more intuitive and empathetic ways. The distinction is simply between a manager's attention to *how* things get done and a leader's to *what* the events and decisions mean to participants.

In recent years, managers have adopted from game theory the notion that decision-making events can be one of two types: the win-lose situation (or zero-sum game) or the win-win situation in which everybody in the action comes out ahead. Managers strive to convert win-lose into win-win situations as part of the process of reconciling differences among people and maintaining balances of power.

As an illustration, take the decision of how to allocate capital resources among operating divisions in a large, decentralized organization. On the surface, the dollars available for distribution are limited at any given time. Presumably, therefore, the more one division gets, the less is available for other divisions.

Managers tend to view this situation (as it affects human relations) as a conversion issue: how to make what seems like a win-lose problem into a win-win problem. From that perspective, several solutions come to mind. First, the manager focuses others' attention on procedure and not on substance. Here the players become engrossed in the bigger problem of *how* to make decisions, not *what* decisions to make. Once committed to the bigger problem, these people have to support the outcome since they were involved in formulating the decision-making rules. Because they believe in the rules they formulated, they will accept present losses, believing that next time they will win.

Second, the manager communicates to subordinates indirectly, using "signals" instead of "messages." A signal holds a number of implicit positions, while a message clearly states a position. Signals are inconclusive and subject to reinterpretation should people become upset and angry; messages involve the direct consequence that some people will indeed not like what they hear. The nature of messages heightens emotional response and makes managers anxious. With signals, the question of who wins and who loses often becomes obscured.

Third, the manager plays for time. Managers seem to recognize that with the passage of time and the delay of major decisions, compromises emerge that take the sting out of win-lose situations, and the original "game" will be superseded by additional situations. Compromises mean that one may win and lose simultaneously, depending on which of the games one evaluates.

There are undoubtedly many other tactical moves managers use to change human situations from win-lose to win-win. But the point is that such tactics focus on the decision-making process itself, and that process interests managers rather than leaders. Tactical interests involve costs as well as benefits; they make organizations fatter in bureaucratic and political intrigue and leaner in direct, hard activity and warm human relationships. Consequently, one often hears subordinates characterize managers as inscrutable, detached, and manipulative. These adjectives arise from the subordinates' perception that they are linked together in a process whose purpose is to maintain a controlled as well as rational and equitable structure.

In contrast, one often hears leaders referred to with adjectives rich in emotional content. Leaders attract strong feelings of identity and difference or of love and hate. Human relations in leader-dominated structures often appear turbulent, intense, and at times even disorganized. Such an atmosphere intensifies individual motivation and often produces unanticipated outcomes.

Senses of Self

In *The Varieties of Religious Experience,* William James describes two basic personality types, "once-born" and "twice-born." People of the former personality type are those for whom adjustments to life have been straightforward and whose lives have been more or less a peaceful flow since birth. Twice-borns, on the other hand, have not had an easy time of it. Their lives are marked by a continual struggle to attain some sense of order. Unlike once-borns, they cannot take things for granted. According to James, these personalities have equally different worldviews. For a once-born personality, the sense of self as a guide to conduct and attitude derives from a feeling of being at home and in harmony with one's environment. For a twice-born, the sense of self derives from a feeling of profound separateness.

A sense of belonging or of being separate has a practical significance for the kinds of investments managers and leaders make in their careers. Managers see themselves as conservators and regulators of an existing order of affairs with which they personally identify and from which they gain rewards. A manager's sense of self-worth is enhanced by perpetuating and strengthening existing institutions: he or she is performing in a role that harmonizes with ideals of duty and responsibility. William James had this harmony in mind—this sense of self as flowing easily to and from the outer world—in defining a once-born personality.

Leaders tend to be twice-born personalities, people who feel separate from their environment. They may work in organizations, but they never belong to them. Their sense of who they are does not depend on memberships, work roles, or other social indicators of identity. And that perception of identity may form the theoretical basis for explaining why certain individuals seek opportunities for change. The methods to bring about change may be technological, political, or ideological, but the object is the same: to profoundly alter human, economic, and political relationships.

In considering the development of leadership, we have to examine two different courses of life history: (1) development through socialization, which prepares the individual to guide institutions and to maintain the existing balance of social relations; and (2) development through personal mastery, which impels an individual to struggle for psychological and social change. Society produces its managerial talent through the first line of development; leaders emerge through the second.

Development of Leadership

Every person's development begins with family. Each person experiences the traumas associated with separating from his or her parents, as well as the pain that follows such a wrench. In the same vein, all individuals face the difficulties of achieving self-regulation and self-control. But for some, perhaps a majority, the fortunes of childhood provide adequate gratifications and sufficient opportunities to find substitutes for rewards no longer available. Such individuals, the "once-borns," make moderate identifications with parents and find a harmony between what they expect and what they are able to realize from life.

But suppose the pains of separation are amplified by a combination of parental demands and individual needs to the degree that a sense of isolation, of being special, or of wariness disrupts the bonds that attach children to parents and other authority figures? Given a special aptitude under such conditions, the person becomes deeply involved in his or her inner world at the expense of interest in the outer world. For such a person, self-esteem no longer depends solely on positive attachments and real rewards. A form of self-reliance takes hold along with expectations of performance and achievement, and perhaps even the desire to do great works.

Such self-perceptions can come to nothing if the individual's talents are negligible. Even with strong talents, there are no guarantees that achievement will follow, let alone that the end result will be for good rather than evil. Other factors enter into development as well. For one, leaders are like artists and other gifted people who often struggle with neuroses; their ability to function varies considerably even over the short run, and some potential leaders lose the struggle altogether. Also, beyond early childhood, the development patterns that affect managers and leaders involve the selective influence of particular people. Managerial personalities form moderate and widely distributed attachments. Leaders, on the other hand, establish, and also break off, intensive one-to-one relationships.

It is a common observation that people with great talents are often indifferent students. No one, for example, could have predicted Einstein's great achievements on the basis of his mediocre record in school. The reason for mediocrity is obviously not the absence of ability. It may result, instead, from self-absorption and the inability to pay attention to the ordinary tasks at hand. The only sure way an individual can interrupt reverie-like preoccupation and self-absorption is to form a deep attachment to a great teacher or other person who understands and has the ability to communicate with the gifted individual.

Whether gifted individuals find what they need in one-to-one relationships depends on the availability of teachers, possibly parental surrogates, whose strengths lie in cultivating talent. Fortunately, when generations meet and the self-selections occur, we learn more about how to develop leaders and how talented people of different generations influence each other.

While apparently destined for mediocre careers, people who form important one-to-one apprenticeship relationships often are able to accelerate and intensify their development. The psychological readiness of an individual to benefit from such a relationship depends on some experience in life that forces that person to turn inward.

Consider Dwight Eisenhower, whose early career in the army foreshadowed very little about his future development. During World War I, while some of his West Point classmates were already experiencing the war firsthand in France, Eisenhower felt "embedded in the monotony and unsought safety of the Zone of the Interior . . . that was intolerable punishment."[6]

Shortly after World War I, Eisenhower, then a young officer somewhat pessimistic about his career chances, asked for a transfer to Panama to work under General Fox Connor, a senior officer whom he admired. The army turned down his request. This setback was very much on Eisenhower's mind when Ikey, his first born son, succumbed to influenza. Through some sense of responsibility for its own, the army then transferred Eisenhower to Panama, where he took up his duties under General Connor with the shadow of his lost son very much upon him.

In a relationship with the kind of father he would have wanted to be, Eisenhower reverted to being the son he had lost. And in this highly charged situation, he began to learn from his teacher. General Connor offered, and Eisenhower gladly took, a magnificent tutorial on the military. The effects of this relationship on Eisenhower cannot be measured quantitatively, but in examining his career path from that point, one cannot overestimate its significance.

As Eisenhower wrote later about Connor, "Life with General Connor was a sort of graduate school in military affairs and the humanities, leavened by a man who was experienced in his knowledge of men and their conduct. I can never adequately express my gratitude to this one gentleman. . . . In a lifetime of association with great and good men, he is the one more or less invisible figure to whom I owe an incalculable debt."[7]

Some time after his tour of duty with General Connor, Eisenhower's breakthrough occurred. He received orders to attend the Command and General Staff School at Fort Leavenworth, one of the most competitive schools in the army. It was a coveted appointment, and Eisenhower took advantage of the opportunity. Unlike his performance in high school and West Point, his work at the Command School was excellent; he was graduated first in his class.

Psychological biographies of gifted people repeatedly demonstrate the important part a teacher plays in developing an individual. Andrew Carnegie owed much to his senior, Thomas A. Scott. As head of the Western Division of the Pennsylvania Railroad, Scott recognized talent and the desire to learn in the young telegrapher assigned to him. By giving Carnegie increasing responsibility and by providing him with the opportunity to learn through close personal observation, Scott added to Carnegie's self-confidence and sense of achievement. Because of his own personal strength and achievement, Scott did not fear Carnegie's aggressiveness. Rather, he gave it full play in encouraging Carnegie's initiative.

Great teachers take risks. They bet initially on talent they perceive in younger people. And they risk emotional involvement in working closely with their juniors. The risks do not always pay off, but the willingness to take them appears to be crucial in developing leaders.

Can Organizations Develop Leaders?

A myth about how people learn and develop that seems to have taken hold in American culture also dominates thinking in business. The myth is that people learn best from their peers. Supposedly, the threat of evaluation and even humiliation recedes in peer relations because of the tendency for mutual identification and the social restraints on authoritarian behavior among equals. Peer training in organizations occurs in various forms. The use, for example, of task forces made up of peers from several interested occupational groups (sales, production, research, and finance) supposedly removes the restraints of authority on the individual's willingness to assert and exchange ideas. As a result, so the theory goes, people interact more freely, listen more objectively to criticism and other points of view, and, finally, learn from this healthy interchange.

Another application of peer training exists in some large corporations, such as Philips N.V. in Holland, where organizational structure is built on the principle of joint responsibility of two peers, one representing the commercial end of the business and the other the technical. Formally, both hold equal responsibility for geographic operations or product groups, as the case may be. As a practical matter, it may turn out that one or the other of the peers dominates the management. Nevertheless, the main interaction is between two or more equals.

The principal question I raise about such arrangements is whether they perpetuate the managerial orientation and preclude the formation of one-to-one relationships between senior people and potential leaders.

Aware of the possible stifling effects of peer relationships on aggressiveness and individual initiative, another company, much smaller than Philips, utilizes joint responsibility of peers for operating units, with one important difference. The chief executive of this company encourages competition and rivalry among peers, ultimately rewarding the one who comes out on top with increased responsibility. These hybrid arrangements produce some unintended consequences that can be disastrous. There is no easy way to limit rivalry. Instead, it permeates all levels of the operation and opens the way for the formation of cliques in an atmosphere of intrigue.

One large, integrated oil company has accepted the importance of developing leaders through the direct influence of senior on junior executives. The chairman and chief executive officer regularly selects one talented university graduate whom he appoints his special assistant, and with whom he will work closely for a year. At the end of the year, the junior executive becomes available for assignment to one of the operating divisions, where he or she will be assigned to a responsible post rather than a training position. This apprenticeship acquaints the junior executive firsthand with the use of power and with the important antidotes to the power disease called *hubris*-performance and integrity.

Working in one-to-one relationships, where there is a formal and recognized difference in the power of the players, takes a great deal of tolerance for emotional interchange. This interchange, inevitable in close working arrangements, probably accounts for the reluctance of many executives to become involved in such relationships. *Fortune* carried an interesting story on the departure of a key executive, John W. Hanley, from the top management of Procter & Gamble to the chief executive officer position at Monsanto.[8] According to this account, the chief executive and chairman of P&G passed over Hanley for appointment to the presidency, instead naming another executive vice president to this post.

The chairman evidently felt he could not work well with Hanley who, by his own acknowledgment, was aggressive, eager to experiment and change practices, and constantly challenged his superior. A chief executive officer naturally has the right to select people with whom he feels congenial. But I wonder whether a greater capacity on the part of senior officers to tolerate the competitive impulses and behavior of their subordinates might not be healthy for corporations. At least a greater tolerance for interchange would not favor the managerial team player at the expense of the individual who might become a leader.

I am constantly surprised at the frequency with which chief executives feel threatened by open challenges to their ideas, as though the source of their authority, rather than their specific ideas, was at issue. In one case, a chief executive officer, who was troubled by the aggressiveness and sometimes outright rudeness of one of his talented vice presidents, used various indirect methods such as group meetings and hints from outside directors to avoid dealing with his subordinate. I advised the executive to deal head-on with what irritated him. I suggested that by direct, face-to-face confrontation, both he and his subordinate would learn to validate the distinction between the authority to be preserved and the issues to be debated.

The ability to confront is also the ability to tolerate aggressive interchange. And that skill not only has the net effect of stripping away the veils of ambiguity and signaling so characteristic of managerial cultures, but also it encourages the emotional relationships leaders need if they are to survive.

Appendix

RETROSPECTIVE COMMENTARY

It was not so long ago that Bert Lance, President Jimmy Carter's budget director and confidant, declared, "If it ain't broke, don't fix it." This piece of advice fits with how managers think. Leaders understand a different truth: "When it ain't broke may be the only time you can fix it."

In the splendid discipline of the marketplace, past formulas for success today contain the seeds of decay. The U.S. automobile industry has been cited so often as the prime example of the suicidal effect of continuing to do what one has been doing in the wake of success that its story borders on the banal. But it's true. Top executives in the automobile industry, along with managers in many other industries in the United States, have failed to understand the misleading lessons of success, revealing the chronic fault of the managerial mystique.

As a consequence of placing such reliance on the practical measure of continuing to do today and tomorrow what had proven successful yesterday, we face the chilling fact that the United States's largest export during the last decade or more has been jobs. We live with the grim reality that the storehouse of expertise called know-how has diminished. Perhaps most dismal of all, our children and our children's children may not be able to enjoy the same standard of living we worked so hard to achieve, let alone enjoy a higher standard of living as a legacy of the generations.

When "Managers and Leaders: Are They Different?" first appeared in the May–June 1977 issue of *Harvard Business Review,* practicing managers and academics, including many of my colleagues at the Harvard Business School, thought I had taken leave of my senses. Don't ordinary people in an organization with superior structure and process outperform superior people operating in an ordinary organization? To those indoctrinated in the "managerial mystique," talent is ephemeral while organization structure and process are real. The possibility that it takes talent to make a company hum counts for less than acting on those variables managers feel they understand and can control.

Talent is critical to continued success in the marketplace. Yet most organizations today persist in perpetuating the development of managers over leaders. Fortunately, however, there may be an awakening. The chairman of IBM, John Akers, startled the business community with his announcement that IBM intended to abandon its long-held course of running its business as one large corporation. Akers intends to break IBM up into a number of corporations. And while "Big Blue" will continue to be big by most standards, the businesses will run under a leadership and not a managerial mentality. The corporation will no longer rest on the false comforts of economy of scale. Nor will executives be preoccupied with coordination and control, with decentralized operations and centralized financial controls. Process will take a backseat to substance, and the power will flow to executives who are creative and, above all, aggressive.

If other large companies follow this lead, corporate America may recharge, and its ability to compete may rebound. But if left to professional management, U.S. corporations will continue to stagnate.

Since "Managers and Leaders: Are They Different?" was first published, strategy has catapulted itself into the number one position on the managerial hit parade. No aspect of corporate life is indifferent to strategy. Every problem leads to strategic solutions, ranging from how to position products to how to compensate executives. We have a plethora of marketing strategies, employee benefit strategies, and executive development strategies. Strategy, it seems, has replaced business policy as the conceptual handle for establishing a corporation's directives.

In relying on strategy, organizations have largely overlooked results. Strategy is an offspring of the branch of economics called industrial organization; it builds models of competition and attempts to position products in competitive markets through analytic techniques. The aggregation of these product positions establishes mission statements and direction for businesses. With the ascendancy of industrial organization in the 1980s, management consultants prospered and faith in the managerial mystique was strengthened, despite the poor performance in the U.S. economy.

To me, the most influential development in management in the last 10 or 15 years has been Lotus 1-2-3. This popular software program makes it possible to create spreadsheets rapidly and repetitively, and that has given form and language to strategic planning. With this methodology, technicians can play with the question, "What if?" Best of all, everyone with access to a computer and the appropriate software can join in the "what if" game.

Alas, while everyone can become a strategist, few can become, and sustain, the position of creator. Vision, the hallmark of leadership, is less a derivative of spreadsheets and more a product of the mind called imagination.

And vision is needed at least as much as strategy to succeed. Business leaders bring to bear a variety of imaginations on the growth of corporations. These imaginations—the marketing imagination, the manufacturing imagination, and others—originate in perceptual capacities we recognize as talent. Talented leaders grasp the significance of anomalies, such as unfulfilled customer needs, manufacturing operations that can be improved significantly, and the potential of technological applications in product development.

Business imaginations are substantive. A leader's imagination impels others to act in ways that are truly, to use James MacGregor Burns's felicitous term, "transformational." But leaders often experience their talent as restlessness, as a desire to upset other people's applecarts, an impelling need to "do things better." As a consequence, a leader may not create a stable working environment; rather, he or she may create a chaotic workplace, with highly charged emotional peaks and valleys.

In "Managers and Leaders: Are They Different?", I argued that a crucial difference between managers and leaders lies in the conceptions they hold, deep in their psyches, of chaos and order. Leaders tolerate chaos and lack of structure and are thus prepared to keep answers in suspense, avoiding premature closure on important issues. Managers seek order and control and are almost compulsively addicted to disposing of problems even before they understand their potential significance. In my experience, seldom do the uncertainties of potential chaos cause problems. Instead, it is the instinctive move to impose order on potential chaos that makes trouble for organizations.

It seems to me that business leaders have much more in common with artists, scientists, and other creative thinkers than they do with managers. For business schools to exploit this commonality of dispositions and interests, the curriculum should worry less about the logics of strategy and imposing the constraints of computer exercises and more about thought experiments in the play of creativity and imagination. If they are successful, they would then do a better job of preparing exceptional men and women for positions of leadership.

Notes

1. New York: Harper-Row, 1973, p. 72.
2. Alfred P. Sloan, Jr., *My Years with General Motors* (New York: Doubleday, 1964), p. 440.
3. Ibid., p. 91.
4. Ibid.
5. Ibid., p. 93.
6. Dwight D. Eisenhower, *At Ease: Stories I Tell To Friends* (New York: Doubleday, 1967), p. 136.
7. Ibid., p. 187.
8. "Jack Hanley Got There by Selling Harder," *Fortune*, November 1976.

5

The CEO As Coach: An Interview with AlliedSignal's Lawrence A. Bossidy

Noel M. Tichy and Ram Charan

In July 1991, Lawrence A. Bossidy became chairman and CEO of AlliedSignal, the $13 billion industrial supplier of aerospace systems, automotive parts, and chemical products. The company's story since then appears to be that of a classic slash-and-burn turnaround: head count has been reduced, assets have been sold, restructurings have occurred, and earnings and market value have risen dramatically. But the view from inside is far more interesting for anyone grappling with what it takes to build and lead a competitive organization capable of sustained performance over the long term.

Bossidy is known as a straight-shooting, tough-minded, results-oriented business leader. But he also is a charismatic and persistent coach, determined to help people learn and thereby to provide his company with the best-prepared employees. In this interview, he discusses what he does to "coach people to win."

The 60-year-old Bossidy is no stranger to corporate transformation. As vice chairman of General Electric, he helped CEO Jack Welch reposition the $65 billion industrial giant. Bossidy's career at GE began in 1957, when he joined the finance staff. In the late 1970s and early 1980s, he led GE Capital Corporation, creating a world-class financial service organization.

This interview was conducted by Noel M. Tichy and Ram Charan late last year at AlliedSignal's headquarters in Morristown, New Jersey.

HBR: How can one person approach the job of changing a large organization?

Lawrence A. Bossidy: I believe in the "burning platform" theory of change. When the roustabouts are standing on the offshore oil rig and the foreman yells, "Jump into the water," not only won't they jump but they also won't feel too kindly toward the foreman. There may be sharks in the water. They'll jump only when they themselves see the flames shooting up from the platform. Chrysler's platform was visibly burning; the company changed. IBM's platform was not visibly burning; it didn't.

The leader's job is to help everyone see that the platform is burning, whether the flames are apparent or not. The process of change begins when people decide to take the flames seriously and manage by fact, and that means a brutal understanding of reality. You need to find out what the reality is so that you know what needs changing.

What was the reality you found at AlliedSignal?

It was a company that had grown rapidly through mergers and acquisitions but whose earnings had stalled. We had 58 business units, each guarding its own turf. It was an inner-directed company, focused mainly on itself. Management made all the decisions, and employees' ideas were rarely solicited and therefore rarely offered.

So what was your burning platform, and how did you use it to get people mobilized?

In 1991, we were hemorrhaging cash. That was the issue that needed focus. I traveled all over the company with the same message and the same charts, over and over. Here's what I think is good about us. Here's what I'm worried about. Here's what we have to do about it. And if we don't fix the cash problem, none of us is going to be around. You can keep it simple: we're spending more than we're taking in. If you do that at home, there will be a day of reckoning.

In the first 60 days, I talked to probably 5,000 employees. I would go to Los Angeles and speak to 500 people, then to Phoenix and talk to another 500. I would stand on a loading dock and speak to people and answer their questions. We talked about what was wrong and what we should do about it. And as we talked, it became clear to me that there hadn't been a good top-down enunciation of the company's problem.

I knew intuitively that I needed support at the bottom right from the outset. Go to the people and tell them what's wrong. And they knew. It's remarkable how many people know what's really going on in their company. I think it's important to try to get effective interaction with everybody in the company, to involve everyone.

It's something I continue to do. Besides talking to large groups, whenever I go to a location I host smaller, skip-level lunches, where I meet with groups of about 20 employees without name tags and without their bosses. I think the combination of talking to a lot of people in an interactive setting and doing skip-levels and conducting periodic attitude surveys gives you a pretty good handle on how people think about things.

Also, there was a context to our burning platform. I mentioned IBM a few moments ago. People here had observed difficulties at IBM, Kodak, and other companies, so the environment was ripe for change. They didn't want what had happened there to happen here. The restructurings and displacements all around us had made people more acutely aware of the value of a good job.

Interestingly, the situation at AlliedSignal was very different from the one that GE faced. Fifteen years ago, GE was preeminent. There was no visible burning platform, but the company had to change. So Jack Welch's idea was to try to make people more humble. At Allied-Signal, our people had been humbled. Our job was to promote our employees' ability to win. But I think that the steps you take to accomplish change aren't dramatically different in either instance.

Can you elaborate a bit more about how you build support in the organization? For example, how do you field tough questions in the large meetings?

First, we want to create an environment in which people will speak up. Every question is interesting and important. When I conduct interactive sessions, I don't walk out after three questions. I make it clear that I'm going to be there until the last question is asked. When employees point out things that aren't right, I'm the first to say, "Yes, that's one we need to do something about, and here's what we're going to do." Or, "I don't know the answer to that, but I'll look into it"—and then I'd better follow up. But let's assume someone asks a question that's critical of what we're doing. The whole room hears it, which I think is positive. That gets it on the table and permits response. And I think it's healthy to let all the frustration get aired. It's good if people go home at night and say, "I told that son of a bitch what I thought about him today."

You have to deal with tough questions honestly. I'll give you an example. A guy in aerospace got up and asked me, "Are we going to have layoffs?" "Here's the issue," I answered. "We're in aerospace. We're in an environment that's weakening. We all know that. Defense expenditures are down. The commercial aviation industry is in recession. And we have too much capacity to begin with. So we're going to have layoffs."

I just try to answer the questions. I don't know if I ever will pull it off, but I think the idea of getting some support from the bottom is powerful. It gets the people in the middle on the horse faster. We need to work on this every day.

During your first 60 days, in addition to getting support from the bottom, you also spent a lot of time team building at the top. Were you focusing on culture change with that group?

I think you don't change a culture. I think you coach people to win. Basically, people want to be successful. They want to go home at night and feel that they've made a contribution. At AlliedSignal, each of our three major sectors had its own history as an independent company, its own distinct culture. We didn't want to change that. It makes the company stronger.

But we had to unite ourselves with vision and values. And that effort begins with the team at the top. In November 1991, we had an off-site meeting with the top 12 managers of the company. We spent two days arguing—and I mean arguing—about values. That was helpful because at the end of the meeting, we not only had the values, we also had a specific definition of each of those values. The seven values we settled on are simple: customers, integrity, people, teamwork, speed, innovation, and performance. They're not unique. But they're important because they give all our people a view of what behavior is expected of them. And if you're a leader in this company, you risk being labeled a hypocrite if you don't behave according to those values. And you're going to get some heat—and I think that's terrific.

Let me explain it another way. We made a major commitment to use total quality as the vehicle to drive change. Everybody in the world has TQ or something like it. I want AlliedSignal to be the people who do it, not the people who talk about it. TQ does not replace goals; it's the vehicle to facilitate progress toward your goals. And here's where the question of values comes in. TQ tests us because we're going to encounter four types of people. We're going to have people who embrace TQ and make their numbers. We're going to want to promote them. We're going to have people who don't like TQ and don't make their numbers. That's easy: we're going to suggest they leave. We're going to have people who love TQ and don't make their numbers. We're going to try to move them someplace so they can continue to contribute. And we're going to have people who don't like TQ and make their numbers. Those are the people who will test our resolve about whether the process is going to go forward, because they have to go, too. Think about it. Anybody who makes his numbers and says, "I don't need TQ," has to walk the plank or change. Some people have changed, and some are gone.

Besides values, you have to have clear goals. People have to know where they're going. What is victory? Where do you want to be? Every year, we set three goals that we put in front of everybody. It creates focus. In 1994, for example, the goals were: make the numbers, reduce cycle times, and make growth happen. Wherever I go in the company, people know what our three goals are. That's important. Because every time I go to a factory, I conduct a review with those three goals in mind. Are we making the numbers? Are we making quantum gains with cycle-time reduction? Are we growing? People need to be focused on what we're trying to do. We want them to believe that the goals we're talking about are real, that we can do it.

The day when you could yell and scream and beat people into good performance is over. Today you have to appeal to them by helping them see how they can get from here to there, by establishing some credibility, and by giving them some reason and some help to get there. Do all those things, and they'll knock down doors.

So you begin by creating values and putting an emphasis on goals. But how do you teach people how to win?

You have to create clarity about the issues you're dealing with, and here I mean the business issues. Before joining AlliedSignal, I looked at the company from afar and thought it had strikingly good market positions in its industries that were not at all matched by margins or profitability. During my first 60 days, I spent a lot of time looking in depth at the businesses and the management processes, and talking to a lot of people. Then I went to the board with my observations, both positive and negative.

I think we all pretty much knew the problems. We were focused internally rather than on customers, and there was way too much organization. Those two generally go hand in hand because layers of organization get in the way. I have the view that you centralize paper and you decentralize people. At AlliedSignal, we had it backward. We had centralized all the people and decentralized all the paper. That created enormous cost. We had far too many purchasing departments, payroll departments, and software systems. In addition, we were being drowned in capital projects—too many projects chasing too little money. The expected payback was unclear. There was no emphasis on margins. We were holding on to underperforming nonstrategic assets.

We felt we could address many of our business issues through TQ. The nice thing about TQ is that it has only three elements: sensitivity to customers, continuous improvement in productivity, and the involvement of all employees. The three are linked, but if we don't satisfy customers, you can pull the curtains. It's over.

TQ can be unifying, it can be positive, it can give self-confidence, and it can get all the players on the field. But to work, it has to yield results. We required every TQ team to have a specific business project to work on and to get something done. So while people are learning new skills, they are also completing projects that make the company better.

In your first 60 days, you also managed to get out and talk to customers. What did you learn, and how did you bring back what you learned to the organization?

I made an effort to talk to customers early on, but that's something you need to do all the time, not just in the first 60 days. I visited a lot of customers, and in my first few months I really got an earful. I tried to get examples in every sector—and I still do. In those early days, we looked at some interesting measurements. While we were saying that we were delivering an order-fill rate of 98%, our customers thought we were at 60%. The irony was, we seemed to think we had to justify why we were right and the customers were wrong, instead of spending time trying to address their complaints. So we changed that. The customers are right, regardless, and we began to use their measurements.

I'll never forget one session in Phoenix with our field salespeople. They were the ones who were getting beaten up every day out there by our customers. We asked them, as a constructive exercise, to tell us what their customers thought about us in each of their territories. I mean, they just colored the air blue.

So we said, "Okay, we're going to do something about this." And we went to the customers and said, "Hey, we have a lot of problems, and we'd like to have you team with us so we can get them identified and solved." Almost to a customer, they agreed to do that. We now have hundreds of multifunctional teams in place, and they have helped give our customers higher-quality products and faster turn-around time.

The benefits of the teams go beyond solving specific problems. People often underestimate the importance of having face time with customers. I noticed that our people in the field weren't asking me to speak with customers. In my former incarnation at GE, I spoke frequently at customer meetings of one sort or another. Why? Because custom ers have events and they need speakers and no one wants to speak. I raised my hand. Why? Because I'm Mario Cuomo? No. Because it gives me two hours to spend with a customer's organization. That's a chance of a lifetime. Invite me, for heaven's sake. I'm not bad. Invite some of the other leaders whose titles can help you. Use us. Don't resent it; don't protect turf. We want a lot of coverage on customers—up and down the organization. We want contacts. Have seminars for them. Have whatever it takes to get quality time with them. And when you visit them, ask, "How are we doing?" You know, they are the only customers we have, so we'd better love them.

Let's get down to specifics about how you've managed change. In your three and a half years at AlliedSignal, you've focused on improving three common core operating processes. In our experience, those three processes—operations, strategy, and human resources—can be bureaucratic, highly staged exercises.

Frankly, we were disappointed with all three of those core processes. We had to strengthen them and make them more robust. As a leader, you can influence only three things. You can influence people, you can influence your strategy, and you can influence operations. In my judgment, that's all you do. And if you don't work on those three things all the time, you might be having fun, but nothing's going to happen.

Anyone reading this interview will say, "Big deal! We have those three processes, too!" But the fact is that 90% of all companies don't work them or push them to the ultimate to get value. So it's not enough just to have the processes. You have to work intensely to make them better and better and involve everybody in them. (For the results, see the exhibit.)

AlliedSignal's Numbers Improve

	Net Income* (in millions)	Operating Margin*	Working- Capital Turns*	Market Value† (in millions)
June 30, 1991	$359	4.4%	4.1	$4,506
June 30, 1992‡	$457	6.0%	4.3	$7,584
June 30, 1993	$592	7.3%	4.5	$9,416
June 30, 1994	$708	8.5%	5.0	$9,792

*For 12-month period
†At period's end
‡Before restructuring charges and accounting changes

Since July 1991, when Lawrence A. Bossidy assumed leadership, AlliedSignal has combined business units, closed factories, increased working-capital turns, and generated substantial free cash flow. Bossidy and his team have maintained capital spending, coordinated companywide functions such as purchasing and information systems, reduced the number of suppliers from 9,000 to 3,000, pruned 19,000 salaried jobs from the payroll, and refocused research and development spending.

How do you become better at managing the operating plan?

One of the first things that struck me when I came here was that it was more or less accepted practice that you put a plan together and then missed it. First revelation: people routinely miss their numbers. We don't need meaningless budgets. We need an operating plan that recognizes that underlying assumptions are often wrong and that provides options when that happens. From day one, I made it clear that the people in this organization will be known for meeting commitments. Period.

Here, as at many other companies, we didn't appreciate the contribution that good finance people can make—good in the sense of well-rounded businesspeople who contribute to business solutions, not just scorekeepers. We had a terrific senior vice president of finance, but his job had been limited to running a good corporate finance function. So we had a lot of financial analysis at the corporate level but very little at the business level. And I wanted the opposite. When he had the chance to broaden his interest and take responsibility for the quality of the finance function throughout the company, dramatic things happened.

Good finance people are the ones who can help give real meaning to operating plans. When you say you're going to get a 6% improvement in productivity, they're the ones who are supposed to ask where. What are the projects? When are they going to be done? How much money are they going to be providing? If we're going to grow by 5%, they ask the tough questions: Where are we going to grow? What products are going to grow by 5%? How are we going to get price increases? Good financial involvement is critical in constructing a sound operating plan; it really drives at the particulars.

And then, if our assumptions are wrong, what are the contingencies? Are we going to have to take out more people? Are we going to have to kill this project? Capable, involved finance people should be monitoring the operating plan constantly. I take it as a given that each one is a good accountant, but they must be more than that. To contribute to the business, they have to interpret financial results in a way that helps us run operations. It's imperative that finance people really understand what's happening in the factories.

Are there specific measures of operating performance that you watch more closely than others?

Productivity is critical. We have to have 6% per year from everybody. Why? Because if we have cost inflation of 3% to 4% per year and little or no ability to raise prices, that can translate into poor margins. That's why productivity is the rule of the day around here. We define productivity change from one year to the next as sales excluding price increases divided by cost excluding inflation. Although initially we worked the cost side hard, we know that eventually you need to get productivity from both unit-volume growth and cost reduction. It isn't easy, but the most successful companies in the world in the 1990s will be those that sustain productivity. It's essential to our survival, not to mention our prosperity.

In my view, productivity is an important part of TQ. TQ must mean results. Managers get results by improving processes, but I'm not interested in process improvement for its own sake. That's where productivity comes in. If we're doing all this stuff and our productivity isn't getting any better, we're kidding ourselves.

We also look at working-capital turnover. Why? Very simple: we need money to grow the company. In 1991, we had a 40% debt-to-capital ratio and no cash. We sold off some assets and cut costs. Working-capital turns were at about four. I said we needed to improve fast. And when we hit five, we raised the hurdle to ten. At first, people asked, "Why is he so interested in cash?" It's just like your checkbook. If there's none there, we can't invest in growth. We worry about cash every day.

Margins are also critical. Every year, we'll miss some plans, not necessarily because we're deficient but because we won't read markets, we won't foresee all the unknowns. That's okay. But in my view, a real professional maintains margins. When you see you're going to miss a plan, I regard it as an obligation to do what you have to do to make your margin commitments.

A lot of people didn't know what their competitors' margins were. I would say to them, "You know, if they have 12 points of margin and we have 8, that's $300 million of cost we have to take out of this business to be competitive. Now, how the hell are we going to do that?" And, bang! You get focused real fast.

Earlier, you mentioned that one of your concerns was that the company was inwardly focused. When you ask about competitors' margins, is that part of a larger effort to get people to look outside?

Absolutely. When we did our large restructuring in 1991, I asked the leadership committee—the top 12—to come back to me with a plan to de-layer the organization and reduce head count. They came back with a plan that I thought was too modest. So I said, "I think you made a sincere effort, but I have to take this public now, and I'm going to make your plan far more ambitious because I don't want to have to come back a year from now and restructure all over again. If we're going to take a charge, I want to take a big one." That was my challenge to them. "As a test," I said, "go back and look at the margins of your best competitors and then see what your margin is, and figure out what you have to do to make that margin." We do that kind of benchmarking continually. You can't say, "Well, we're done. We benchmarked." You have to say, "We benchmark every day."

Our people have worked hard to improve working-capital turnover. But now we have to do even better. If someone says, "I don't know how to do it," my job is to say, "Wait a minute. Let's talk about that." Again, I go to the competition. "Ford Motor turns working capital more than 20 times. Now, what's the difference between its business and yours?" I carry charts around showing who has made the particular goals we're working on; they don't have to be in our businesses. I ask people to get out there and talk with these folks and figure out what they're doing, and then come back and we'll talk.

We have to assume that every company does at least one thing better than we do. Benchmarking is not industrial tourism. It is looking at specific practices, getting the benefit of expertise, bringing it back, and having no inhibitions about adopting it and letting people know where it came from.

We bounce around depending on where we think the expertise is, and we benchmark many companies. For new-product development, 3M has done a good job. For acquisitions, it might be Emerson Electric. In manufacturing and inventory management, we've looked at Motorola; and for receivables, American Express.

I ask my senior managers to go to as many companies as they can, and I also do it myself.

What about another of those core operating processes—strategic planning? What sorts of things have you done to improve that process?

The strategic planning process was under way when I arrived, so rather than try to change it, I let it happen. It was the kind of thing I'm sure everyone has seen before: a series of big books, show and tell, and then the books were relegated to the shelf and life went on. It was all highly orchestrated. During the sessions, I listened a lot, but then we talked about it and agreed we wanted something different.

I don't believe strategic planning should be a one-time annual event. It's important to have a good, concentrated thought period. But then you have to live with that strategy every day. Whenever we do an operating review, we have to be calibrating against our strategy. When we talk about competition or market share in our operating reviews, we're working on strategy in real time. That means we ask ourselves whether we're doing what we said we'd do and, if we aren't, what happened.

Today the business heads make the presentations and answer the questions. And look, there's no rocket science to strategy, but you're supposed to know where you are, where your competition is, what your cost position is, and where you want to go. If you don't know those four things, you're not going to have a very effective effort. We needed a better database—key measures such as market share over time, for example—followed by issue identification and some options for solutions.

So we put together a corporate training program to expose people to a more external way of approaching strategy. The result is a much more exciting conversation. And after every strategy review we have,

I write a three- or four-page letter to the business head that solidifies our agreement about what the issues are and what we're going to do about them.

I brought in a new person to take charge of the strategic plan, and an important part of his job is to make sure people are learning how to do strategy better. I did the same with the two other important management processes: I put the CFO in charge of the operating plan, and the head of human resources is responsible for the management-resource review. We continually rethink what we want those three processes to yield. We also want to make sure we have good coaching in all of them so that we can continue to improve.

That brings us to the third process: human resources. What do you do to strengthen it?

One of the worst things we do in corporate America is not tell people what we think of them. Every appraisal looks the same. Basically, you get a star if you don't say anything offensive. That's no way to foster development. I think you have a responsibility to make people as good as you can make them. And if you identify a trait that interferes with their being better, you have an obligation to point it out and to try to do something about it with them. I don't think you should approach the job gingerly. I don't want people dreading the day they get their appraisals. But I do say to myself, Gee, if I think John Doe is as good as I'm going to get in that job, then I have to see if I can make him as good as I can make him.

People tend to flinch when it comes to certain words to describe employees: saying that they're not aggressive enough or not results-oriented enough or not outgoing enough, or that they don't have communication skills or they're not analytically inclined or they don't like customers. But you have to say those things if you want to help them.

Describe what you do in performance appraisals.

I don't have a sophisticated appraisal. I write down what I think is good and what should get better. Pluses and minuses. The first thing I do is give you a copy and ask you to read it. Then I talk frankly, spending more time on the areas for improvement. The sessions usually take about an hour. Then I give the appraisal to you and say, "If you want to think about it and come back and talk again, that's fine." Most don't; some do.

I want to stress how important it is to put the appraisal in writing. I don't want people to go home and say, "He said something else—I just heard him wrong." Some people are complicated and want to rationalize these things. Putting it in writing helps them learn to live with it.

When I sit down with someone 6 or 12 months later, I want to see some of those minuses erased. Sometimes that doesn't happen. Recently, one guy said, "Well, I don't care if I'm going to limit my potential; I've gone as far as I want to anyway." I said, "No, no, you've got it wrong. You have to keep growing just to stay where you are. And you've demonstrated that you can't do it yourself, so you have to get some help." Then I offered him some suggestions and said, "We're not going to sit here and have the same discussion every year."

Since you took over at AlliedSignal, how many of the key players have you changed?

Of the top 12, 4 have left; the other 8 are still here. But of the 140 senior managers, about 75% are new to their jobs. We hired 40 new people from the outside, and the rest were moved from other jobs in the company. I didn't replace the head of finance, as I mentioned earlier, but we needed an enormous number of new finance people. I told the people filling a corporate role that they had to be involved in the field. I said to the CFO, "I'm going to measure you not just on who works for you here at headquarters. Every finance person in the business who doesn't perform, I'm going to blame on you."

If you don't have the best people, you hurt everyone in the organization. You have to be sensitive and compassionate to people, and you have to extend your hand to help them, but you have to have the best people.

As tough as it is to cut a lot of employees, I kept coming back to one item that showed up in our employee attitude survey. People in great numbers were saying that we tolerated mediocrity. Now, that's quite an indictment. So at every review meeting, we talk about people and whether they are meeting their goals, and what they are doing to fix weaknesses that have been pointed out. Do they like our values, share our enthusiasm? Do they support TQ? And what's their understanding of the businesses? Do they understand strategy, people, and operations? So I wasn't the one saying, "It's time for Joe to go." Instead, they'd say, "Hey, look. Joe's not going to make it." And I told them, "Let's get this done sooner rather than later. Because no matter how well it's done, it's negative, and you might as well get it behind you and get positive."

Another tendency we've changed was to take people who weren't cutting it and move them somewhere else in the company. We've stopped doing that. I think you have to get those people out of the organization. Give them some time—not a pink slip on Friday afternoon. Err on the side of giving them more time. But get them out of here. Credibility matters.

If having the best people is so important, can you describe what kind of people you're looking for?

Today's corporation is a far cry from the old authoritarian vertical hierarchy I grew up in. The cross-functional ties among individuals and groups are increasingly important. They're channels of activity and communication. The traditional bases of managerial authority are eroding. In the past, we used to reward the lone rangers in the corner offices because their achievements were brilliant even though their behavior was destructive. That day is gone. We need people who are better at persuading than at barking orders, who know how to coach and build consensus. Today, managers add value by brokering with people, not by presiding over empires. That has a big impact on how you think about who the "best" people are.

Don't get me wrong. We're not looking for backslapping nice guys, however dumb they might be. Competition is tough, and it takes brains to win. But today we look for smart people with an added dimension: they have an interest in other people and derive psychic satisfaction from working with them.

I am convinced that nothing we do is more important than hiring and developing people. At the end of the day, you bet on people, not on strategies. Strategies are intellectually simple; their execution is not. Your strategies will not make you a better company. Of course, you want to have a good idea of where you're going, but that's not enough. The question is, Can you execute? That's what differentiates one company from another.

To execute, you need people who can lead. Managers have to understand that they don't *manage* anybody. That is especially true in a freedom-loving country like the United States. We all hate to be managed. I like the way Teddy Roosevelt put it: "The best executive is the one who has sense enough to pick good men to do what he wants done, and self-restraint enough to keep from meddling with them while they do it."

You've invested a lot of money and management time on training, and you've accomplished it at a faster pace and wider scope than anyone else we've seen. Why?

The only way to bridge the gap between where we are and where we want to go is education. We put every one of our 80,000 people through TQ training within two years. All our business leaders, including me, go through all the training. And I visit as many classes as I can whenever I'm on location. We want people on the factory floor to feel as good about training as top-level managers do.

Beyond formal training programs, we also need to provide tools. Let me give you an example. We need to be more global. Specifically, we want to be major factors in China, India, and Mexico. In order to get there, people need help in understanding those markets. For example, we've put together an Asia council so that the people who are undertaking initiatives at the business-unit level have an opportunity to get together, share market intelligence, and compare notes. It gives people access to information they need, and it helps them stay current about what people in other sectors are doing in that country. So there's a support network to help people tackle something new.

Everyone has to get on board with the importance of learning new skills. I'll give you an example. When I go to a factory, I always look up the union leader and say, "Look, you're responsible for keeping these jobs as much as I am. If you turn down TQ, you're refusing to let these people be trained, and you're going to have to be accountable for it." They don't want to hear that. They know that jobs are an important factor in their life. I don't do it to excoriate them, but I make sure everyone understands.

You've mentioned a number of times the reviews you have for each of the three core management processes. How do they work?

Each process review is separate, so each business leader can expect to go through three reviews with me a year—one for people, one for strategy, and one for operations. Right now, I want to get to a lot of employees, so we tend to include more people in the meetings. I want everyone to know what we think about market share and productivity. When you pack the room, you lose some candor. You have to be more careful. You don't want to embarrass anybody. But you do get to communicate with five times as many people.

How do the review sessions work? Take operations, for example. Before the review, I send the business leader a letter to explain what I want him to emphasize. Then we have the review. It covers both my issues and his. It's a candid discussion about operations and not about people or strategy. When it's over, I write a letter setting down what the goals are. Then the head of the business writes me a letter telling me what he is doing to meet those goals. That closes the loop—and serves as a starting point for the next review.

The process is the same for strategy and for human resources. I don't want to make too much of the letters. They aren't a bureaucratic exercise. But they are a useful operating mechanism. They eliminate a lot of questions and tension and misunderstandings about what we agreed to do. They save us from spending the first half hour of every meeting trying to determine who said what to whom. They help us focus on the work we need to get done.

Then, coming off the meetings, my mantra is, Make the numbers. By that I mean not just financial targets but all the goals we agreed on.

Where are you today in the change process?

People's mind-sets have changed. Employees are interested in our stock price now. You go into the lobbies where we've installed monitors, and people are tracking AlliedSignal. Not just their sector but the whole company. The chief achievement of all that we're talking about, and it's not finished yet, is that people are thinking differently about their jobs. We still have a long way to go. We're still far from achieving our vision of becoming a premier company, but I think our people are now motivated to get there and, more important, they know what they have to do to get there.

I think you have to position organizations to continue to take steps up. Companies don't change incrementally. They change in quantum jumps. If you shoot for anything less, you don't get any change. You may fall short, but still you've made a big difference.

I think that the closer you come to the customers, the more you appreciate the need to change. And the more inwardly focused you are, the less you understand that need. As we get more and more customer focused, we don't have to preach about the need to change. People know it.

The Eye of the Storm: The Force at the Center

James Champy and Nitin Nohria

Reviving the debate about whether history is driven by great men and women or by great events—and without any knowledge of meteorology—consider the following question: Does the eye of a hurricane exist because of the storm or does the storm exist because of the eye of a hurricane? The answer lies in recognizing the inherent duality of cause and effect. In our introduction to this book, we examined the external forces driving the storm. We were looking outside in. In this epilogue, we want to look inside out. We want to look from the perspective of the managers and leaders who sit in the eye of the storm, shaping and being shaped by it.

Throughout this book we have extolled change. Change brings renewal: It reshapes organizations, revives businesses, creates industries, alters the nature of work, and fuels the engine of progress. But change brings destruction, as well: massive displacement of workers, the decimation of traditional middle management, and the life struggle of icons of American business. To the extent it generates fear and cynicism, it not only halts progress, it takes us backward.

Change also leads to a need—indeed a powerful search—for greater personal connectedness and meaning in our work.

Finally, change displays in sharp contrast the essential traits of *personal character* that leaders must possess to manage change successfully. Leaders

- are driven by a higher ambition;
- maintain a deep sense of humility;
- undertake a constant search for the truth;

- don't flee from ambiguity, uncertainty, or paradox;
- take personal responsibility for consequences of their actions;
- are highly disciplined in their everyday lives; and
- are always authentic

These character traits are the hallmarks of leaders cited in this book.

Storms create vacuums, and business change has created a strong demand that all managers, to one degree or another, demonstrate those characteristics of leadership. Too often, managers have taken the easy road. They have been quite willing to embrace change intellectually. Indeed, one can hardly think of a company that has not refocused, right-sized, reengineered, or restructured. Yet there is an element of faddishness in this that leads cynics to conclude that an appearance of progressiveness—not necessarily renewal—is what is desired.

The result, of course, is that many change initiatives have failed. Surveys of almost any change effort—whether it be TQM, reengineering, mergers and acquisitions, or restructurings—suggest a lower-than-acceptable success rate. There is so little to show for the pain. As a result, many question their sacrifices in these times of violent change.

Under the headline "Lost Jobs, Found Directions," the *New York Times* examined the aftermath of once fast-track managers who were victims of downsizing. "We talk more about cosmic realities," noted the husband of one of two former IBM managers. "How are we all linked together? I never gave these questions much thought five years ago. I was too damn busy."[1] *Fortune* magazine ran a related feature on women managers and executives who are leaving in mid-career. "I wasn't fulfilled," one said. Many had started entrepreneurial ventures to find a new center for their work lives; others had taken sabbaticals. But the phenomenon of wanting to bail out was found to be surprisingly widespread. Eighty-seven percent said they were contemplating a career change; 40% said they felt trapped. "There is some kind of profound something going on—a reassessment, a rethinking, a big gulp, whatever," explained a Yankelovich researcher. "It has to do with self-image and the workplace."[2]

Without wishing to appear too facile in our conclusions, it feels as if people have lost a broader sense of purpose. They have an elemental need for meaning and connectedness that their managers have failed to provide. If this continues for too long, they lose confidence in their managers' abilities.

Meaning and connectedness are particularly necessary when the agony of change is destroying people's commitment to their jobs, causing burnout and despair. Meaning and connectedness are critical at a time when business is demanding of people a greater level of creativity, autonomy, and decision making than ever before.

It is surprising that one of the best expressions of the great potential that could be released by this almost universal longing for self-fulfillment comes from a poet, David Whyte.

Whyte's book, *The Aroused Heart,* is subtitled *Poetry and the Preservation of the Soul in Corporate Life.* It is showing up in corner offices these days. His thesis is that the old form of organization required workers to surrender their souls to the corporation. But the new employer-employee "contract" will be based more on equality. Here is an excerpt:

> It seems that all the overripe hierarchies of the world, from corporations to nation states, are in trouble and are calling, however reluctantly, on their people for more creativity, commitment and innovation. If these corporate bodies can demand those creative qualities, which by long tradition belong so directly to our being, to our soul, they must naturally make room for their disturbing presence within their buildings and their borders. But the human ability to innovate and follow an individual vision depends also on a sure foundation of continuity and community. The corporation must make room for an equally strong need for stability and tradition, reverence and respect, continuity and contemplation. Above all, the corporation demanding creativity from its own employees has as much changing to do as [its] workforce.[3]

The profound changes we are witnessing are indeed demanding a new organization—an adaptive, networked organization with a soul to energize it and principles to guide it. This is the challenge. Managers must rise to it, for they are the force at the center of the storm.

Notes

1. Trip Gabriel, "Lost Jobs, Found Directions," *New York Times,* September 7, 1995.

2. Betsy Morris, "Executive Women Confront Midlife Crisis," *Fortune,* September 18, 1995.

3. David Whyte, *The Aroused Heart: Poetry and the Preservation of the Soul in Corporate Life* (New York: Doubleday, 1994).

About the Contributors

Anthony Athos is a former independent consultant to top management of middle-sized professional organizations. He was the Jesse Isador Straus Professor at the Harvard Business School from 1968 to 1982 and is the coauthor with Richard Pascale of *The Art of Japanese Management*.

Christopher A. Bartlett is a professor of business administration at the Harvard Business School, where his interests focus on the general management challenges faced particularly by multinational corporations. He serves both as a board member and as a consultant/management advisor to several large corporations. Professor Bartlett is the author or coauthor of five books, including *Managing Across Borders: The Transnational Solution* with Sumantra Ghoshal (Harvard Business School Press) and has written articles for various management journals.

James D. Berkley was a research associate at the Harvard Business School at the time of his article's publication. He is currently a doctoral student in comparative literature and philosophy at the University of California, Los Angeles.

James Champy is CEO and chairman of CSC Index, a management consulting firm based in Cambridge, MA, and a leading authority and strategist on business reengineering. He consults extensively with CEOs, presidents, and senior executives of multinational companies seeking to improve business performance dramatically. Mr. Champy is the author of *Reengineering Management: The Mandate for New*

Leadership, coauthor with Michael Hammer of *Reengineering the Corporation: A Manifesto for Business Revolution,* and featured in the Harvard Business School Management Productions video "Managing Successful Reengineering."

Ram Charan is a Dallas-based consultant and advisor to executives of several Fortune 50 companies on corporate transformation and on linking business strategies to bottom-line results through the use of "social technology." He contributes to several university and in-house executive programs and has been the recipient of best teacher awards at General Electric and Northwestern University's Kellogg Graduate School of Management. He is the author of articles appearing in such publications as *Directorship, The Corporate Board,* and the *Harvard Business Review.*

Peter F. Drucker is the Clarke Professor of Social Science & Management at the Claremont Graduate School in Claremont, California, where he has been teaching since 1971. He also consults to businesses and non-profit organizations on strategy and policy. Professor Drucker has been writing on management since he published *The Future of Industrial Man*—his second book—in 1943, and is a frequent contributor to the *Harvard Business Review.* His latest book is *Post Capitalist Society.*

David A. Garvin is the Robert and Jane Cizik Professor of Business Administration at the Harvard Business School. His research focuses on the areas of general management and strategic change, with a particular interest in organizational learning, business and management processes, and the development of leading-edge organizations. Professor Garvin is the author of *Operations Strategy: Text and Cases* and coauthor with C. Roland Christensen and Ann Sweet of *Education for Judgment: The Artistry of Discussion Leadership* (Harvard Business School Press).

Sumantra Ghoshal holds the Robert P. Bauman Chair in Strategic Leadership at the London Business School. His research, writing, and consulting focus on the management of large worldwide firms. He has published a number of books, articles, and award-winning case studies, including *Managing Across Borders: The Transnational Solution* with Christopher A. Bartlett (Harvard Business School Press), *Organisation Theory and the Multinational Corporation* with Eleanor Westney, and *The Strategy Process: European Perspective* with Henry Mintzberg and J.B. Quinn.

Tracy Goss is president of Goss Reid Associates and cofounder of The Center For Executive Re-Invention, both in Austin, Texas. She is an expert on transformational leadership and the originator and leading exponent of the concept of "Executive Re-Invention." Ms. Goss specializes in consulting to CEOs and their executive teams throughout the world to "re-invent" themselves and their leadership body to successfully design and implement an "impossible" future for the organization. Her recent publications include *The Last Word on Power: Re-Invention for Leaders Who Must Make The Impossible Happen.*

Michael Hammer is president of Hammer and Company, Inc., based in Cambridge, MA, and a leading proponent of the concept of reengineering. Named by *Business Week* as one of the preeminent management thinkers of the 1990s, Dr. Hammer regularly addresses senior executives of the world's leading companies, while also educating through reengineering seminars and videotapes. He is the coauthor with James Champy of *Reengineering the Corporation: A Manifesto for Business Revolution.*

Rosabeth Moss Kanter holds the Class of 1960 Chair as Professor of Business Administration at the Harvard Business School. Her many books include *World Class: Thriving Locally in the Global Economy*, the award-winning *When Giants Learn to Dance*, and *The Change Masters*. An advisor to leading companies worldwide, she also served as editor of the *Harvard Business Review* from 1989 to 1992 and hosts "Rosabeth Moss Kanter on Synergies, Alliances, and New Ventures" in the Harvard Business School Video Series.

John P. Kotter is Konosuke Matsushita Professor of Leadership at the Harvard Business School, where he teaches in both MBA and executive programs, and is a frequent speaker at top management meetings around the world. He is the author of several best-selling business books, including most recently *The New Rules: How to Succeed in Today's Post-Corporate World* and coauthor with Jim Heskett of *Corporate Culture and Performance*. Professor Kotter was the recipient of the Exxon Award for Innovation in Graduate Business School Curriculum Design and the Johnson, Smith & Knisely Award for New Perspectives in Business Leadership.

Nitin Nohria is an associate professor of business administration at the Harvard Business School. His current research focuses on the dynamics of organizational change in large industrial Fortune 100 companies, including their efforts during the last fifteen years to change their strategic scope, structure, governance, and culture. Professor Nohria is the author of *Beyond the Hype: Rediscovering the Essence of Management* (Harvard Business School Press) and *Building the Information Age Organization,* and he is the coeditor with Robert G. Eccles of *Networks and Organizations: Structure, Form, and Action* (Harvard Business School Press).

Richard Normann is founder of the SMG Group, a European management consulting firm specializing in strategy and business systems design. He is the author of *Management for Growth* and *Service Management.*

Richard Pascale is a leading business consultant worldwide and was a member of the faculty at Stanford's Graduate School of Business for twenty years. He has served as adviser to top management and architects of corporate transformation programs for several Fortune 100 companies and participated in the reorganization of the Executive Office of the President. Dr. Pascale is the coauthor with Anthony Athos of *The Art of Japanese Management* and author of *Managing on the Edge: How the Smartest Companies Use Conflict to Stay Ahead.*

Rafael Ramírez is an associate professor of management and human resources at Groupe HEC in Paris and vice president of the SMG Group, a European management consulting firm specializing in strategy and business systems design. Professor Ramírez focuses his work on value-creating systems and reconfiguration, as well as aesthetics.

Robert H. Schaffer is the head of Robert H. Schaffer & Associates, a consulting firm based in Stamford, CT. He is the originator of the firm's results-driven change management process, which is described in his book, *The Breakthrough Strategy: Using Short-Term Successes To Build the High Performance Organization.* He was a founding director of the Institute of Management Consultants and chairman of its Professional Development Committee for four years, and he is currently editor of the *Journal of Management Consulting.*

William Taylor is cofounder of *Fast Company,* a business and management magazine that focuses on the New Economy. A former associate editor of the *Harvard Business Review,* he is a coauthor of *No-Excuses Management* and *The Big Boys: Power and Position in American Business.*

Harvey A. Thomson is head of the Toronto office of Robert H. Schaffer & Associates. Before joining the consulting firm, he was an associate professor of organizational behavior at McGill University's

Faculty of Management. Dr. Thomson is author of several articles on organization effectiveness and the management of change.

Noel M. Tichy is a professor at the University of Michigan's School of Business Administration in Ann Arbor and director of its Global Leadership Program. He is coauthor of *Transformational Leader: Molding Tomorrow's Corporate Winners* and *Control Your Destiny or Someone Else Will.*

Abraham Zaleznik is the Konosuke Matsushita Professor of Leadership, Emeritus at the Harvard Business School and a consultant to business, corporations, and government. He is known internationally for his research and teaching in the field of social psychology in the business setting and for his investigations into the distinguishing characteristics of managers and leaders. Dr. Zaleznik is the author of thirteen books, the latest being *Learning Leadership*, and has written numerous award-winning articles.

INDEX